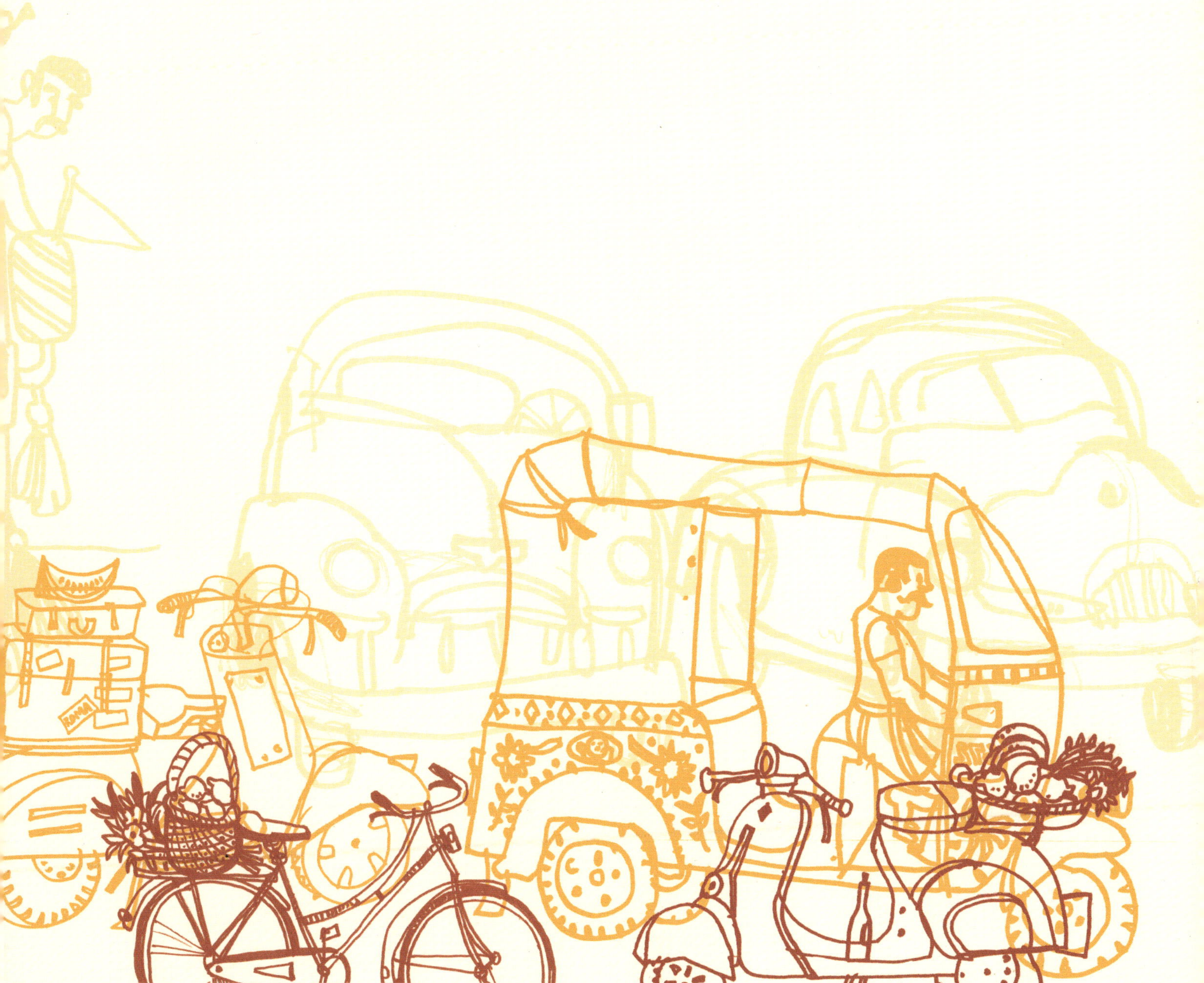

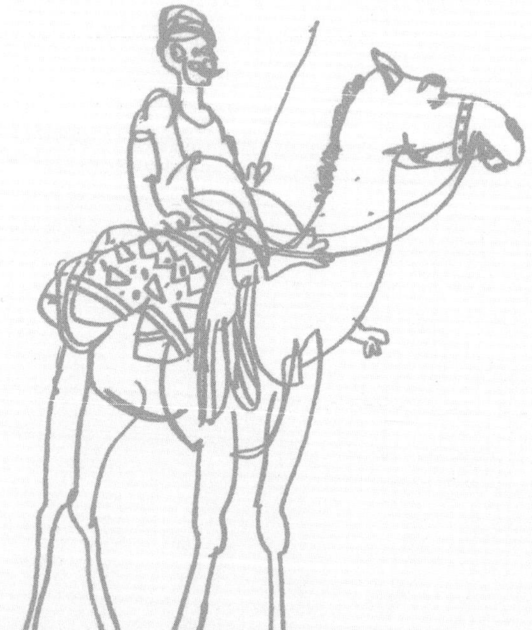

LEON MORROCCO

A PAINTER'S JOURNEY

This book is dedicated to my wife Jean, whose unwavering support and encouragement over the years will never be replaced.

Jean Morrocco 1944-2016

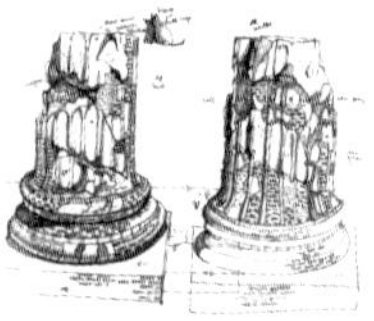

LEON MORROCCO

A PAINTER'S JOURNEY

Published in 2017 by Unicorn,
an imprint of Unicorn Publishing Group LLP
101 Wardour Street
London W1F 0UG
www.unicornpress.org
and by
John Martin Gallery
38 Albemarle Street
London W1S 4JG
www.jmlondon.com

ISBN
Trade Edition: 978-1-910787-93-9
(Collectors Edition: 978-0-9932195-8-0)

Designed by Studio Gualtiero Gualtieri London
Printed in Slovenia for Latitude Press Ltd

LEON MORROCCO

A PAINTER'S JOURNEY

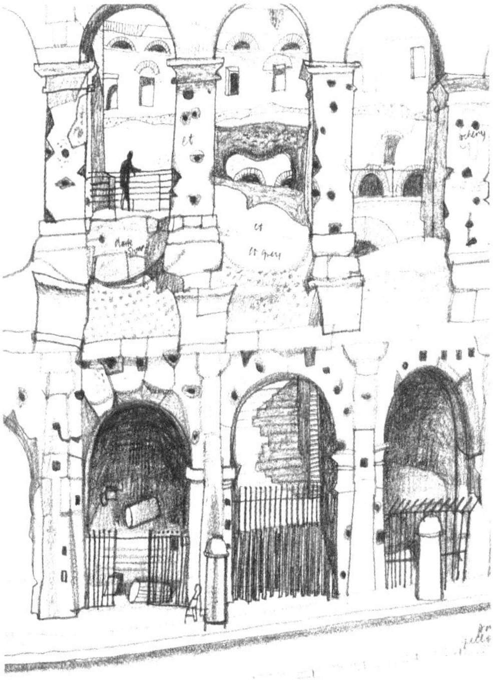

UNICORN

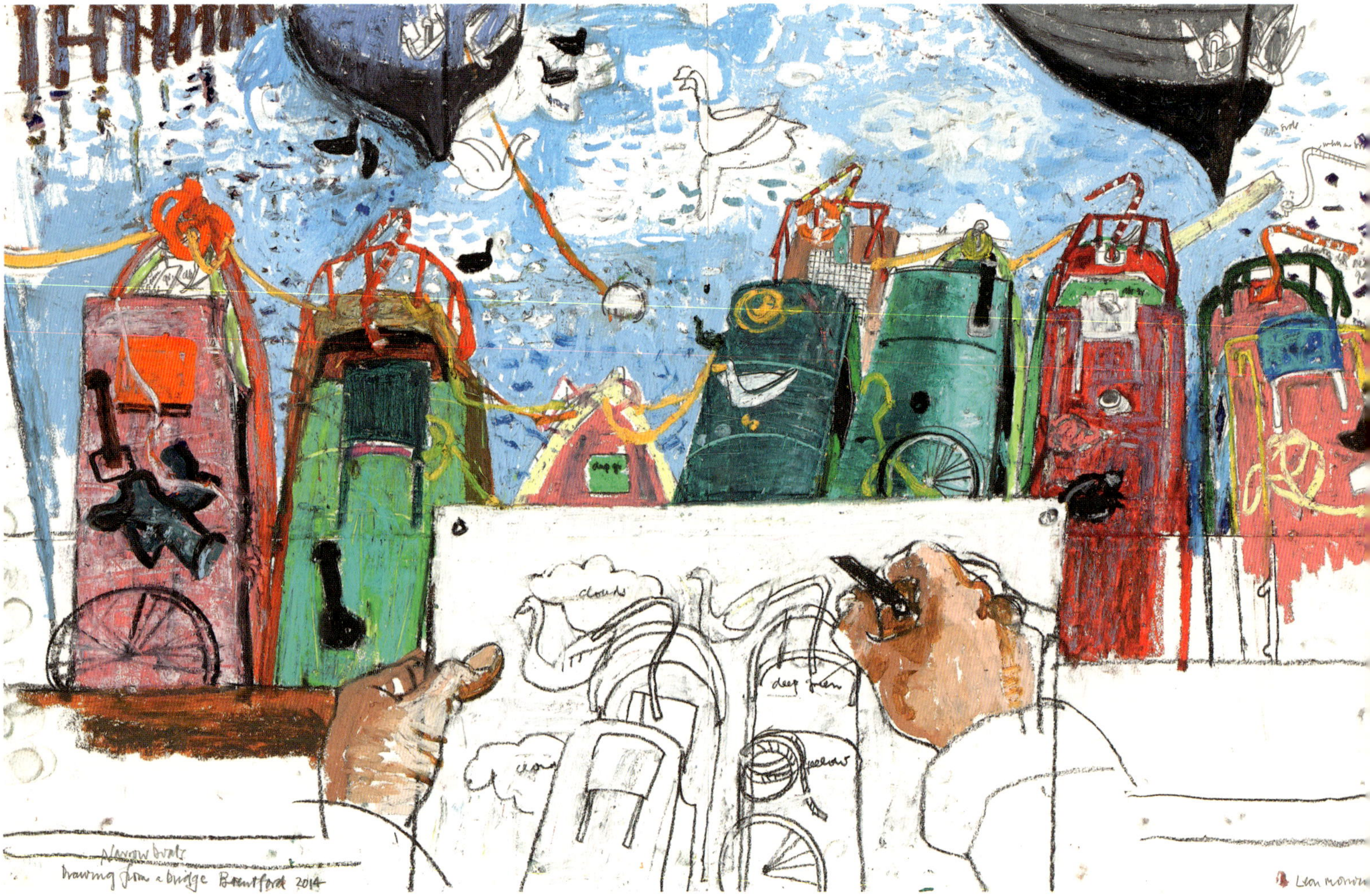
Narrow boats
Drawing from a bridge Brentford 2014

LEON MORROCCO, CELEBRATED PAINTER FOR MANY YEARS, IS SOMETHING OF AN ENIGMA. He is not quite a complete outsider but nor is he a fully paid-up member of the contemporary art club. He does not use his success to voice social concerns, global issues or climate change, nor does he even vaguely attempt to pander to the constructs of conceptual art.

Why, then, does he find himself out on a limb when attendance figures for public exhibitions of contemporary art are at a record high? The answer may lie in his reluctance to accept the tired and outdated statement that painting is dead.

Leon is obviously not totally alone; many figurative painters feel marginalised by the art world hierarchy who favour the practitioners of conceptual and peformance art. We are in an era where it seems all artwork worth its salt must not only be challenging but must also have the added ingredient of shock and sensationalism.

Leon does not belong in that world, He is concerned with beauty, a term seldom used in contemporary art speak. His beauty is the beauty of the backyard, of the peeling plaster of neglected façades – the exterior equivalent of the kitchen sink. He is a visual sleuth constantly searching for the subject matter we overlook in our quest to get from A to B as quickly as possible.

However, what sets him apart from his painter peers and is the key to the core of his art is in his adherence to the historic principles of draughtsmanship. This is fundamental to him and without this his trademark use of colour and cleverly constructed composition would not be possible.

We should all embrace the varied aspects of original contemporary art and realise the importance of each individual body of work. With this in mind we should celebrate the work of Leon Morrocco who has consistently proven throughout his career that it is perfectly possible to produce work which is highly original, challenging and experimental without the need for shock and awe.

Thomas Wilson, October 2016

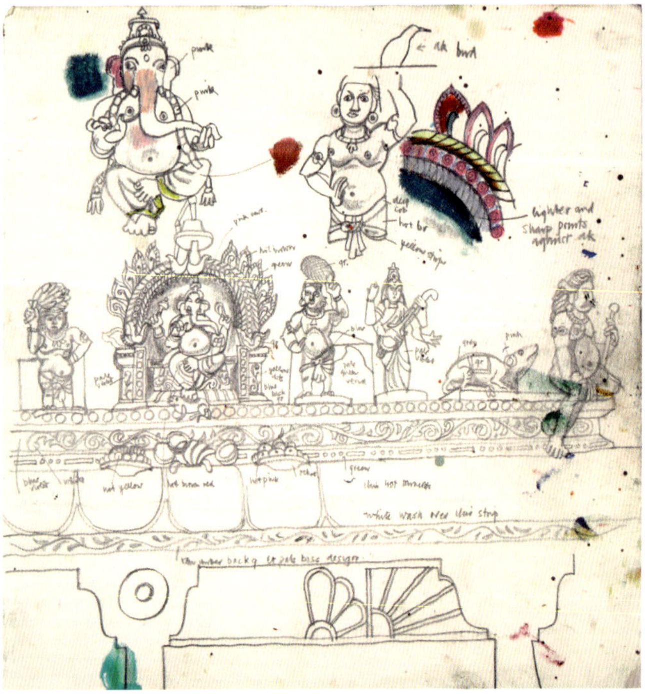

Page 4: **Drawing Narrow-boats from a Bridge 2014** pencil & oil pastel on paper 81.5 x 49.5 cm
Page 6: **Temple Sculptures, Chennai 2009** pencil on paper 28.5 x 30 cm
Page 7: **Zapatos 2006** oil on canvas 76 x 81 cm
Page 8: Leon Morrocco in his studio, 2017
Photograph by Dan Weill

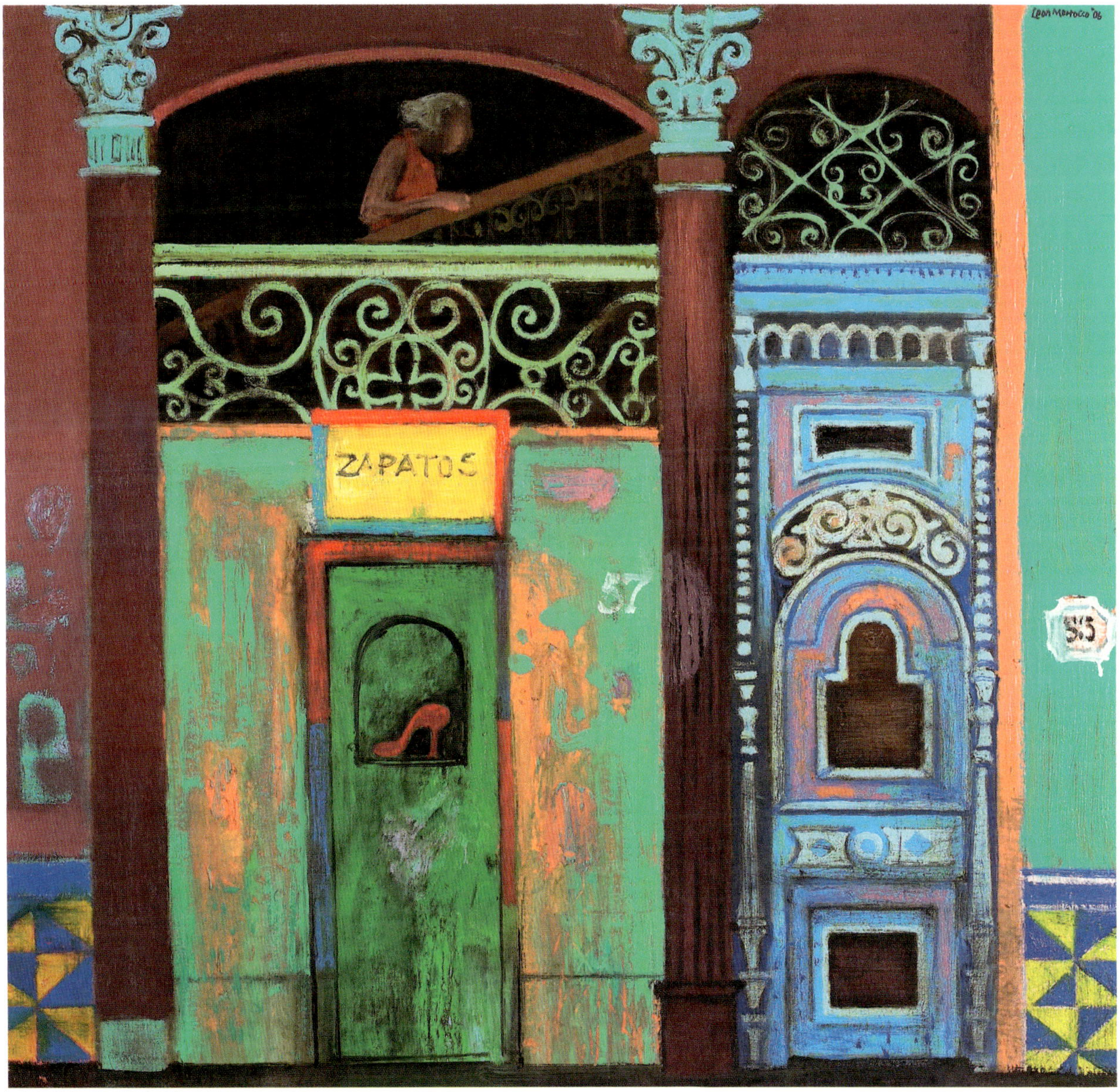
ZAPATOS
57
55

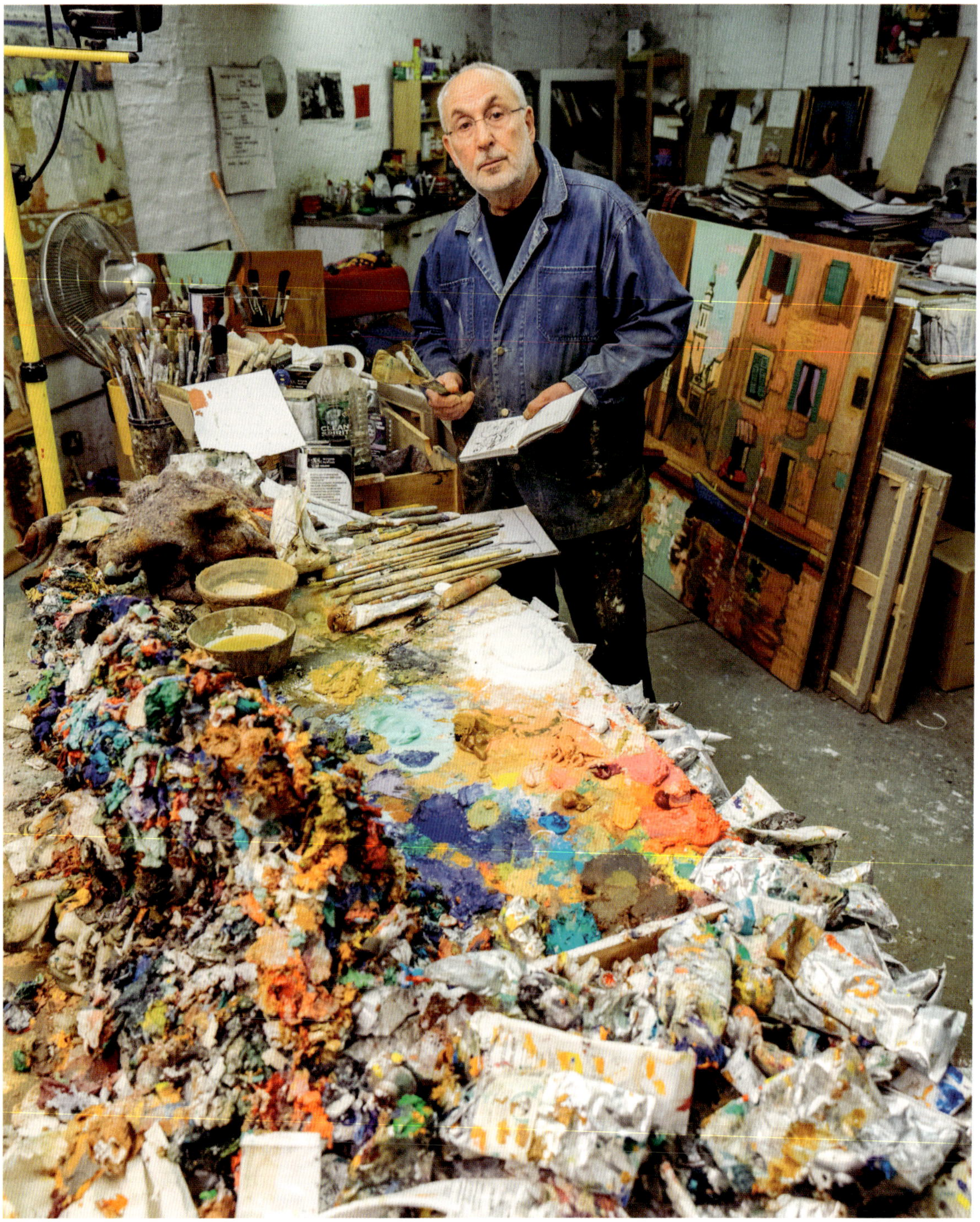

MY FRIEND, THE PAINTER LEON MORROCCO, INSISTS HE IS A REALIST. NOTHING MORE, NOTHING LESS.

I'm taken aback by this for a moment. Realism? Painstaking photographic likeness? Deadly, dogged, verisimilitude? I've always associated the term 'realism' with that arid kind of art I have no interest in whatsoever and there is, thank goodness, absolutely none of this here in Leon's studio. None of my delight is anything whatsoever to do with how accurate a depiction any of it is.

This studio: how to describe it? Well, it's in this unremarkable north London mews, next door to a joiner's. Ring the bell at the green front door, or shout up to the window to be let in. Ignore, for now, the ground floor with its interestingly crammed racks and stacks of archived unfinished or abandoned paintings, blank canvases, panels of wood and thick cardboard, rolls of heavy paper and a few old frames. Just go straight up those steep, slightly rickety ladder-like stairs to the clutter and sprawl of the upper floor and find an old-fashioned ideal of an artist's studio, straight out of central casting.

There's a comfy old battered leather office chair; as a guest I'll be given that one and he'll move over for himself that uncomfortable metal one from over there near that desk. On it there are random bits of business letters and a wee pile of paperwork weighted down under an old telephone, a right ancient-looking non-cordless model. Over there an every bit as paint-spattered old ghetto-blaster-CD-and-radio as house-painters always bring along with them to a job; then there's a kettle, a fridge that possibly has a rather nice bottle of white in it, some bits and pieces of ill-matched crockery, a few assorted wine glasses, mugs and tilting plates that have been long drying on that old plastic dish rack beside the sink and the teabag tin. Ranged around there are the half-dozen-or-so big canvases Leon's currently working on, either propped up against the wall or on the easel.

There, centrally, is that big painting table. It's in lieu of a palette and no visitors can ever take their eyes off it, not from the fresh fat worms of squeezed out oil paint all around the table's edge, nor from the great multicoloured high-arching wall made of yesterday's and the day-before's and the day-before-that's scrapings; a wall around the almost-burnished surface of the clean, cleared mixing-centre. The palette knives are to hand, the brushes soaked overnight and now cleaned, cared for and ready.

Sketchbooks. Here are leaning towers of sketchbooks I'm encouraged to rifle through freely. So now I'm looking at swift, sure, line drawings: here in pencil, 4 or 5B, a whole page of knock-kneed, supercilious camels; turn the pages and here are all ages and varieties of human beings in full colour sunning themselves by the sea; there rickshaws, bicycles with precarious baskets of lemons, Vespas, Lambrettas, all manner of motorini, the hardworking marketplaces of many nations. These might be mainly in monochrome with wee passages of colour notes executed in oil pastels and strong graphite blacks.

It's all far from minimal or tidy looking, this studio, but I am to learn that in fact everything is to hand exactly where it is needed. Even those wee card-board boxes and boxes of pastels are colour-coded and neatly labelled. And this whole place is redolent of that long ago, so familiar to me, smell of oil paint, linseed oil and turps – a smell that instantly takes me back the best part of 50 years to the Department of Drawing and Painting at the Glasgow School of Art.

This is where Leon and I glancingly crossed paths way back in 1970, in the last days of what he calls 'the atelier system', when he was in his first year as a tutor in the Department of Drawing and Painting. The tutor who, along with one other, actually talked to us about our work. A tutor who was known to be sympathetic, not scathing, about the struggles of the students.

I was a student in my last year and most definitely struggling. Quite lost. Actually thinking of dropping out this late in the day, except for fear of what Mum and Dad, who'd had big doubts in the first place about my trying for art school, would say. In one consultation Leon gave me that one single vital bit of encouragement I've always remembered and been grateful for. It got me through my diploma at the time. 'It's your sketchbooks!' he said, 'Keep the life and interest that's going on in them alive in your paintings.'

Our paths didn't cross again for over 45 years. Since our chance re-acquaintance at his exhibition three years ago in Edinburgh's Open Eye Gallery at Festival time, he's once again been generous in encouraging me, after what has turned out to be my life's work of making pictures out of nothing but words, to just get on with my unexpected and lately revived need to shut up and draw.

I know what a privilege these days of occasional studio visits here are. Perhaps over some M&S sandwiches I've brought and a nice glass of wine from that fridge, we'll wonder what the correspondences and differences between writing and drawing might be. Unapologetic about being old-fogeys, we'll deplore together the – to us – terrible tendency to ask art students to write an essay about what they wish to achieve before they do the bloody painting and for them to be evaluated on the 'idea', not the actual work. We despair for the poor art school Leon visited lately that doesn't smell like oil paint, but is full of students working on computers.

We'll talk about creativity itself, about the problem of how, amidst the inevitable griefs and terrible losses we confront as we age, to keep it alive for as long as we are. A serious, though not at all solemn, conversation. Mixed in there will be a lot of gossip about things from that scrap of time our lives so briefly overlapped. There will be a lot of laughter over occasionally conflicting memories of ridiculous characters and failed student pranks, our recollections of the fabled '60s that were only really getting going in Glasgow by 1970.

Nowadays, still drawn to the romance of backstage in the theatre, to the control room in recording studios, to dressing rooms, to scuzzy overheated or draughty rehearsal rooms, to all the places where all the interesting work gets done, I better remind myself that for Leon this is his everyday, workaday, place. On a rare good day when it's flowing, I know how much I resent being torn away from my desk. He's got to get on with it, I better not overstay my welcome, better not try cadge too many of these invitations to visit.

Apparently it's a mere by-product that these initial sketchbook drawings I'm looking at are so lovely, among my favourite things of his. Often with wee written notes-to-self on them ('paler', 'spiky', 'grey-green water') for him at the time they were all about, and only about, getting down the info. Drawing for Leon is the basis of everything, always, he says; his only way of understanding the form, of owning it. Ah, in the end it seems all Leon meant by the 'Realist' remark is that everything for him has to start with a purely visual, visceral response to something real. When something sparks off the impulse to draw he doesn't analyse, conceptualise, verbalise or, perish the thought, explore 'ideas', but just gets on with it, obeys his instinct and imperative – just for himself and his own future use – to get down on paper vital information that records as much as possible of his five-sound-senses pleasure and interest in the actual it. He says he doesn't care to make things up.

I'd guess he doesn't have to. His glad eye for workplaces, fishermen's huts, beaches, barges, back-yards, smokehouses, potting sheds, boathouses, garages, bits of maritime machinery, for rags and streaks, crumblings and flakings, stains and graffiti on walls, has always given him more than enough to be getting on with. He glories in colour wherever he may find it, relishing the contrast and the clash of complementary spectrum-opposites as much as the buzz of two exactly-the-same tone-values of different hues in the zing of juxtaposition.

You could call it an old-fashioned method, though I'd rather call it a time-honoured one. Armed with all he has recorded outdoors, back here in the studio the next stage is him looking hard at these studies, conjuring them up in memory all over again, changing bits around if he needs to, re-composing the elements, posing himself problems to solve on canvas in these big easel paintings of his. Aesthetic, essentially abstract and painterly problems. Lots of scraping down and starting again. Leon says he's not interested if there are no problems, if there's no struggle, nothing to prove. This, though, is for him to know and the subsequent owner of his work never to find out. Such confident 100 per cent sensuous paintings. It's no struggle for us to simply and directly respond to their, to us, apparent spontaneity and joie de vivre.

Scribbling this down now, as this book is about to go to press, I am of course very curious to know which ones of the hundreds of possible images have finally made the cut and been included in this book you now have in your hand. 'A Painter's Journey'. Well, this painter has done a lot of these. Throughout his one big metaphorical lifelong journey he's always been stimulated by his travels, compelled to make image upon image as he goes. There'll no doubt be a lot of Italy, the home-from-homeland of his sketchbooks. Rome, Sicily, Sardinia, Morocco, places all around the Mediterranean hold a permanent fascination for him. There'll be Cuba too. India, that assault on all the senses, its street life brash with people and their animals, alternately spice-fragrant and stinking, rendered in gold and emerald, loud with turmeric yellow and blaring pink. These will all, surely, contrast greatly with images made here in Scotland, the place he was born and grew up in. The son of Alberto, a Scots-born Italian, and of Vera, Scottish through and through, Leon has always been secure in his twin cultural identity –

whilst, in all his journeying, there's always that genetic pull to sunlight, the South.

Here is what sparked off that 'Realism' conversation in the first place. Early in 2015 I saw a tremendous exhibition devoted purely to drawing. Three monumental finished works by Leon took up a whole room at the Royal Scottish Academy Gallery in Edinburgh. Far, far, from any sketchbook in scope and scale, each finished work was formed of four or five huge paper panels mounted on board, the honest joins clearly visible. It was tour de force, but just part of a series of very large drawings and paintings from an ongoing project of Leon's called 'Drawing the River'. During the long hot summer of 2013, armed with melting Sennellier oil-pastels, he had spent several weeks in situ daily documenting some of the quirks, crooks and elbows of the Thames, the interesting lives, locales and riverside workplaces of its people. Full of verve, joy and curiosity, detailed and delighted, they were brilliant in colour, gorgeous in texture, luxuriating in the lushness of the summer, mining for the tiny jewels of glint and light in the grunge and garbage among the mucky swans.

Up here in Leon's London studio, having seen these pieces, that whole gallery wall in Edinburgh just the week before, I'm asking him what he thinks of this trio of drawings being described by the exhibition's curator as 'fantastical'. He is astonished. Nothing 'fantastical' about them! He is a Realist. OK. But it strikes me how very often, given his vigorously enthusiastic nature about . . . och, great painters of the past, Passolini films, saxophone music or the book on Picasso by Françoise Gilot he is currently re-reading and offers to lend me when he's done – how very often, 'Fantastic!', in its colloquial, affirmative sense, is a word he comes out with.

I'm not much of a critic. I once truthfully and cheerfully admitted in an essay for the Glasgow School of Art magazine of critical studies I'd been leant upon to contribute to: 'With the exception of some few words written down by artists I revere, I hate all writing about art.' Still feel the same. If it's not from the horse's mouth, I can't really be bothered with it. No fan of the current impenetrable art-speak theoretics, I heartily concur that good wine needs no bush, a good play no epilogue. When I hear a bit of music I love, I just want to say, 'hey, listen to this'. A great meal? 'Have a taste, it's delicious.'

So, what are you doing wasting your time reading these words? The images in this book by the Realist Morrocco are certainly not fantastical, but, oh boy, what fantastic drawings these are, aren't they? And fabulous paintings? What a bonny picture book this is going to be. Wow, just look, enjoy.

Liz Lochhead,
poet and playwright,
Glasgow, March 2017

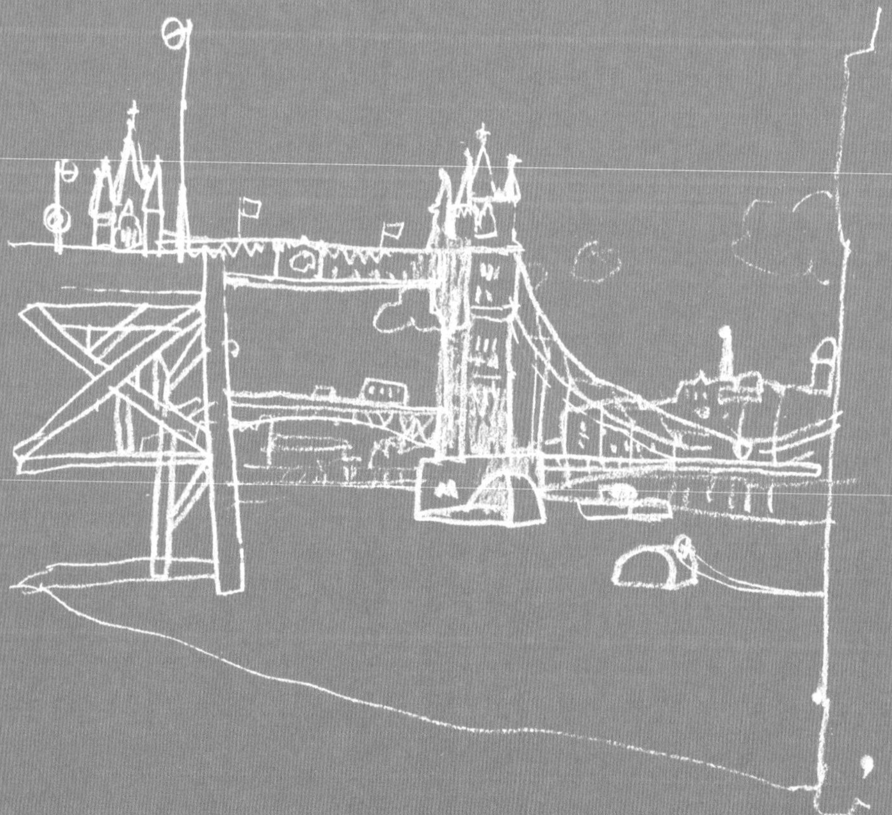

HOME

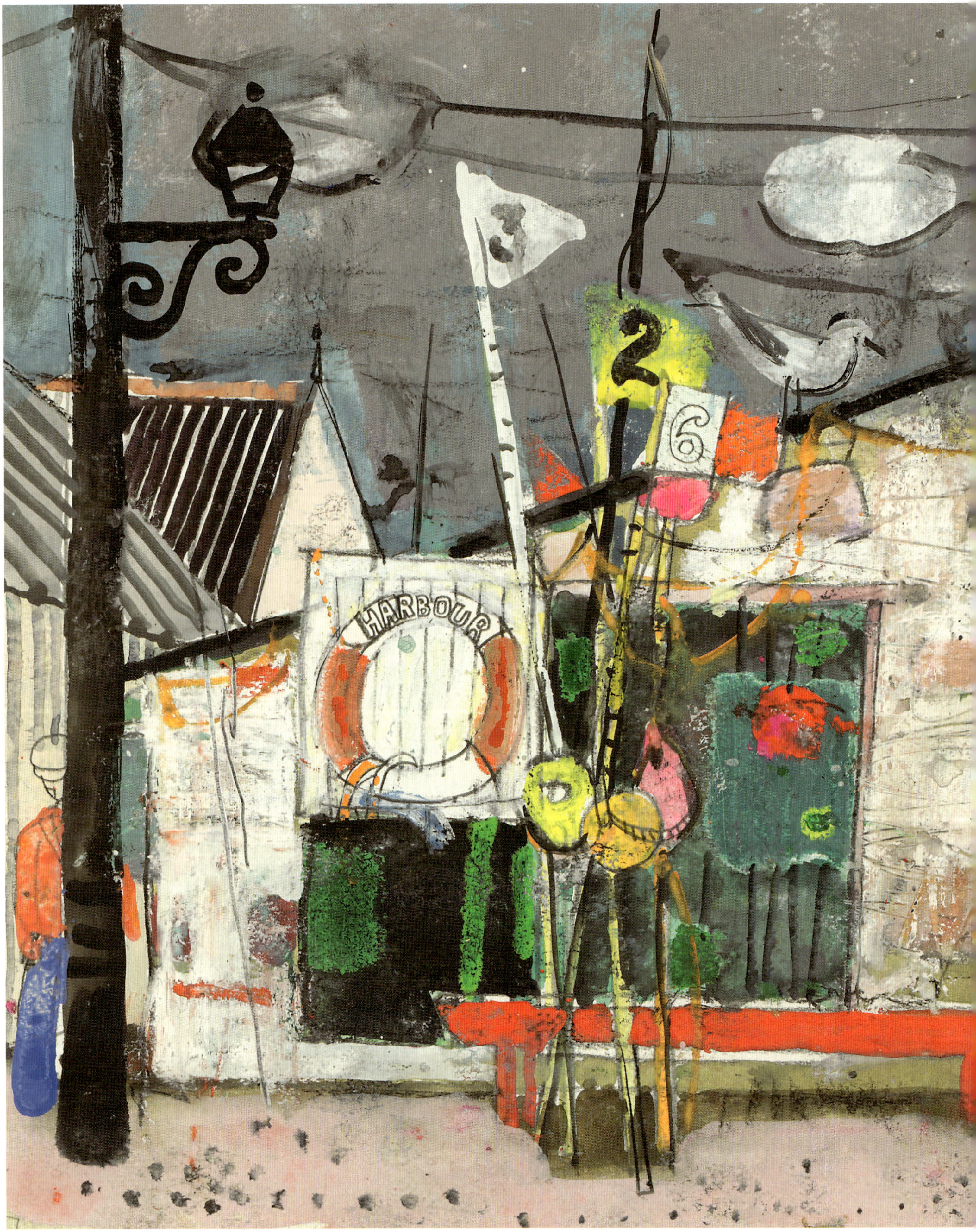
HARBOUR
3
2
6

BECAUSE OF MY FAMILY CONNECTIONS, ITALY – AND, IN FACT, THE WHOLE OF the Mediterranean basin – has held great fascination for me throughout my working life. However, I do not underestimate the contribution to the creative process of my upbringing in Scotland. My father was Italian but my mother was a Scot and this I am convinced has genetically led me to feel that I have a foot in each cultural camp.

All my schooling and a substantial part of my training as a painter occurred in Scotland. When I attended the Edinburgh College of Art, in the 1960's the Scottish Art Schools had a long-established tradition of offering a strong, skill based training where drawing underpinned the whole curriculum. Painting, by and large, was taught with due reference to Post-Impressionism and a 'feel' for paint and its manipulation was encouraged. I absorbed all this as a fledging painter and to a degree it continues to preoccupy me today.

At the Edinburgh College of Art, a day a week was allocated to something called 'compositional drawing' where it was expected that students would prepare 'working drawings' (from any visual source) with the intention of developing these as paintings. My interpretation of this was to go out into the city and draw. I suppose it would be true to say that drawing remains of fundamental importance to me today.

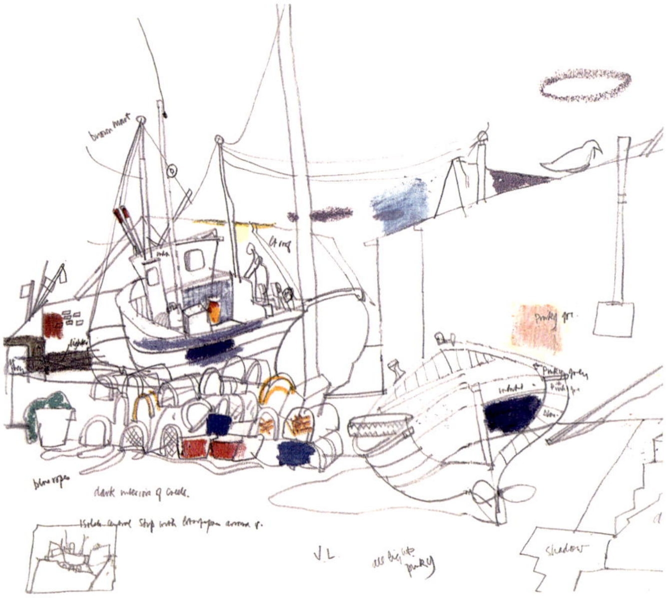

Page 16: **Harbour Hut, Arbroath 2012** gouache 36 x 43 cm
Page 18: **Sketch for Boat Repair, Gourdon 2012** pencil on paper 18 x 23 cm
Page 19: **Gourdon Boat Repair 2012** pencil & oil pastel on paper 43 x 66 cm

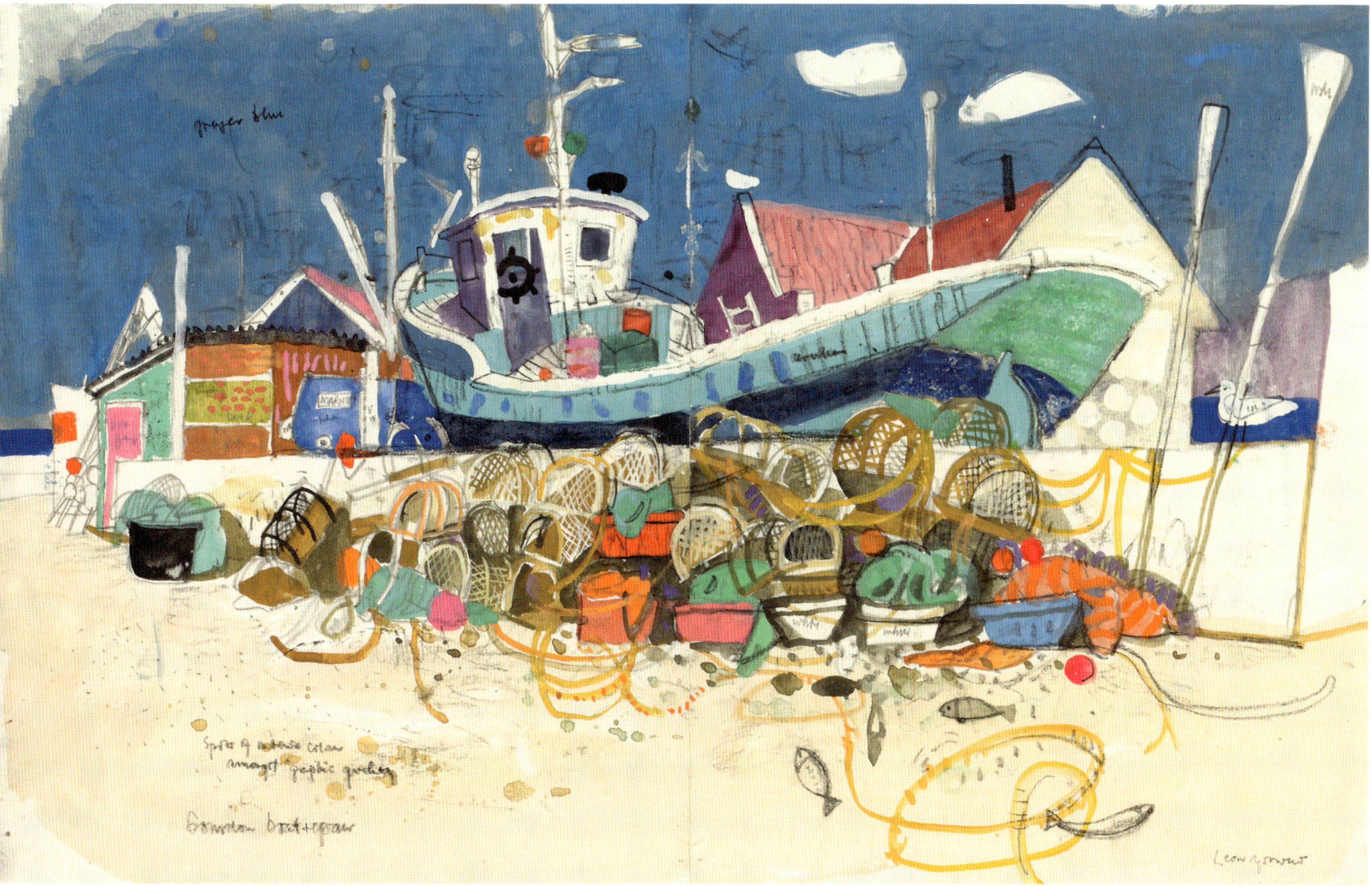

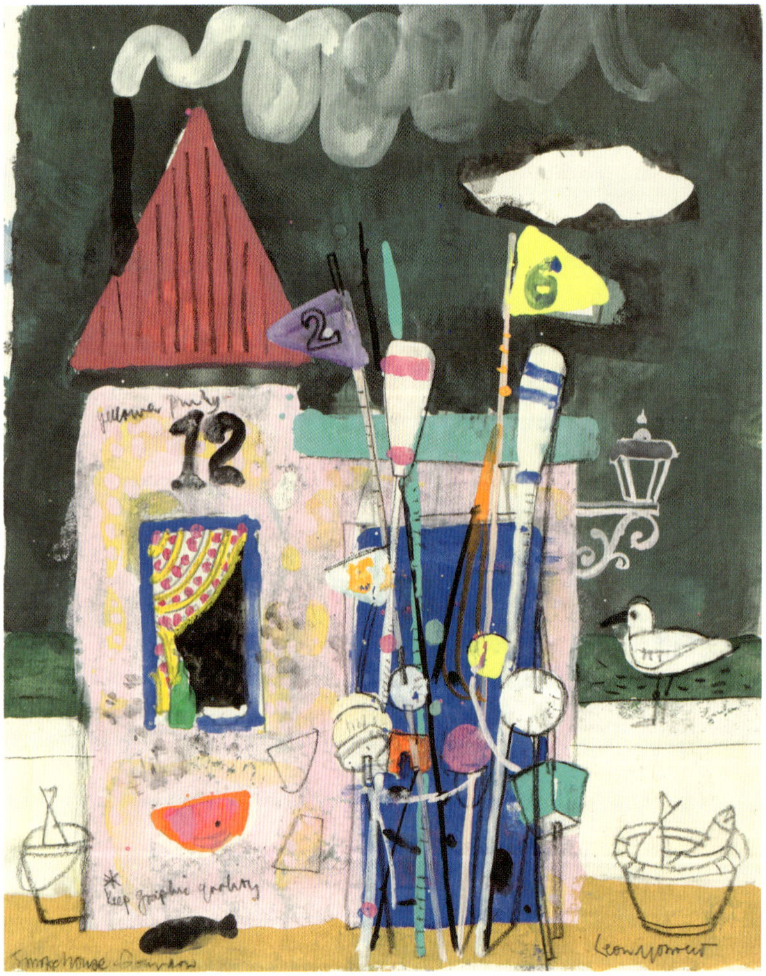

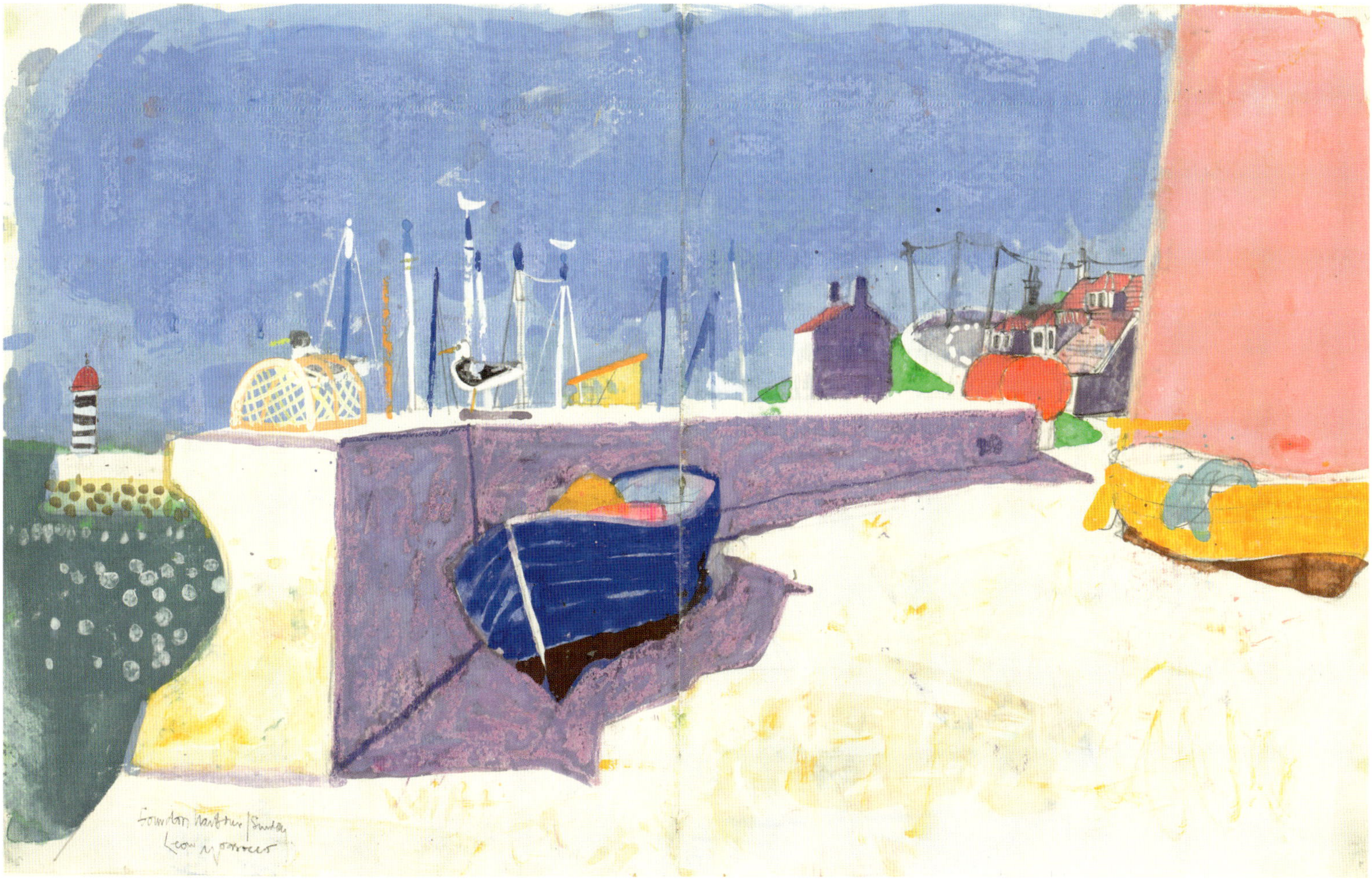

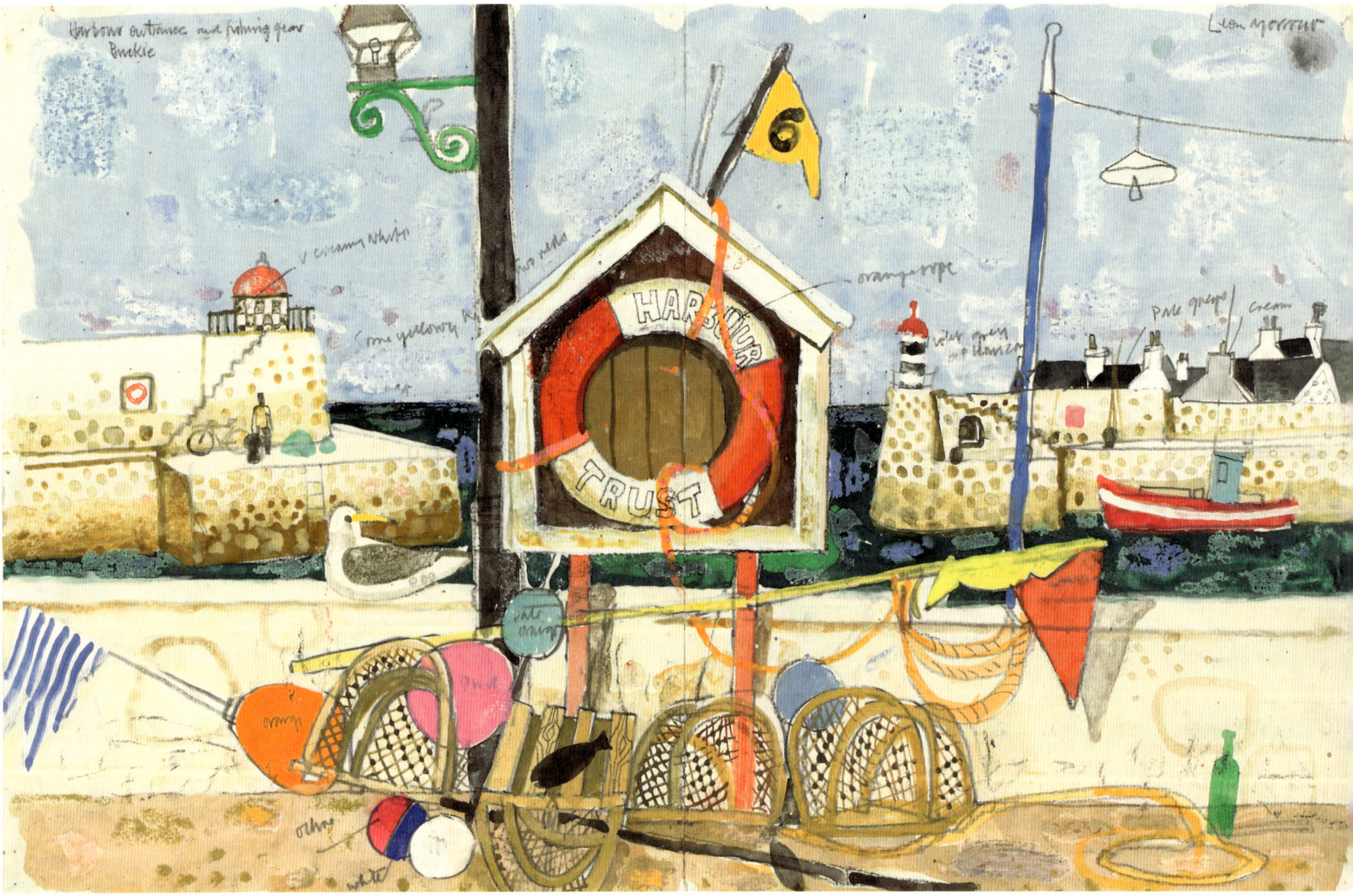
Harbour entrance and fishing gear
Buckie
HARBOUR
TRUST
6
orange rope

Page 20: **Smokehouse, Arbroath 2012** pencil & gouache on paper 43 x 36 cm
Page 21: **Gourdon Harbour, Sunday 2012** gouache 43 x 66 cm
Page 22: **Harbour Entrance and Fishing Gear, Buckie 2012** gouache 43 x 66 cm
Page 23: **End of the Pier and Smokehouse 2012** gouache 36 x 43 cm

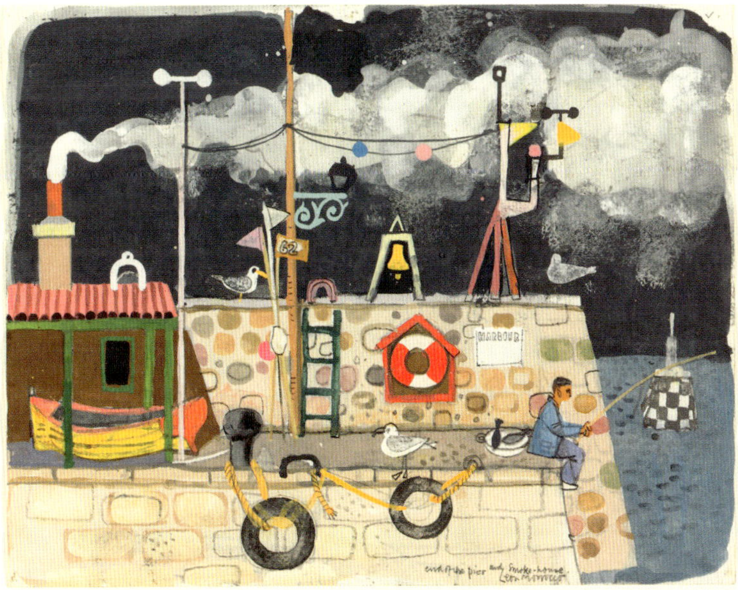

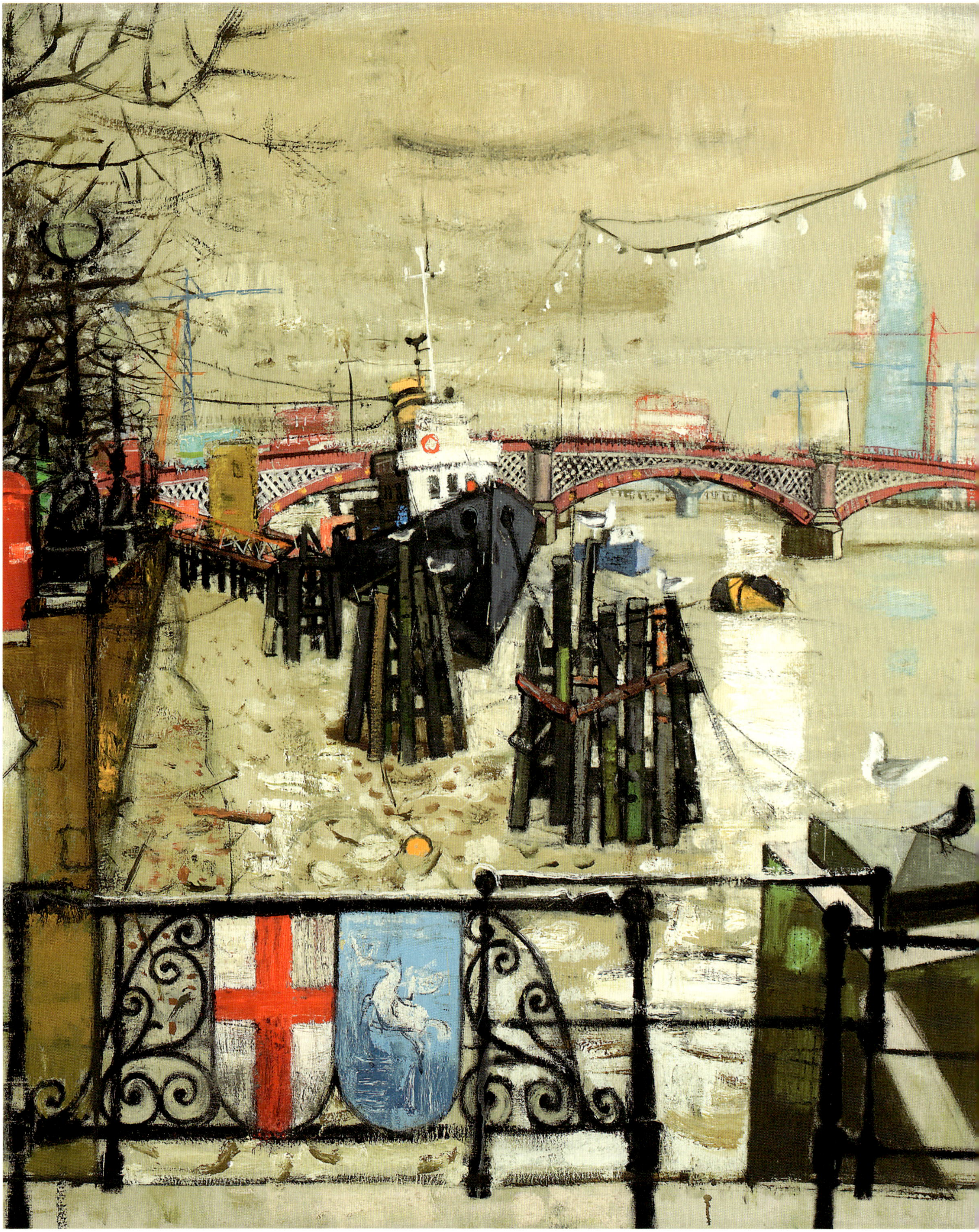

SEEKING OUT EXOTIC LOCATIONS AS A SOURCE FOR PAINTING CAN have its drawbacks. It is easy to fall into a kind of superficiality. Too little time spent in the chosen locality can result in a failure to get under the skin of a place.

I am always keen to achieve a sense of 'place' in my work but to arrive at this I have to spend days drawing my way to that position. For example, in India, I spent three weeks in Madurai traversing and exploring the town and putting down on paper everything that interested me, be it markets, temples, rickshaws, animals, etc. This method is hard but exciting work and really the only way I can connect with a place and its people. These drawings, colour-notes and ideas are then brought back to my studio in London, there the process of editing and translating all this visual information into paintings takes place.

I do not paint outside directly from a point of reference, preferring (and finding it easier) to work from my drawings. This enables me to avoid too literal an interpretation of the subject. In contrast, my recent fascination with London and the river is an attempt to steer away from the 'exotic' and force myself to find the formal possibilities in visual situations that are obviously less attractive than Cuba, India or Morocco. In this context, I am reminded of Vincent van Gogh's paintings of an old pair of peasant boots and a pile of humble potatoes. The lesson being, I think, is that it is perhaps not the subject matter which is of prime importance but the artist's ability to see a way of painting it.

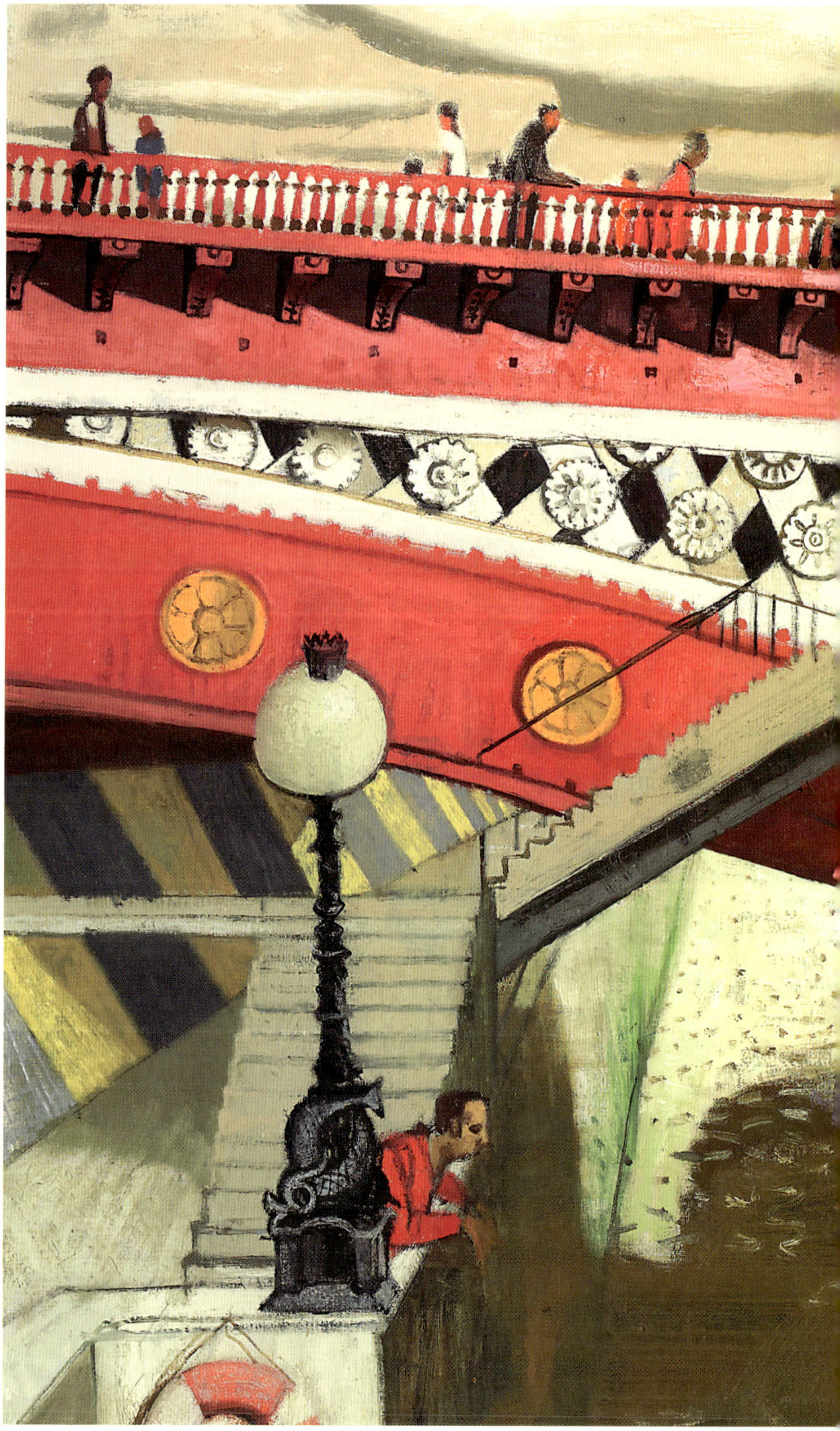

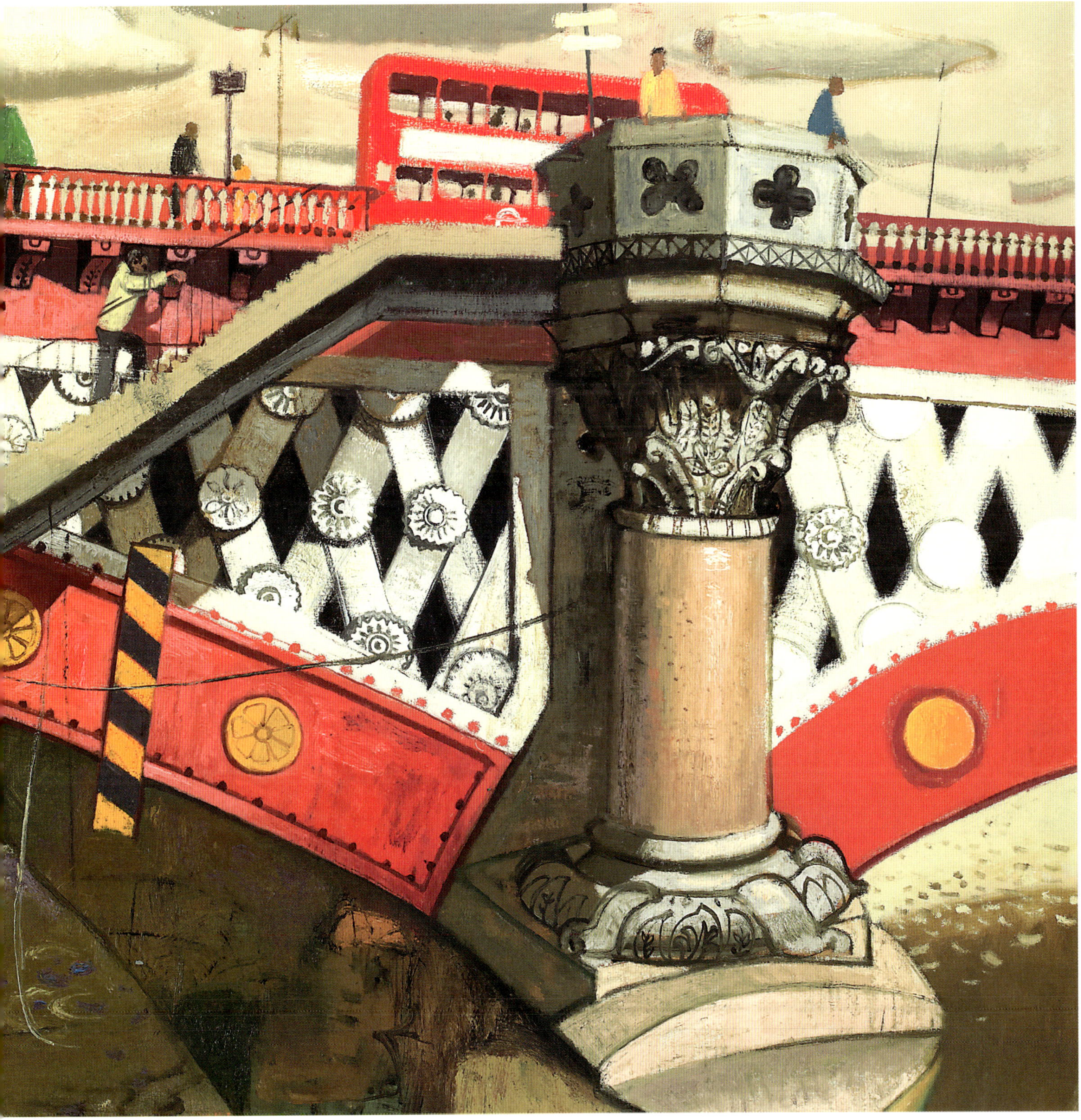

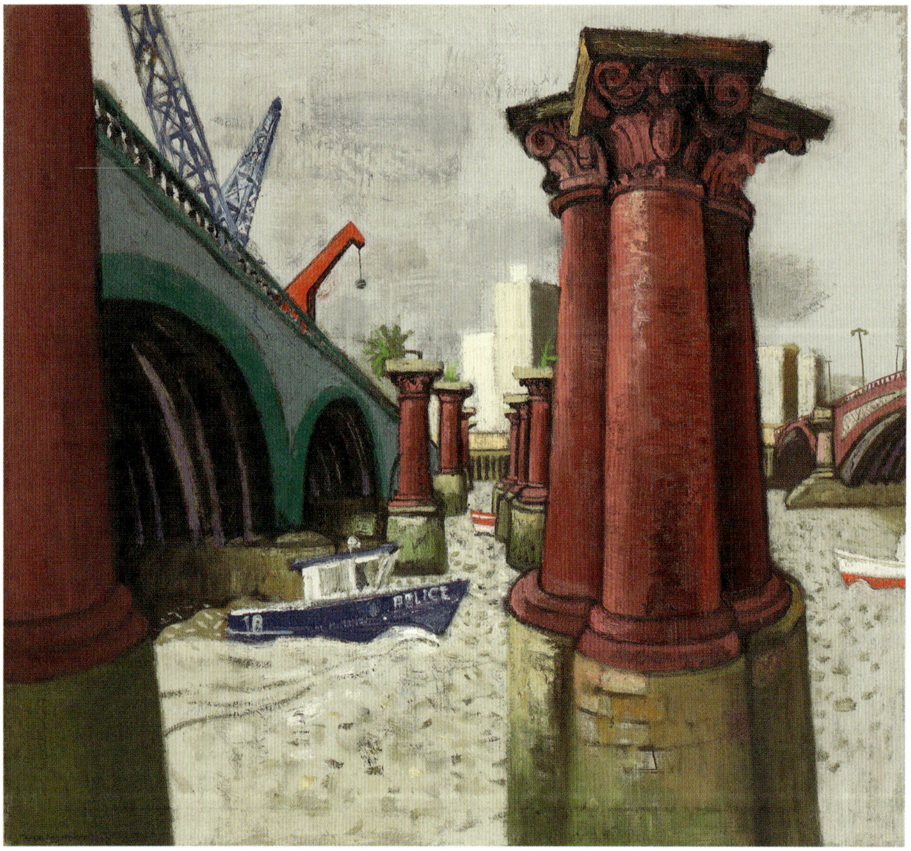

Page 24: **Temple Pier with Resting Birds 2012** oil on linen 147 x 152 cm

Page 26: **Watching the River, Blackfriars Bridge 2012** oil on linen 127 x 183 cm

Page 28: **Red Crane and Columns** oil on linen 2012 91 x 101 cm

Page 29: **Dolphin Lamp and Columns, Old Blackfriars Bridge 2012** oil on linen 127 x 183 cm

Page 30: **Cranes and Arches, Borough Market 2012** oil on linen 127 x 183 cm

Page 32: **Battleship at Rest 2012** oil on linen 127 x 244 cm

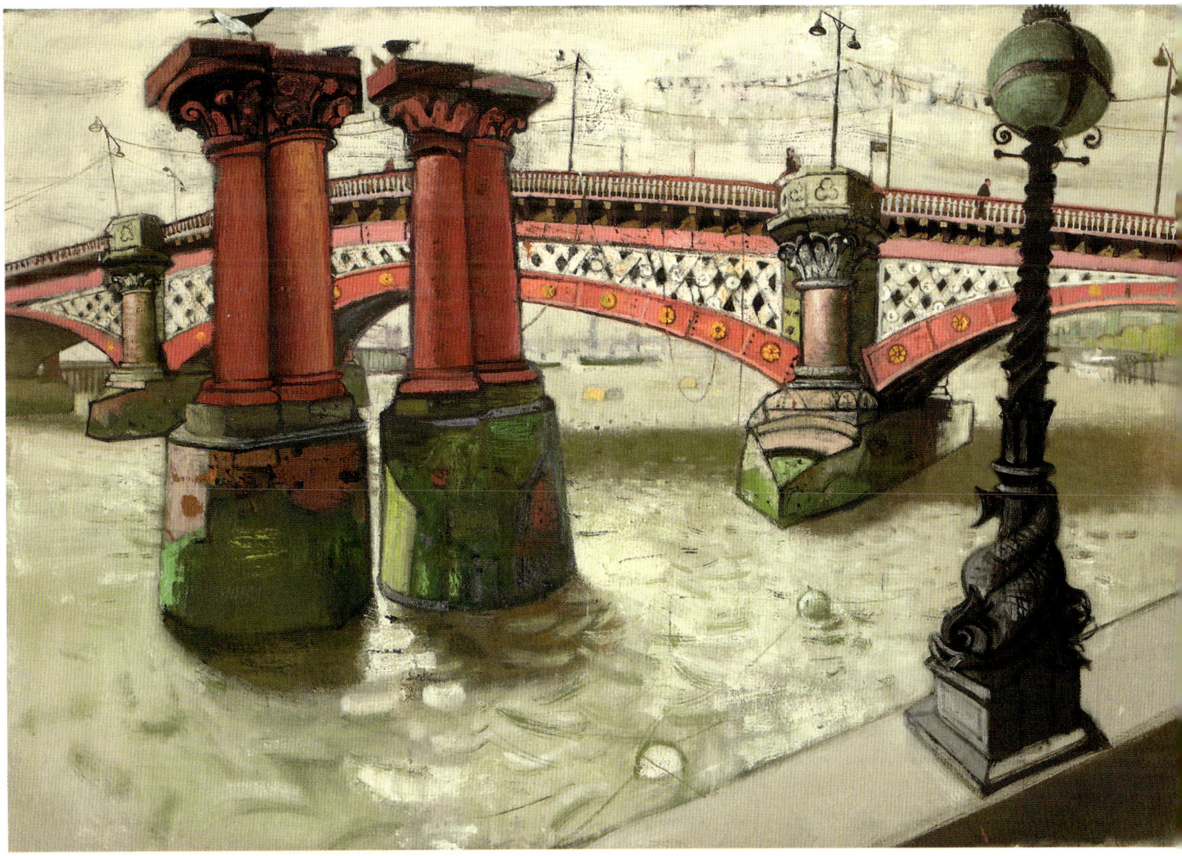

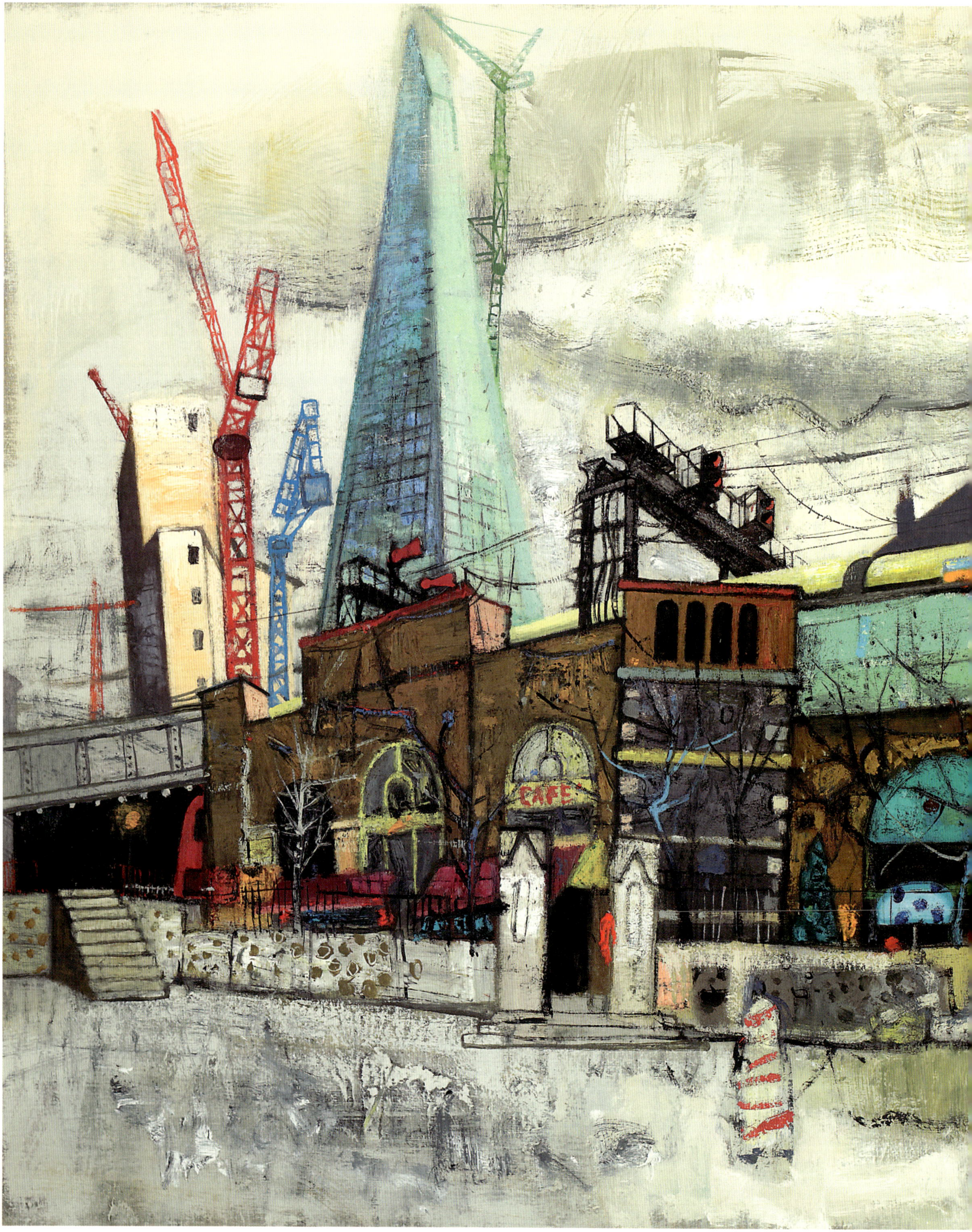
CAFE

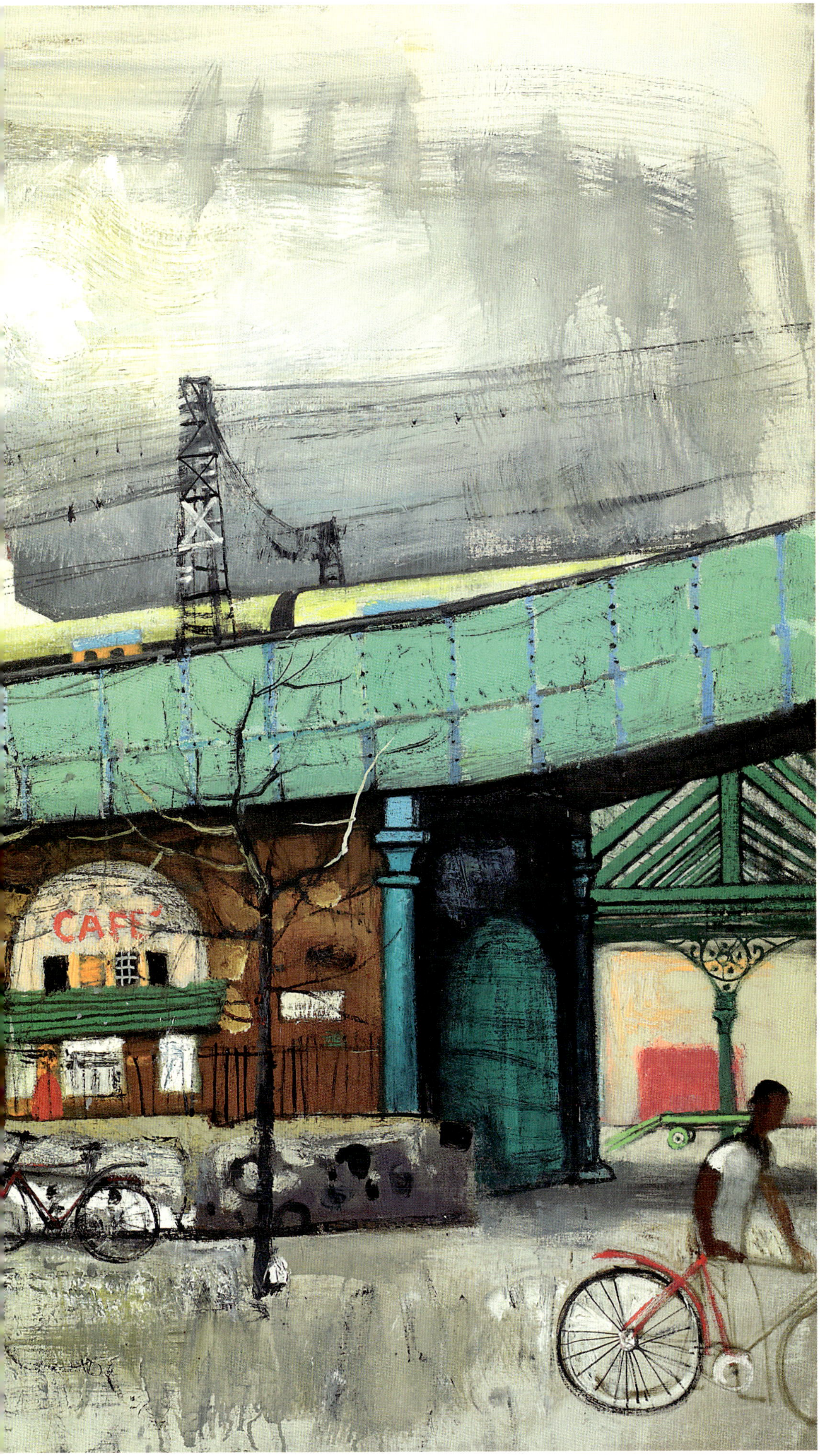
CAFE

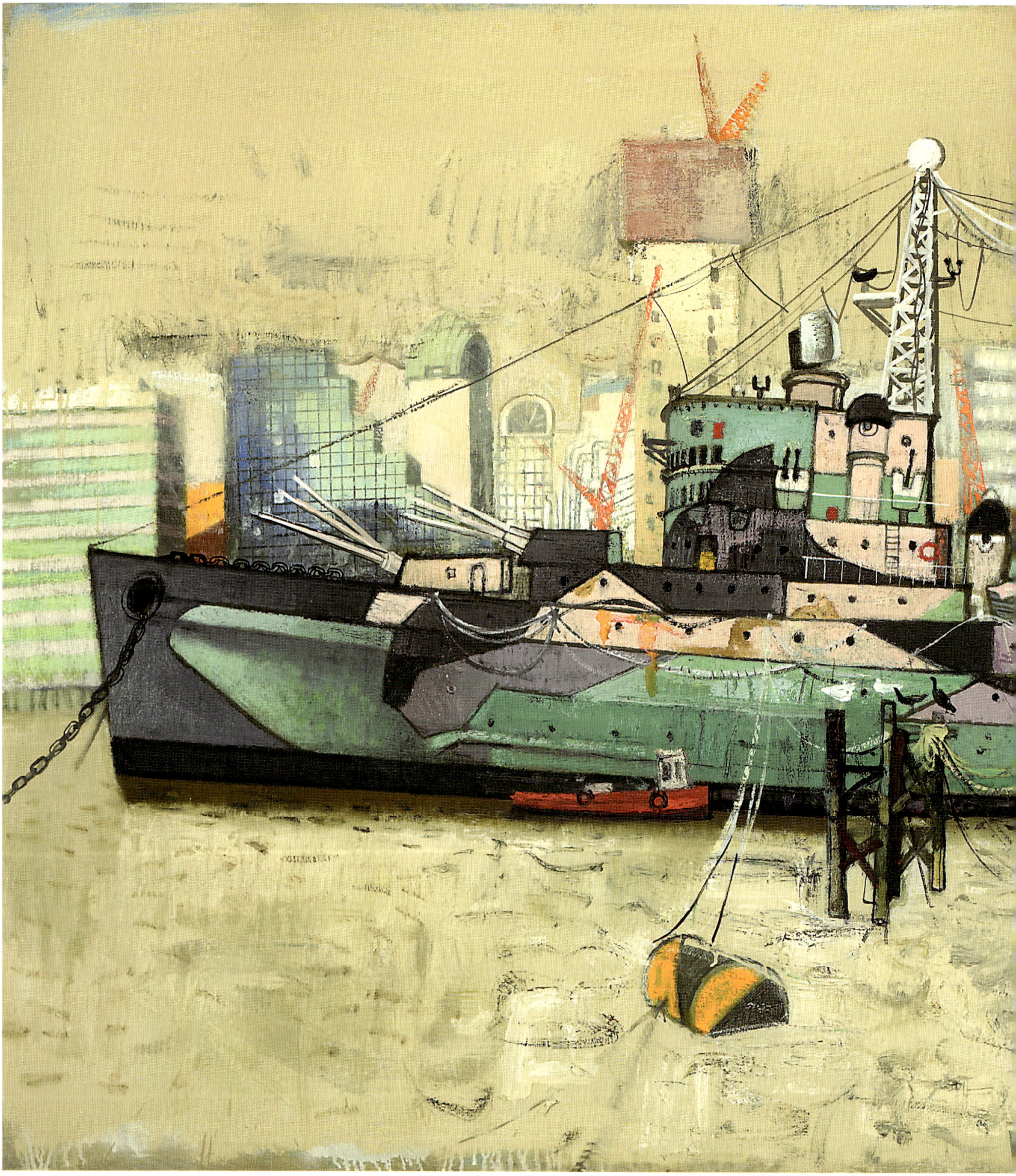

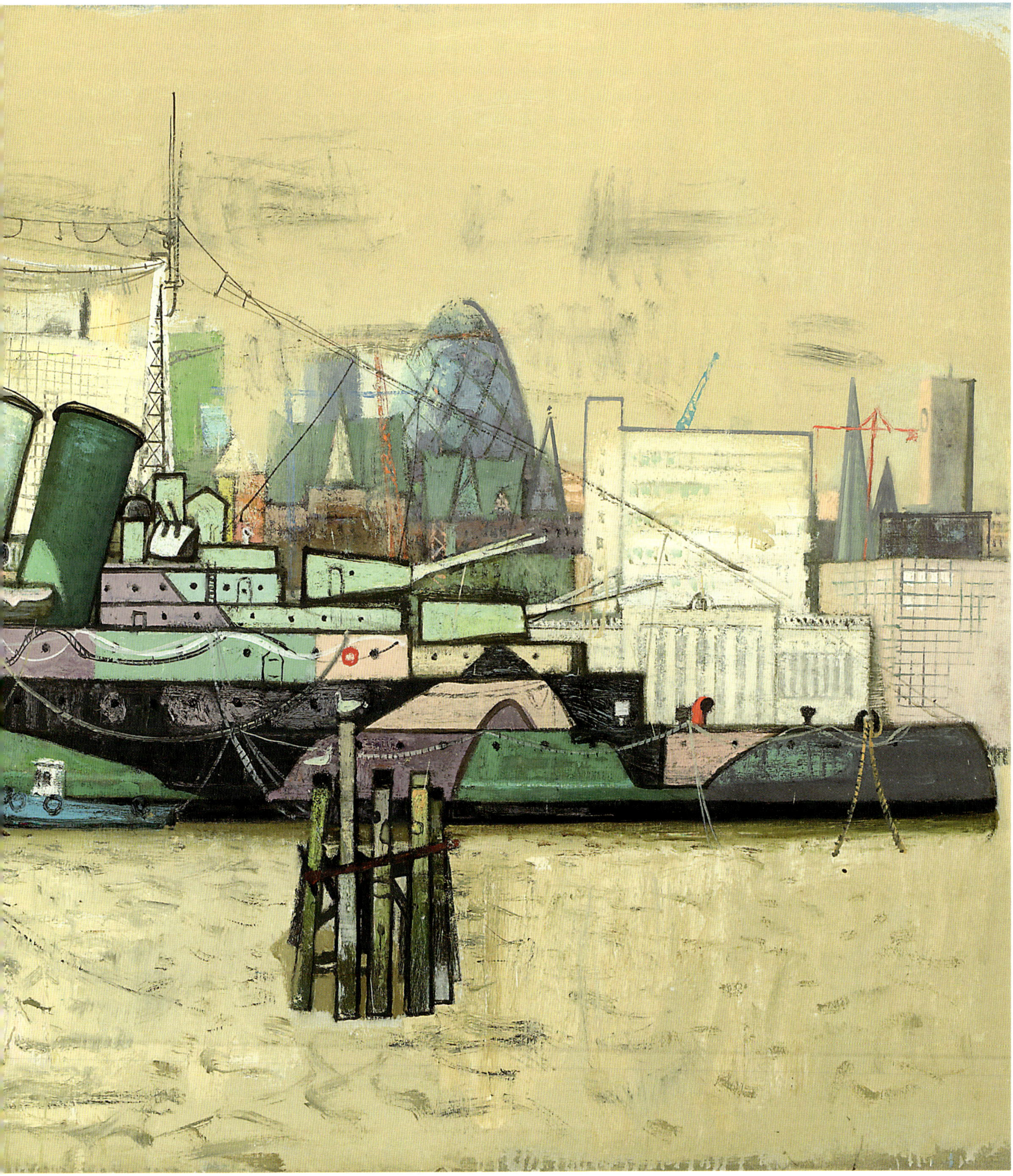

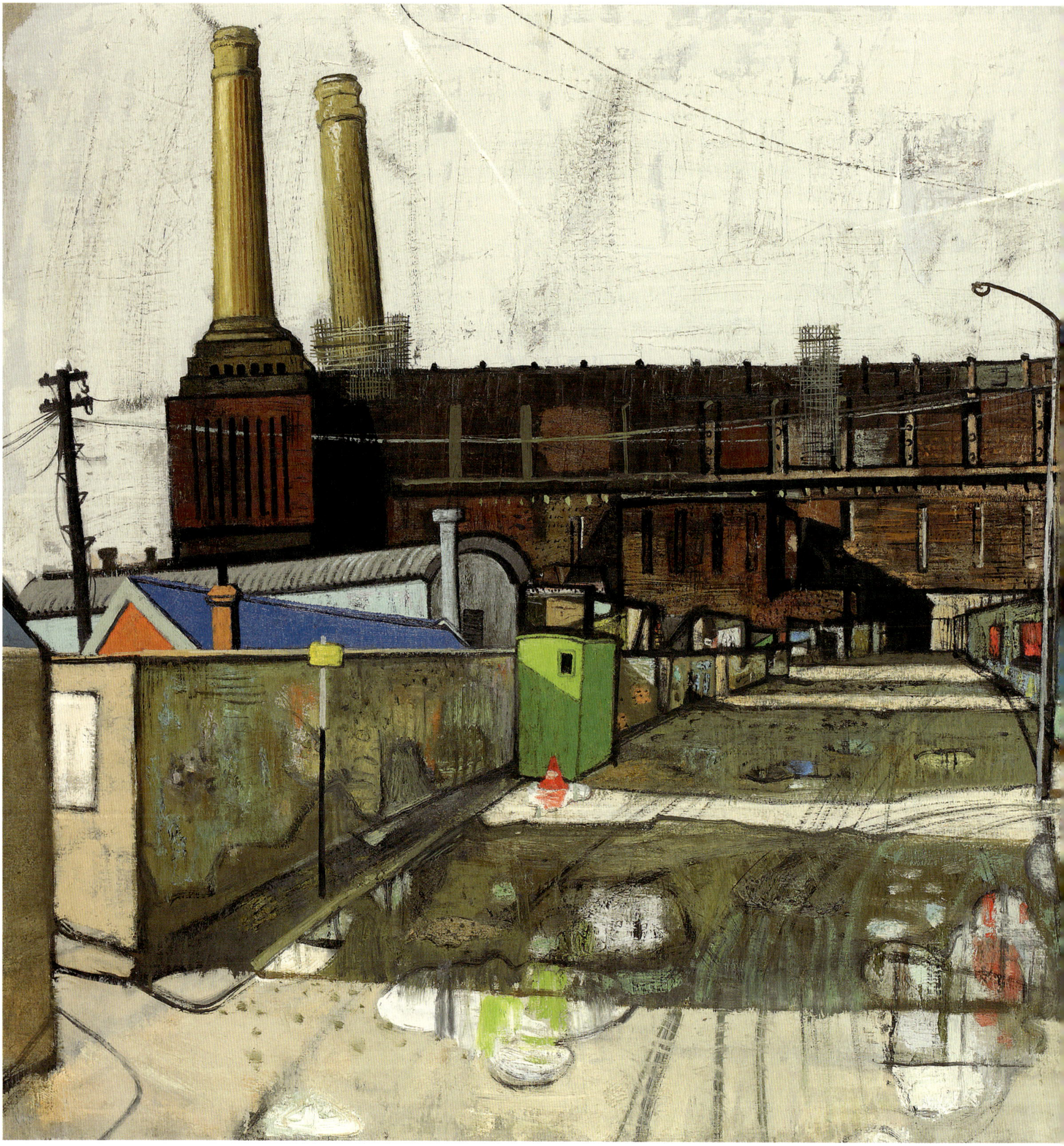

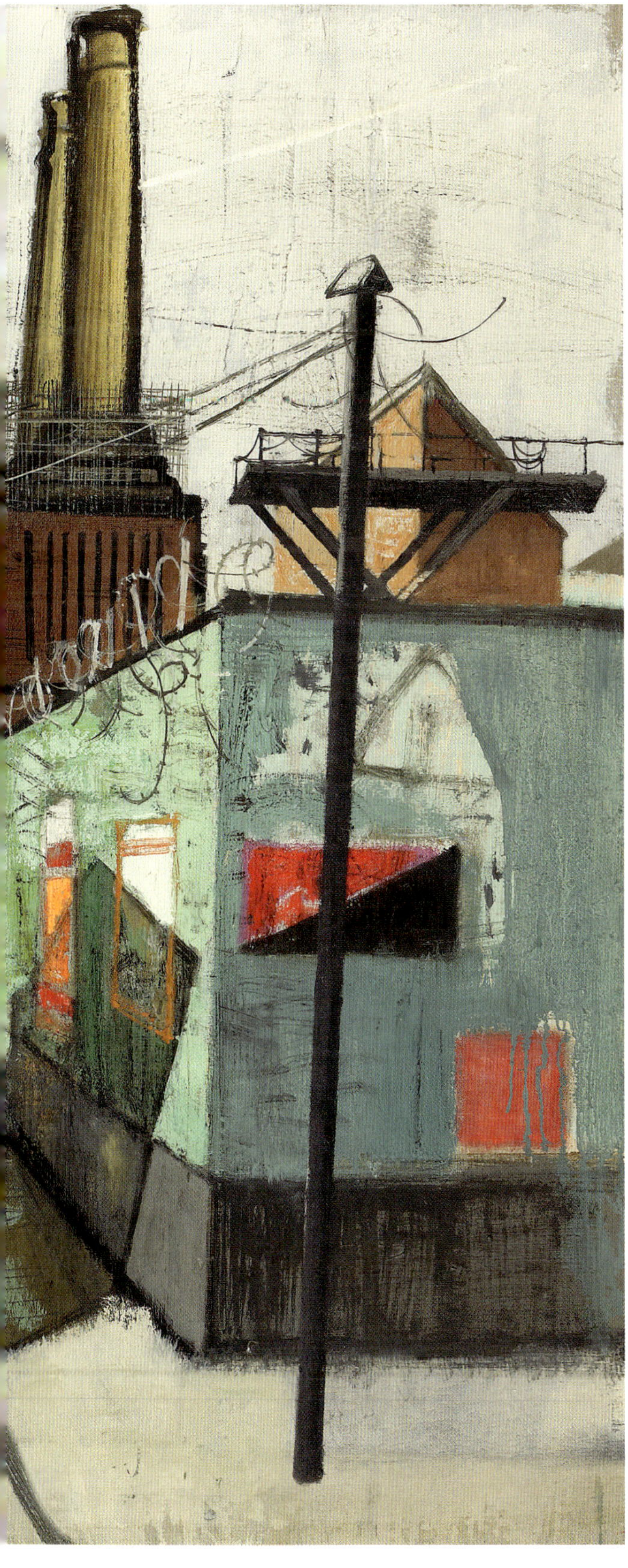

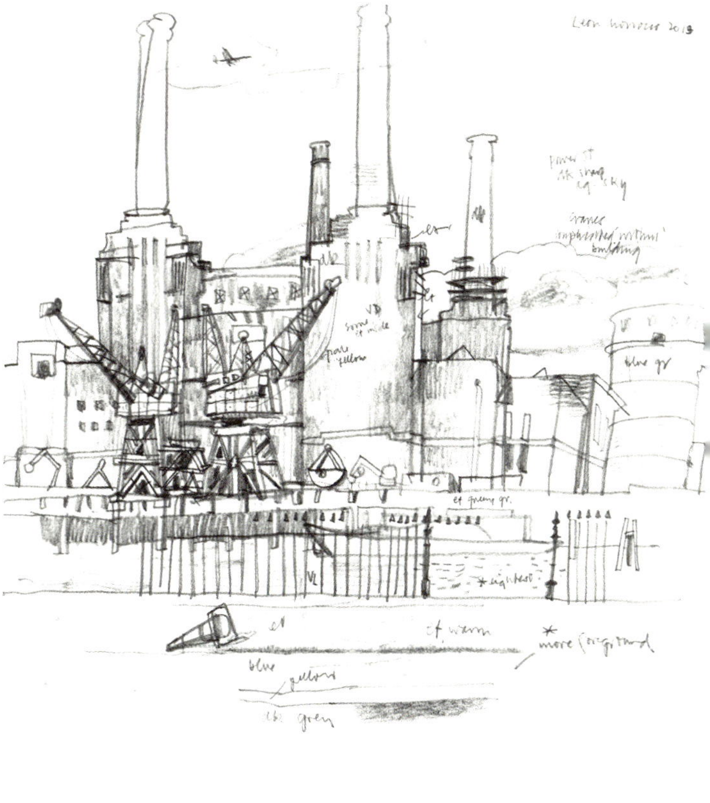

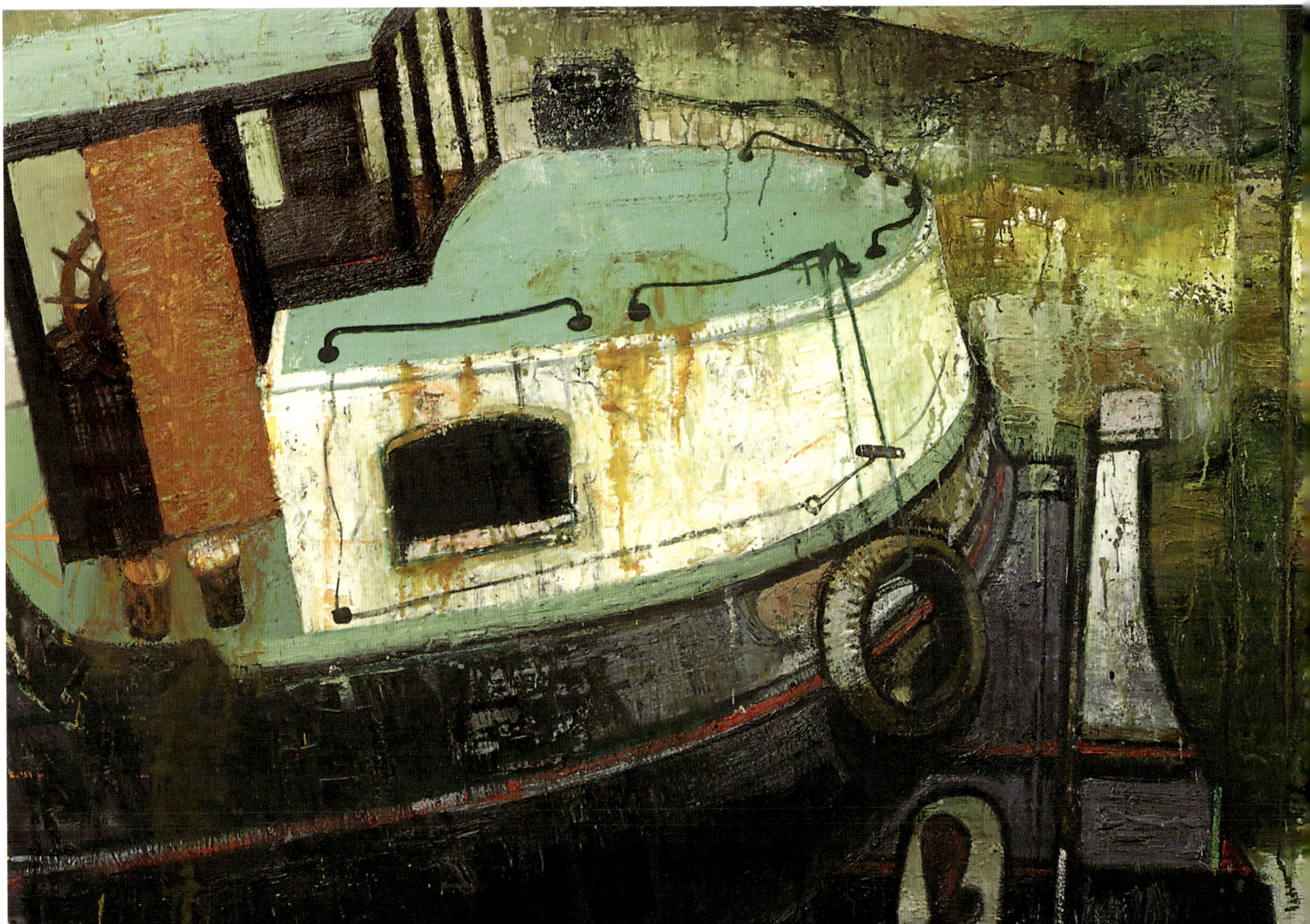

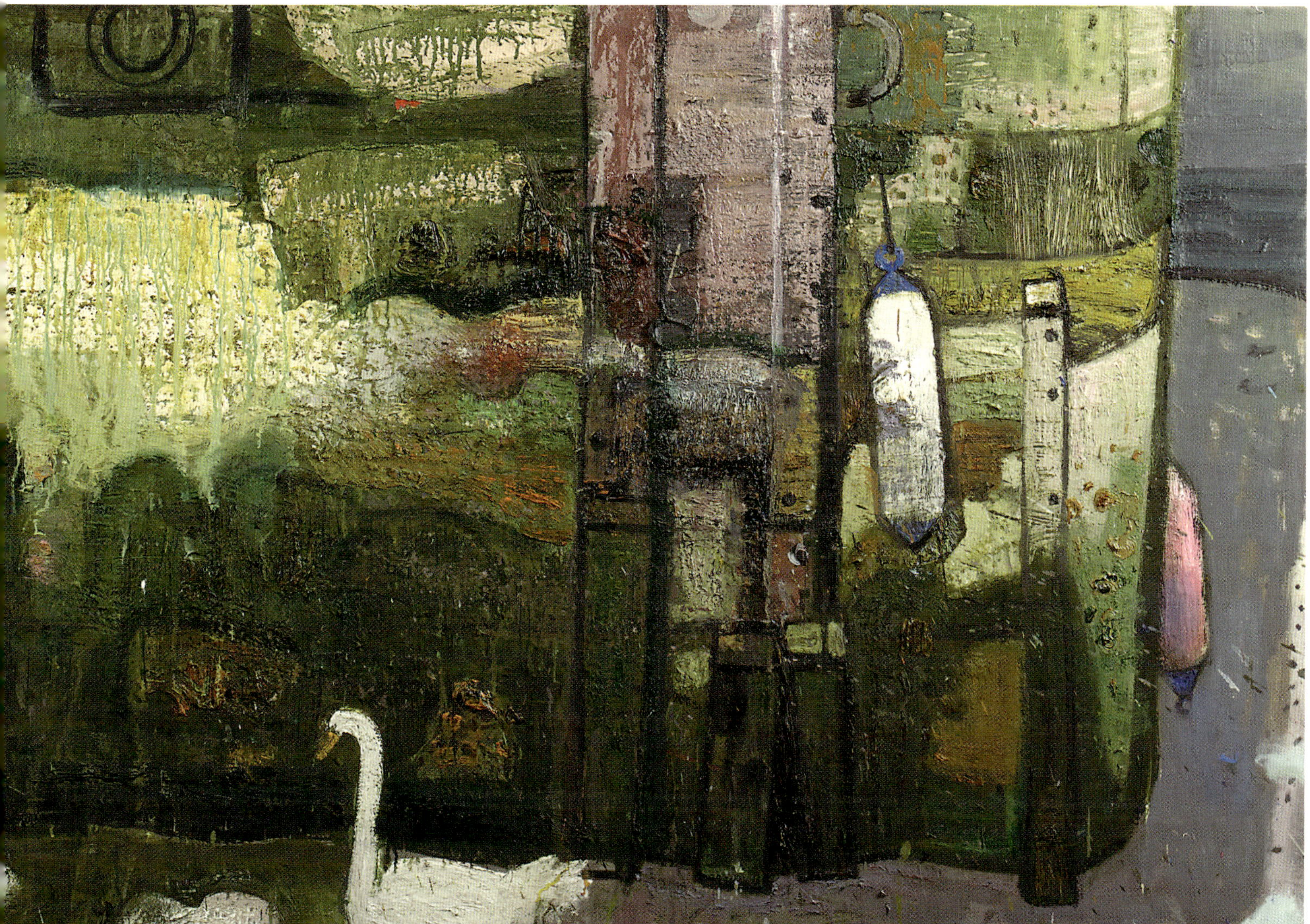

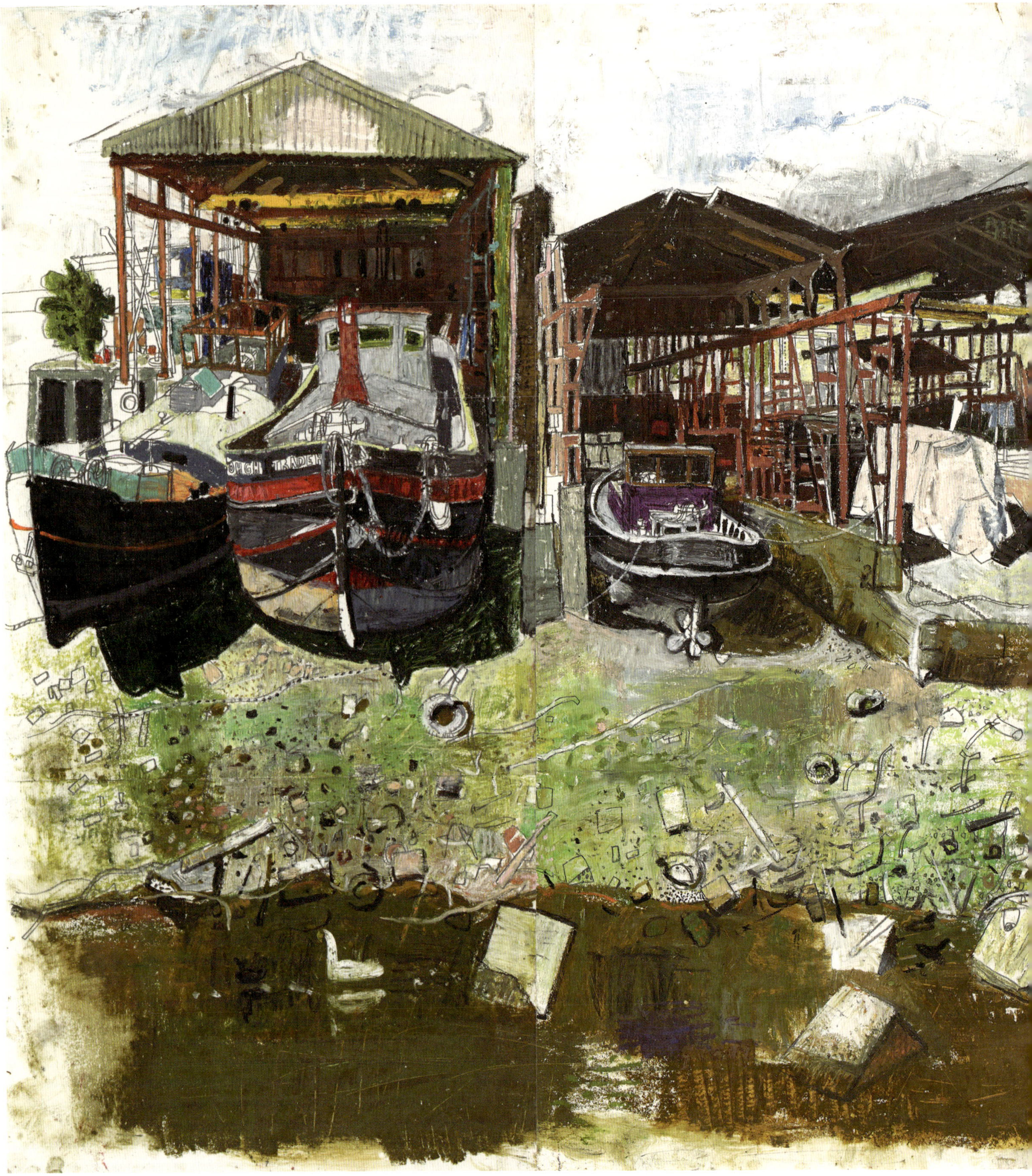

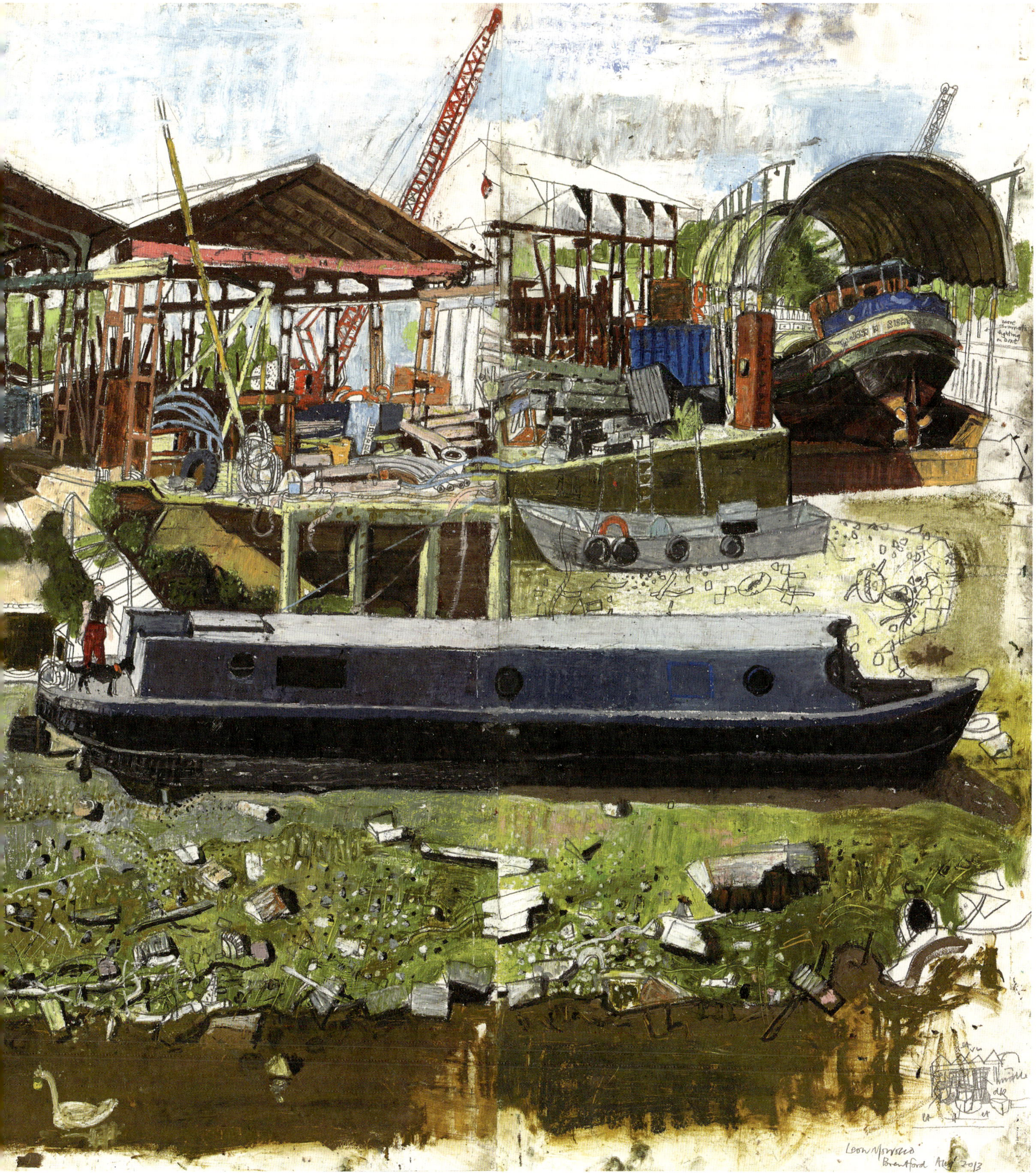

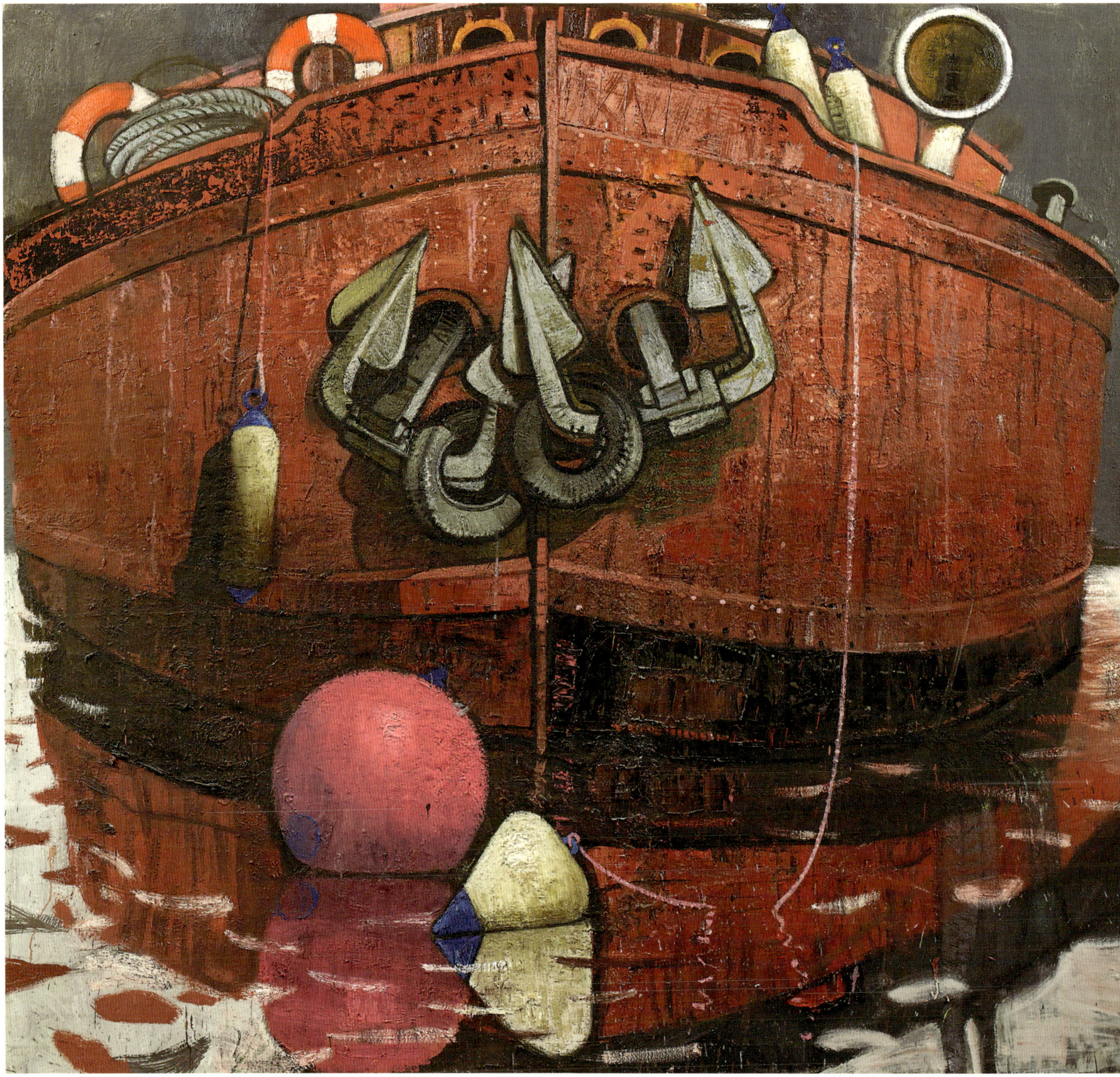

Page 34: **Composition I with Power Station 2012** oil on linen 122 x 152 cm

Page 35: **Corner of Battersea Power Station from Across the River 2012** pencil on paper 30.5 x 30.5 cm

Page 36: **Barge-stern & Mooring Wall 2015** oil on canvas 109 x 285 cm

Page 38: **Boat-Repair Sheds at Low Tide, Brentford 2012** pencil & oil pastel on paper 42 x 168 cm

Page 40: **Anchors & Floats 2015** oil on canvas 83 x 168 cm

Page 42: **Moored Narrowboat 2013** oil on linen 71 x 76 cm

Page 43: **Sterns & Floats, Grand Union Canal 2014** oil on linen 76 x 76 cm

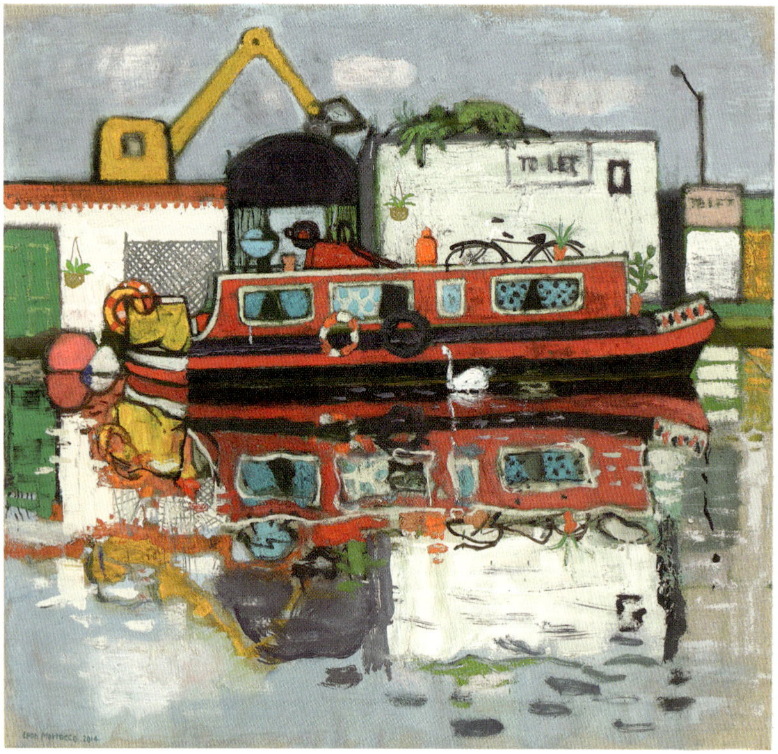
TO LET

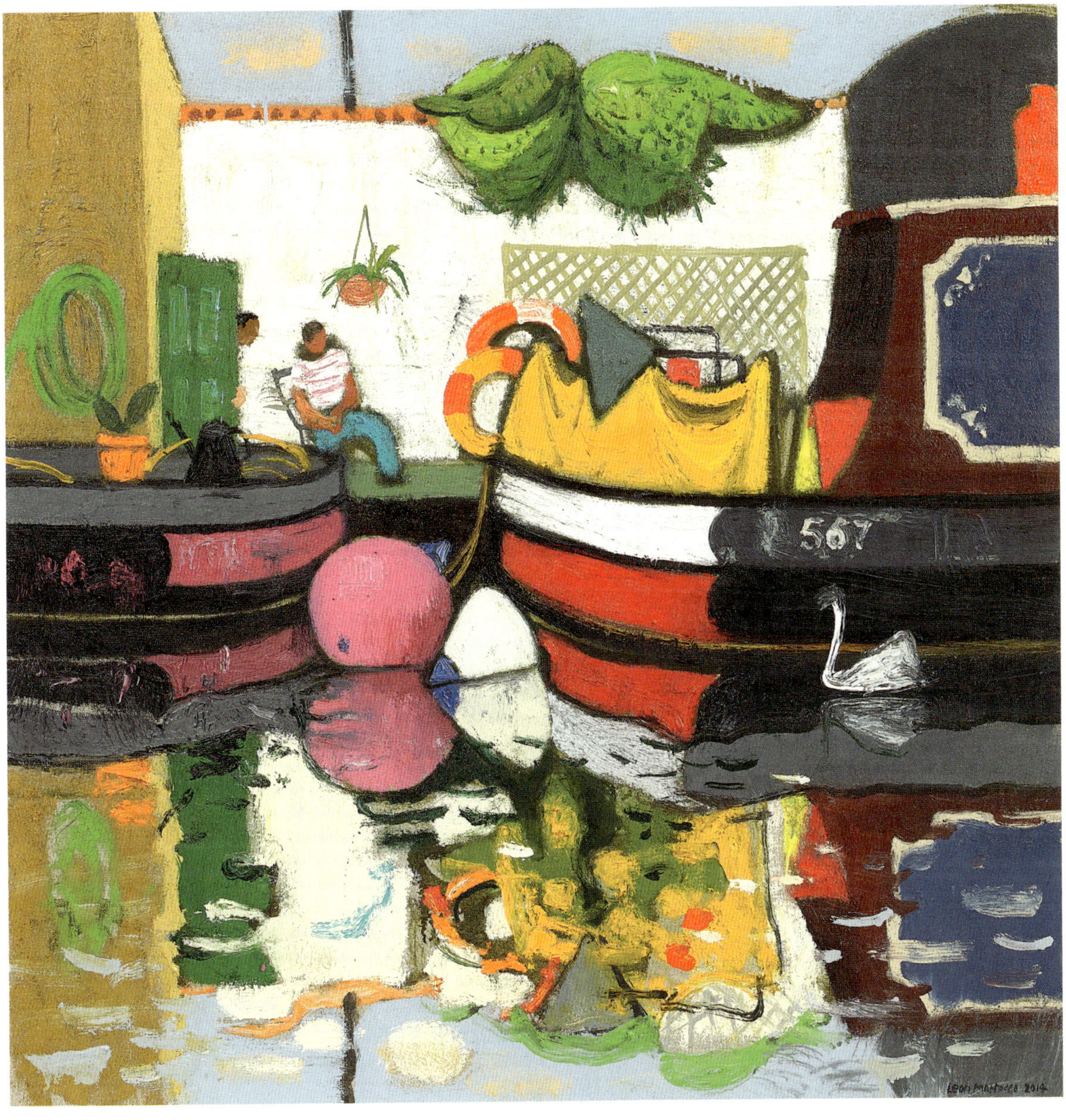
567

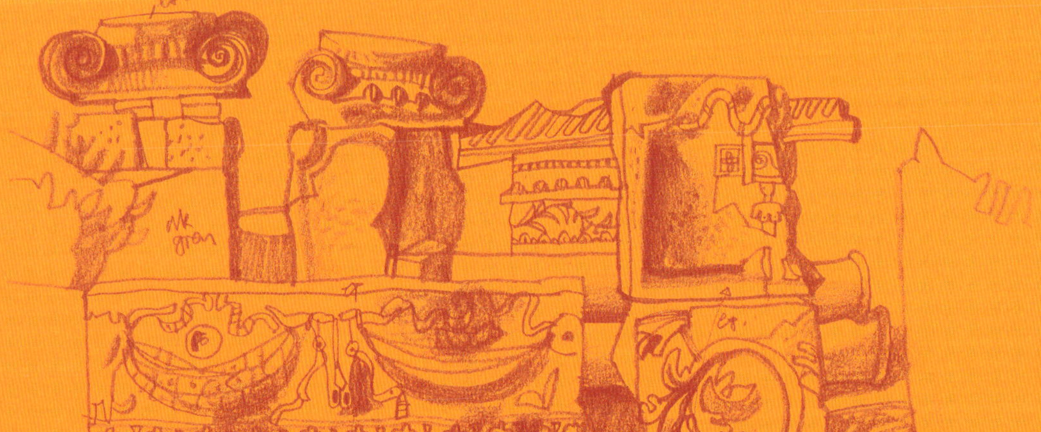

ROME

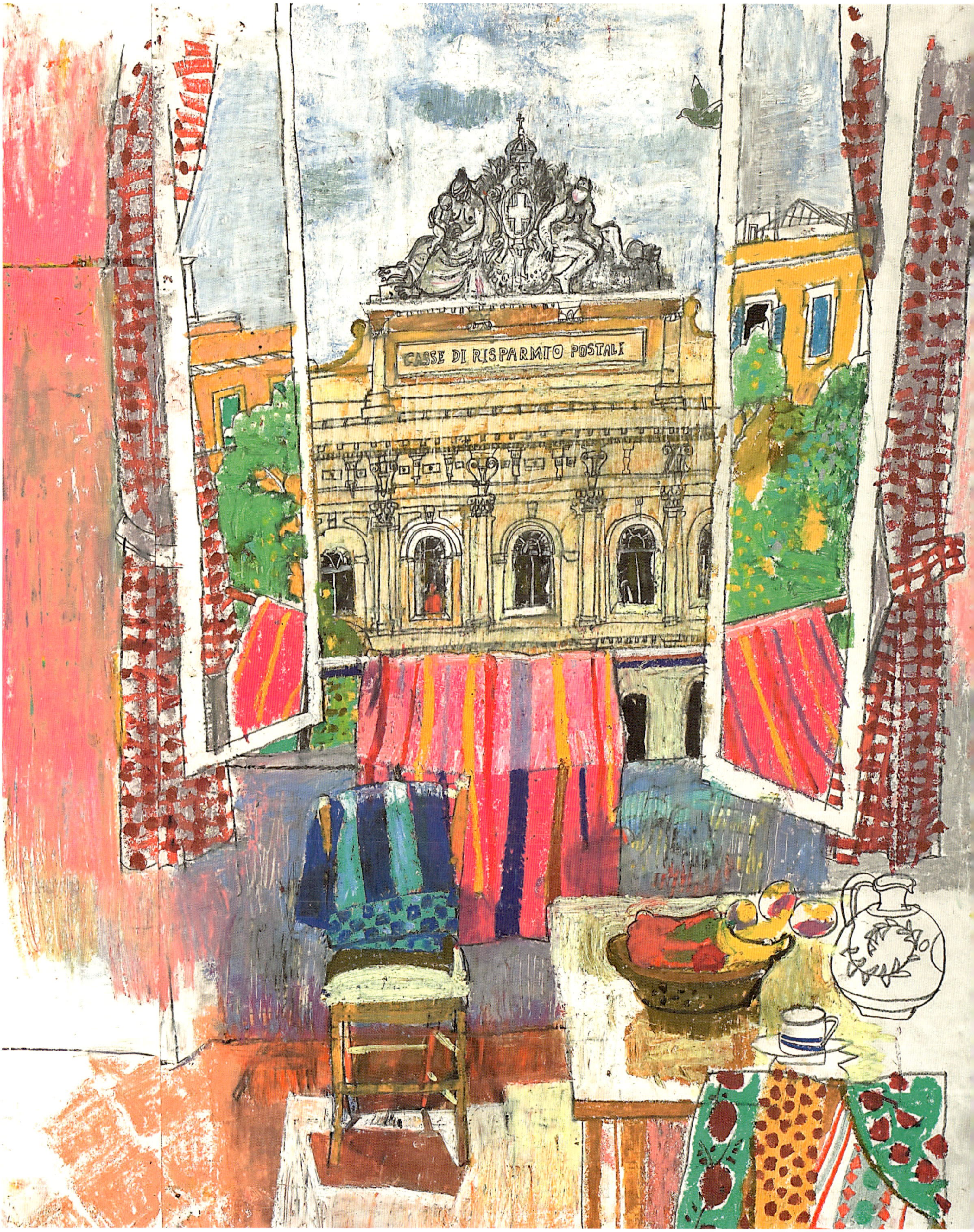
CASSE DI RISPARMIO POSTALI

ITALY HAS BEEN A CONSTANT IN MY LIFE SINCE CHILDHOOD WHEN MY father took my family from Scotland to Italy every summer. We mostly spent two months in Anticoli Corrado, a hill village east of Rome and near Tivoli. My father painted there throughout the summer and it was there in the 1950's that I made my first serious attempts at drawing.

Aged 15 and bored, I took to accompanying him into the hills on his painting trips and began to draw all the aspects of rural peasant life that still existed at that time – donkeys, mules, pigs, farm buildings, washerwomen at the river and so on. I still have some of those early efforts and they differ surprisingly little in the basic approach to my present work.

These summer sojourns from the cold northern climes of Scotland, to the heat of the Roman hills must have had an unconscious but profound affect on me as a child and adolescent, and instilled in me a love of sunlight, something I find almost impossible to exclude from my work. Of course, a love affair with Italy and the Mediterranean ensued and although living and teaching in Scotland (1966–69) at the Edinburgh College of Art and from 1969–79 at the Glasgow

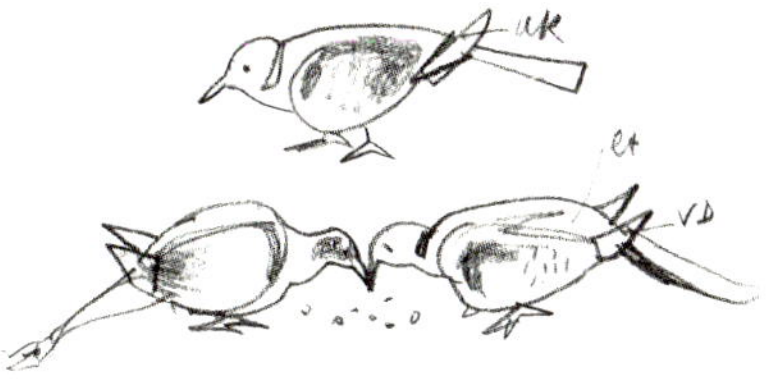

School of Art, numerous trips were made to Italy and much of my work was developed from drawings done there.

In 1980 I was offered and accepted the position of Head of Fine Art at an art school in Melbourne, Australia which meant a 12 year gap in my trips to the Mediterranean. On returning to the UK in 1992 I was once again drawn to Italy and the Med as a source for painting ideas and I also spent some time in Greece.

Renting an apartment in Antibes (1997–2000) led to three years work there as well as in Nice, Juan-les-Pins, Mewton and into Italy – Ventimiglia and Bordighera. I also spent time drawing in Corsica. The resulting work was shown in London at the John Martin Gallery and at the Open Eye Gallery, Edinburgh. By the year 2000 I was desperate to obtain a more permanent base in Italy and took an apartment/studio in Rome. It was a return to the city with which I had become familiar on those early family summers in the 1950s.

This was both an exciting and productive period. I immersed myself in drawing the remains of ancient Rome alongside a modern Rome, and the relationship between its history and its people. I soon built up a large group of drawings which constituted a kind of portrait of the city and from which I was able to develop a series of large paintings, culminating in the largest – some 18 x 7 feet – of the Colosseum.

During this period I was able to explore other parts of Italy and found lots to interest me in Terracina, Naples and Sicily.

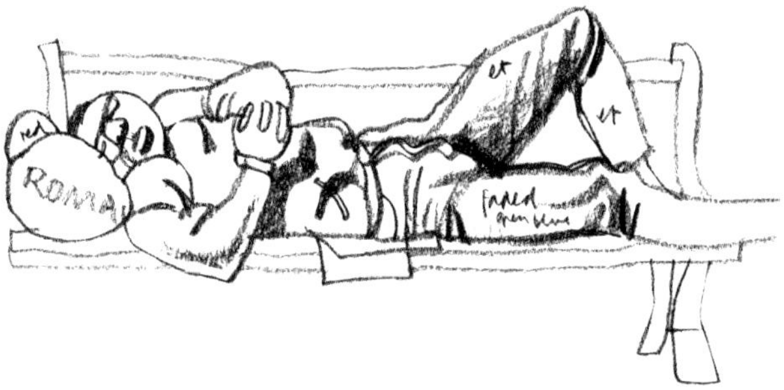

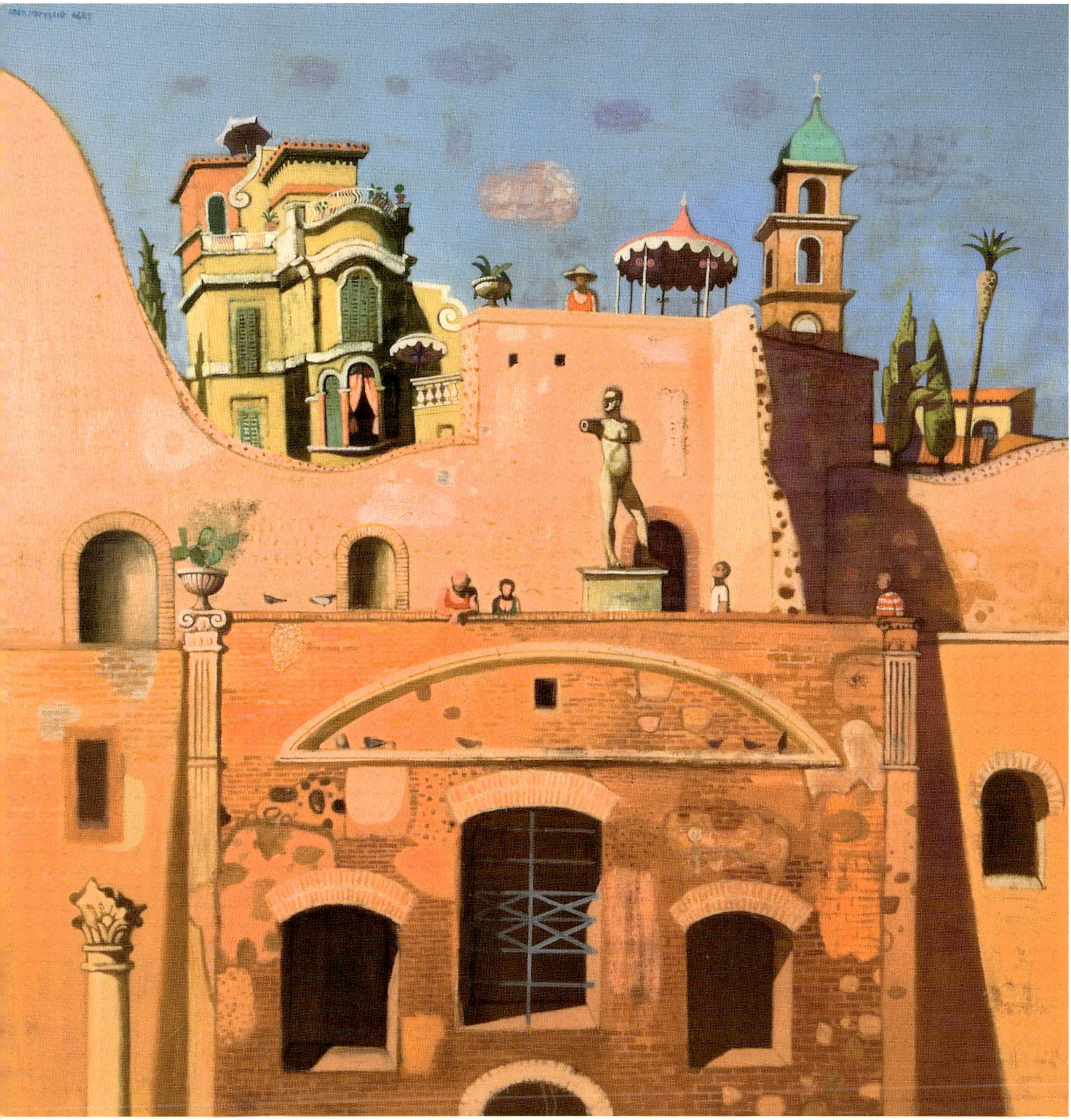

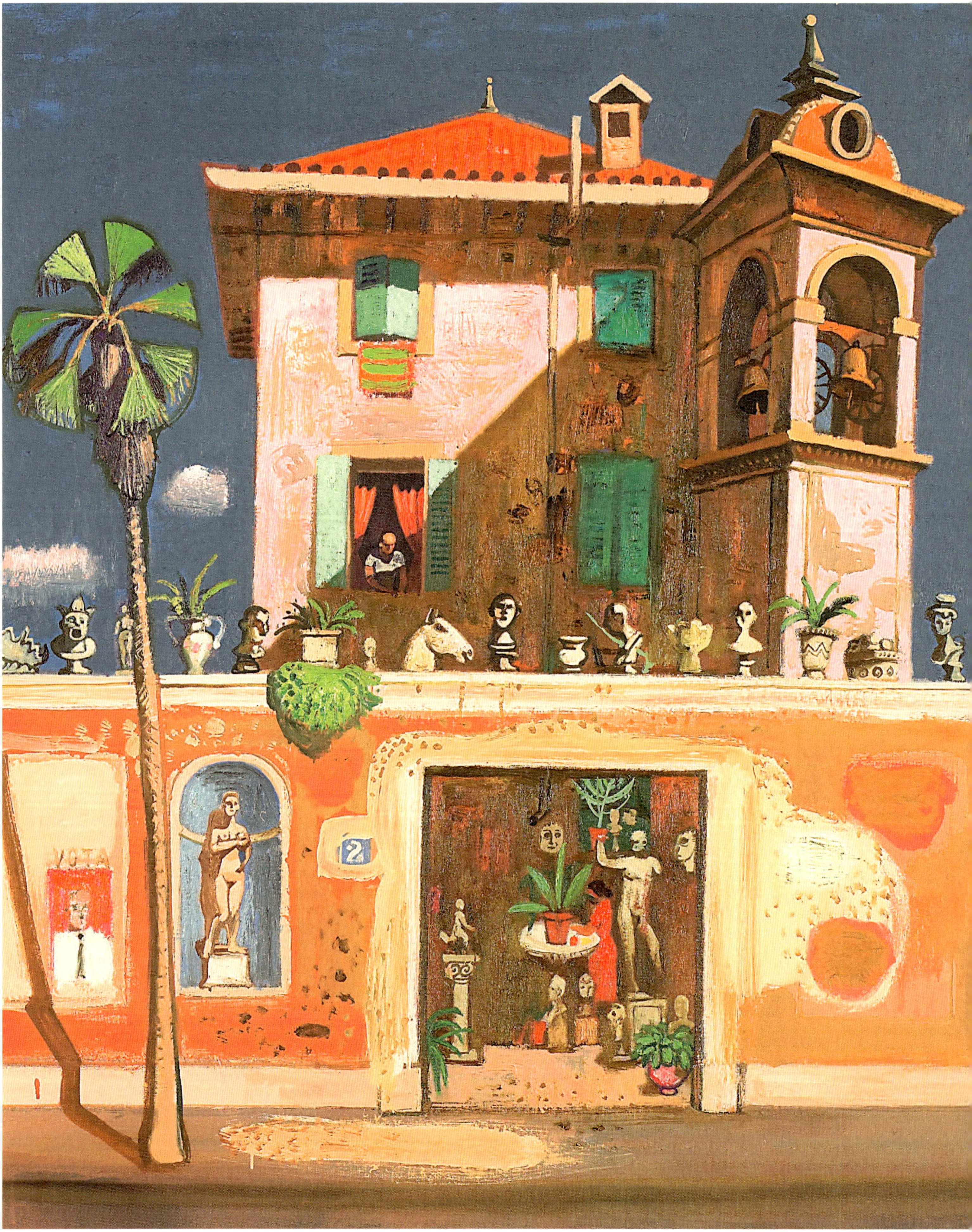
VOTA
2

Page 46: **View From the Kitchen Window, Piazza Dante, Rome 2001** pencil & oil pastel on paper 66 x 56 cm
Page 49: **At the Exhibition 2003** oil on canvas 152 x 183 cm
Page 50: **Sculptor's House 2005** oil on canvas 106.5 x 101.5 cm
Page: 52 **Ristorante Ulpia Sketch with Columns 2005** pencil on paper 25.5 x 25.5 cm
Page 53: **The Newsreader, Piazza Farnese 2003** oil on board 60 x 122 cm

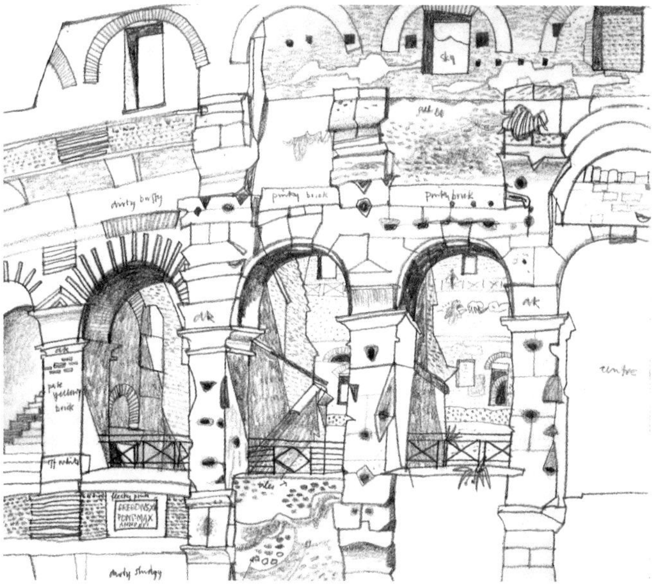

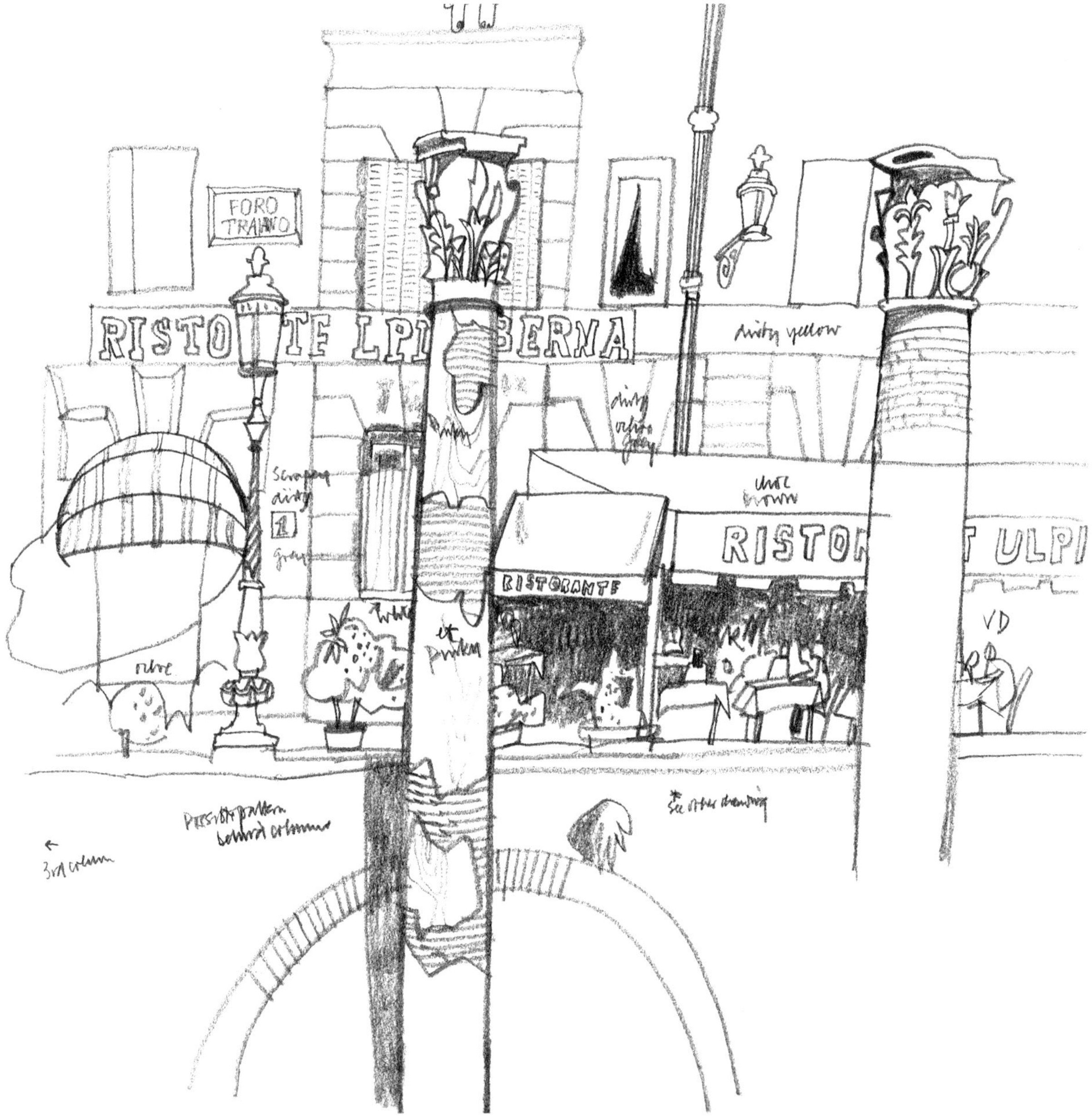
FORO
TRAIANO
RISTO TE LPI BERNA
dirty yellow
RISTOR
T ULPI
RISTORANTE
VD
see other drawing
3rd column

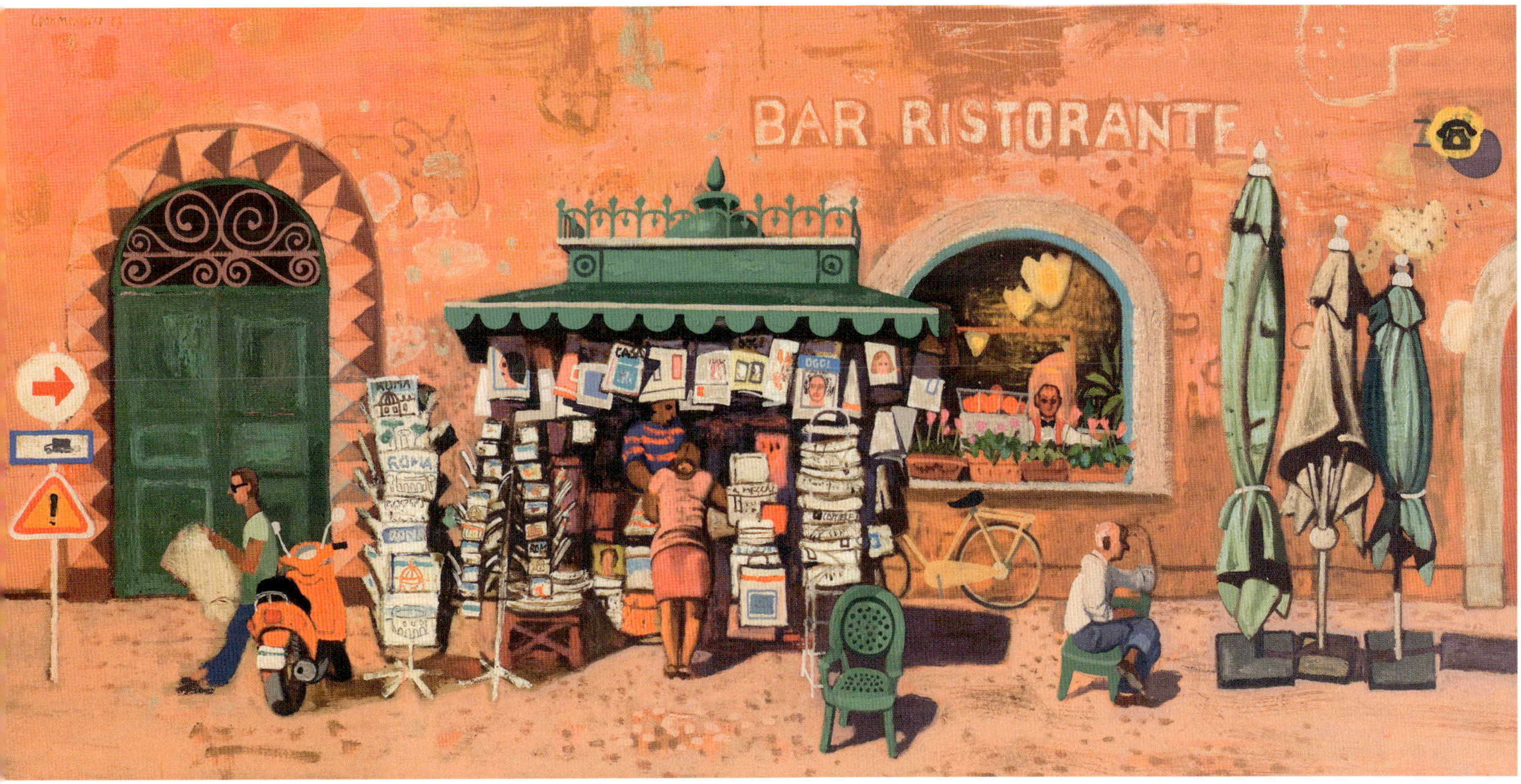
BAR RISTORANTE

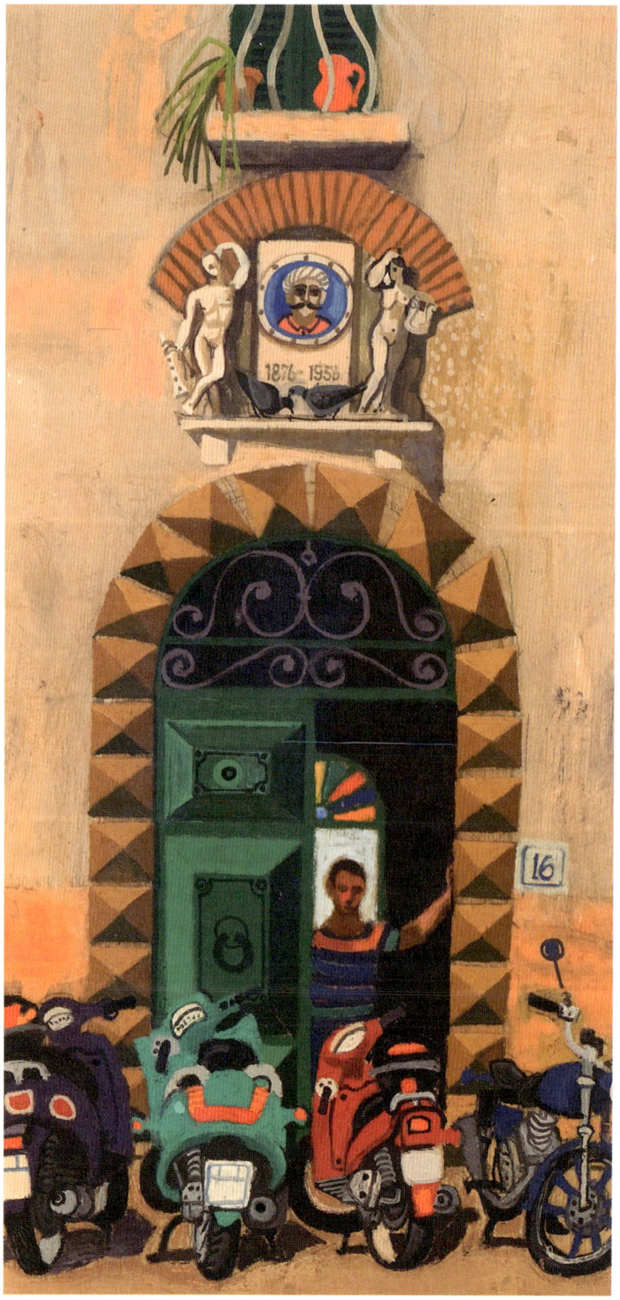
1876 - 1956
16

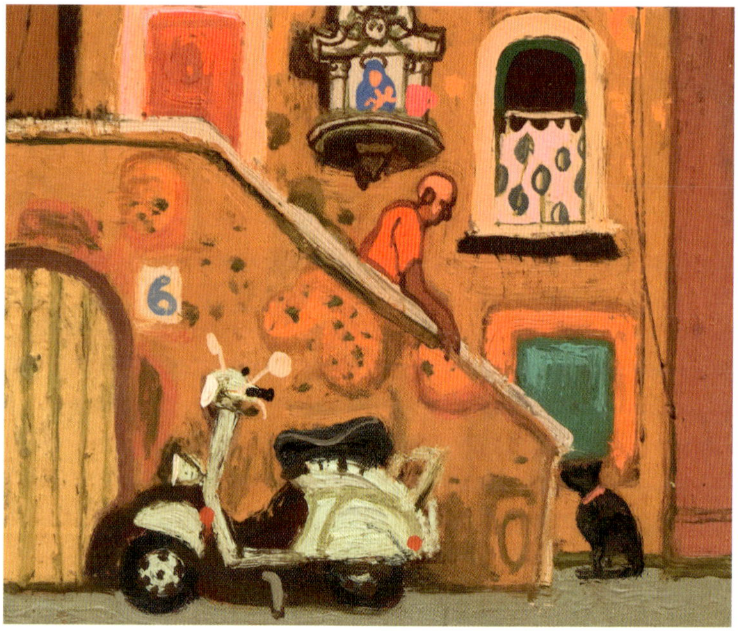
6

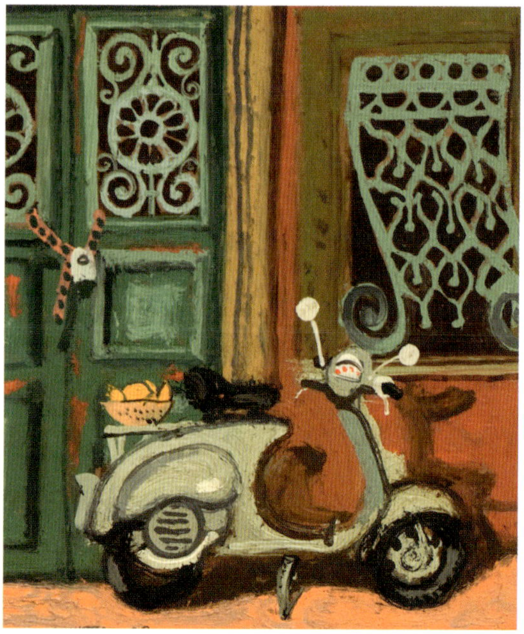

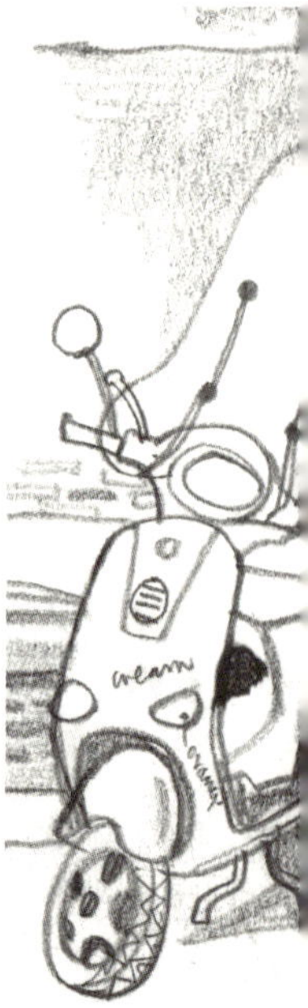

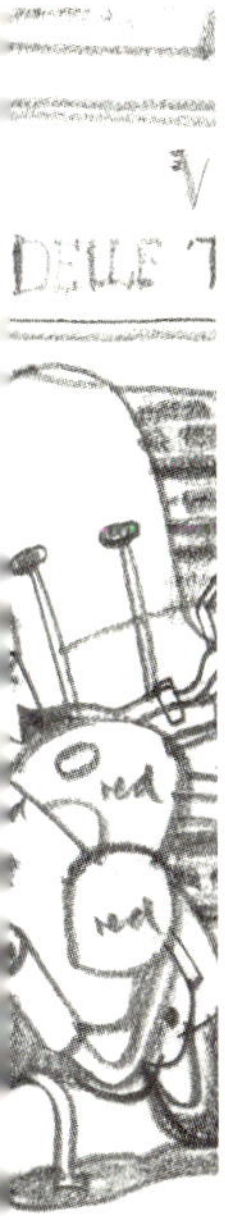

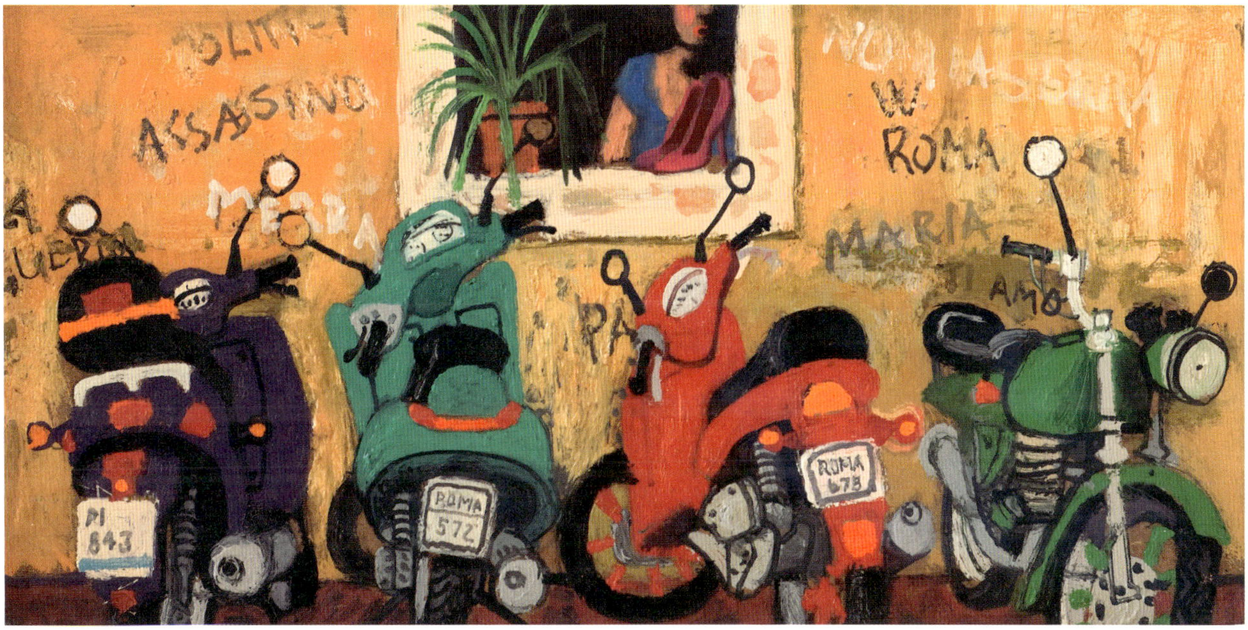
ASSASSINO
ROMA
MARIA
PI 843
ROMA 572

ROMA 690

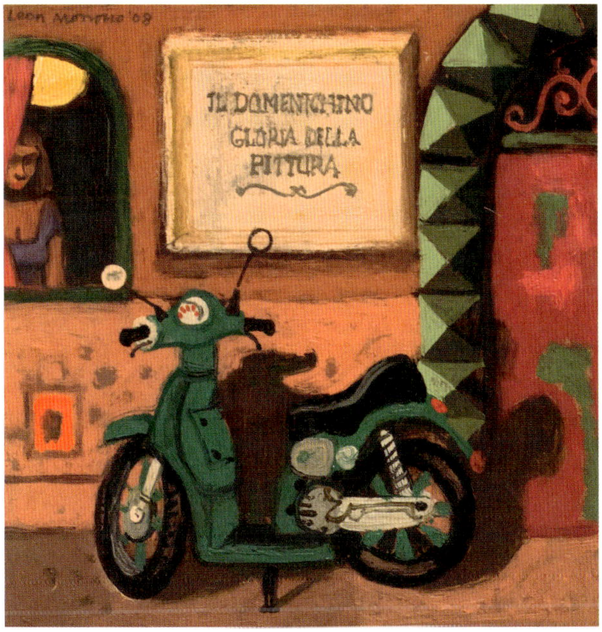
IL DOMENICHINO
GLORIA DELLA
PITTURA

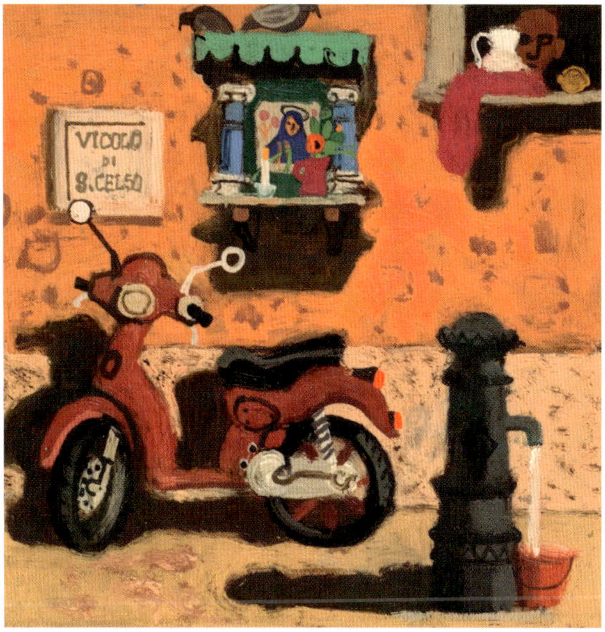
VICOLO
DI
S.CELSO

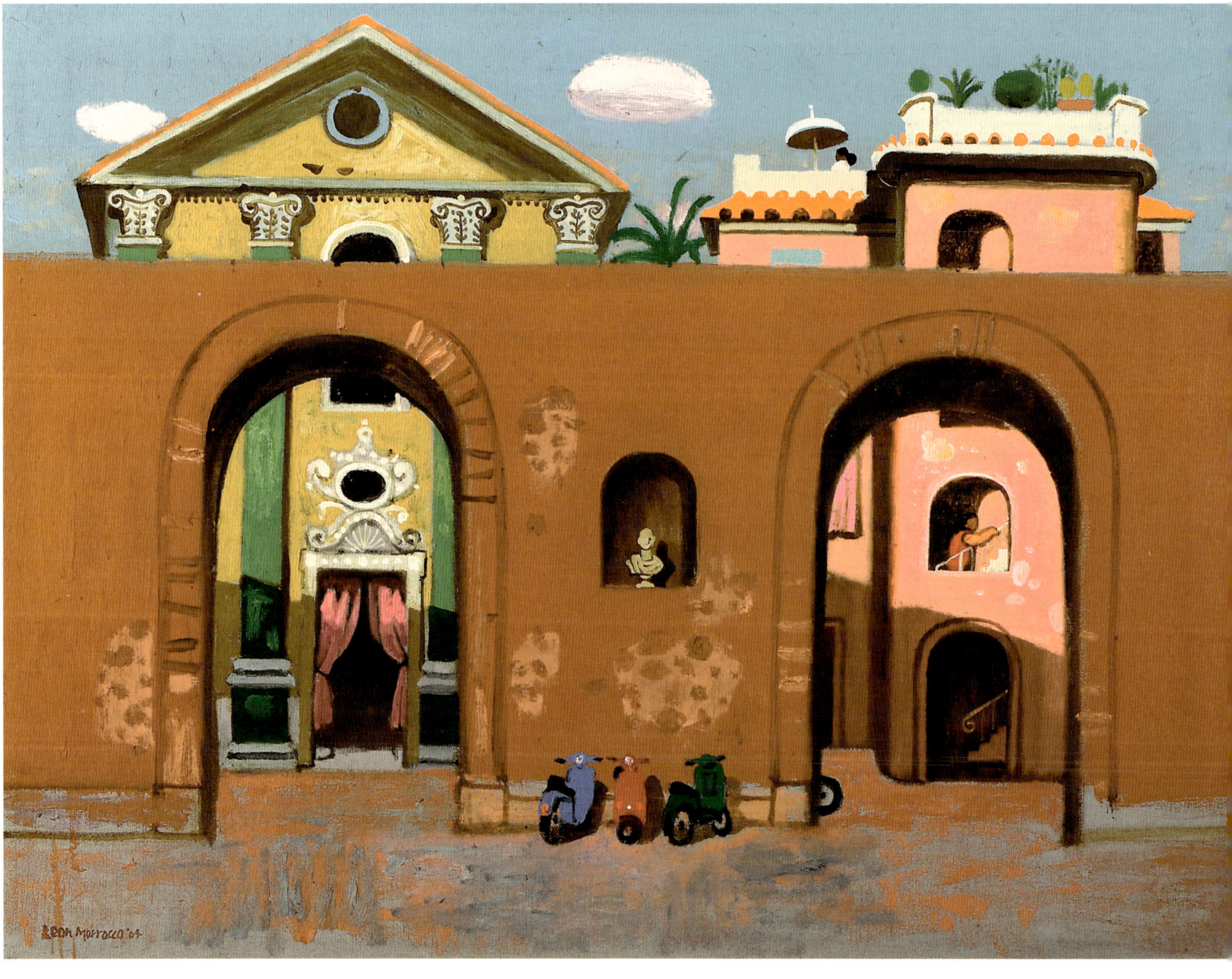
Leon Morrocco '04

Page 54 *clockwise from left*:
Numero Sedici 2008 oil on canvas 20 x 20 cm
Reluctant Dog Walker 2008 oil on canvas 20 x 20 cm
Return to the Eternal City 2008 oil on canvas 18 x 46 cm
Roadside Shrine 2008 oil on canvas 20 x 20 cm
Casa del Domenichino 2008 oil on canvas 20 x 20 cm
No Visitors 2008 oil on canvas 20 x 20 cm
Page 56: Two Archways – Three Scooters 2005 oil on canvas 61 x 81 cm
Page 59: Resting Archaelogist & Ristorante Ulpia 2005 oil on canvas 96.5 x 91.5 cm

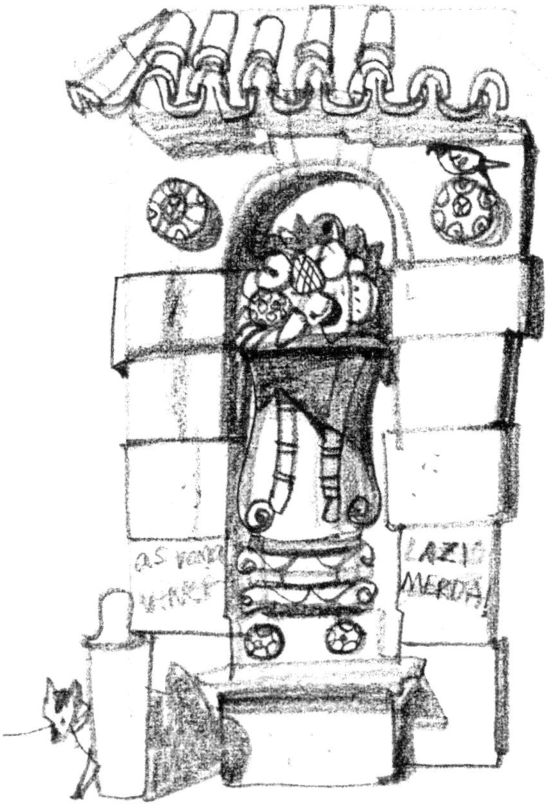

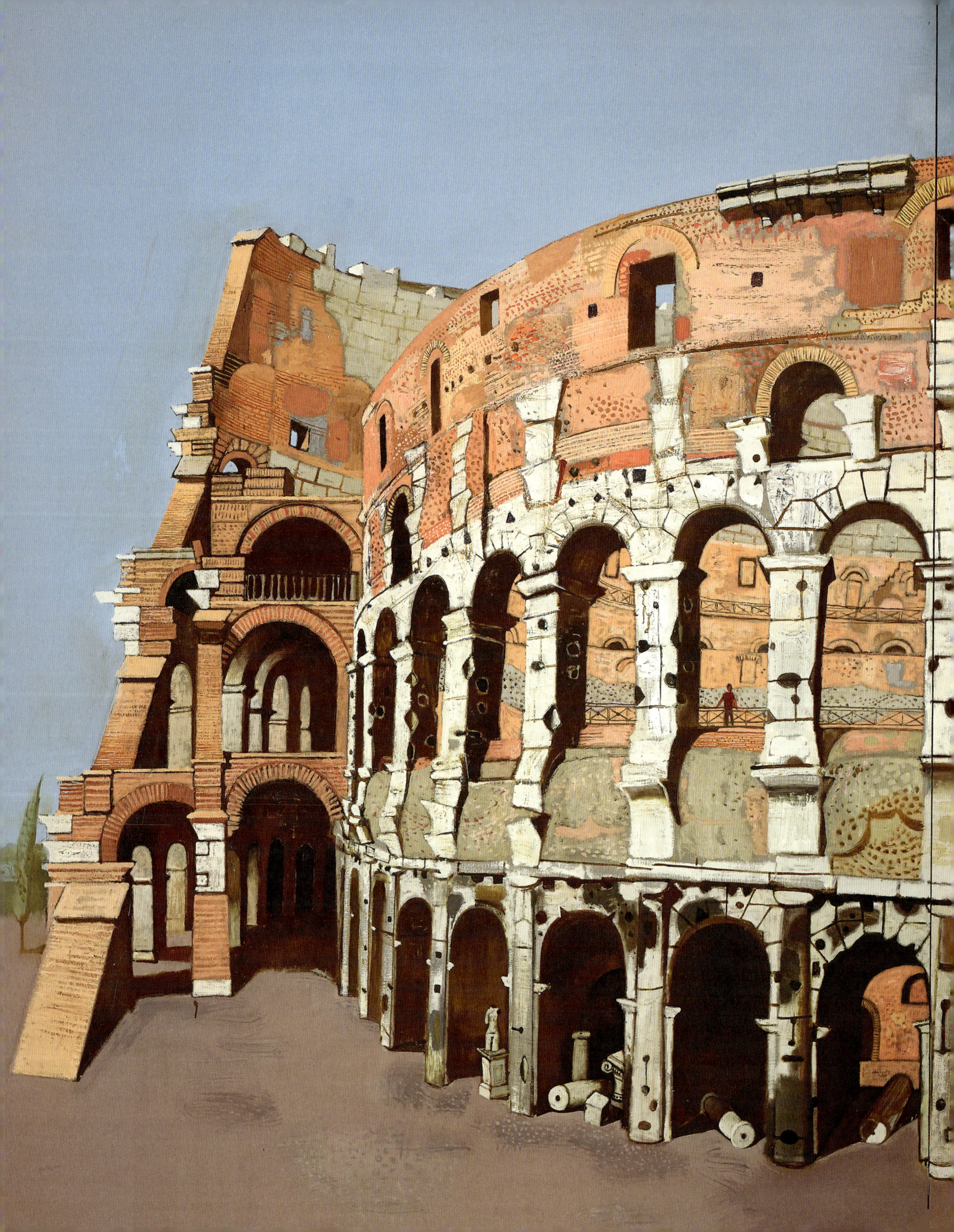

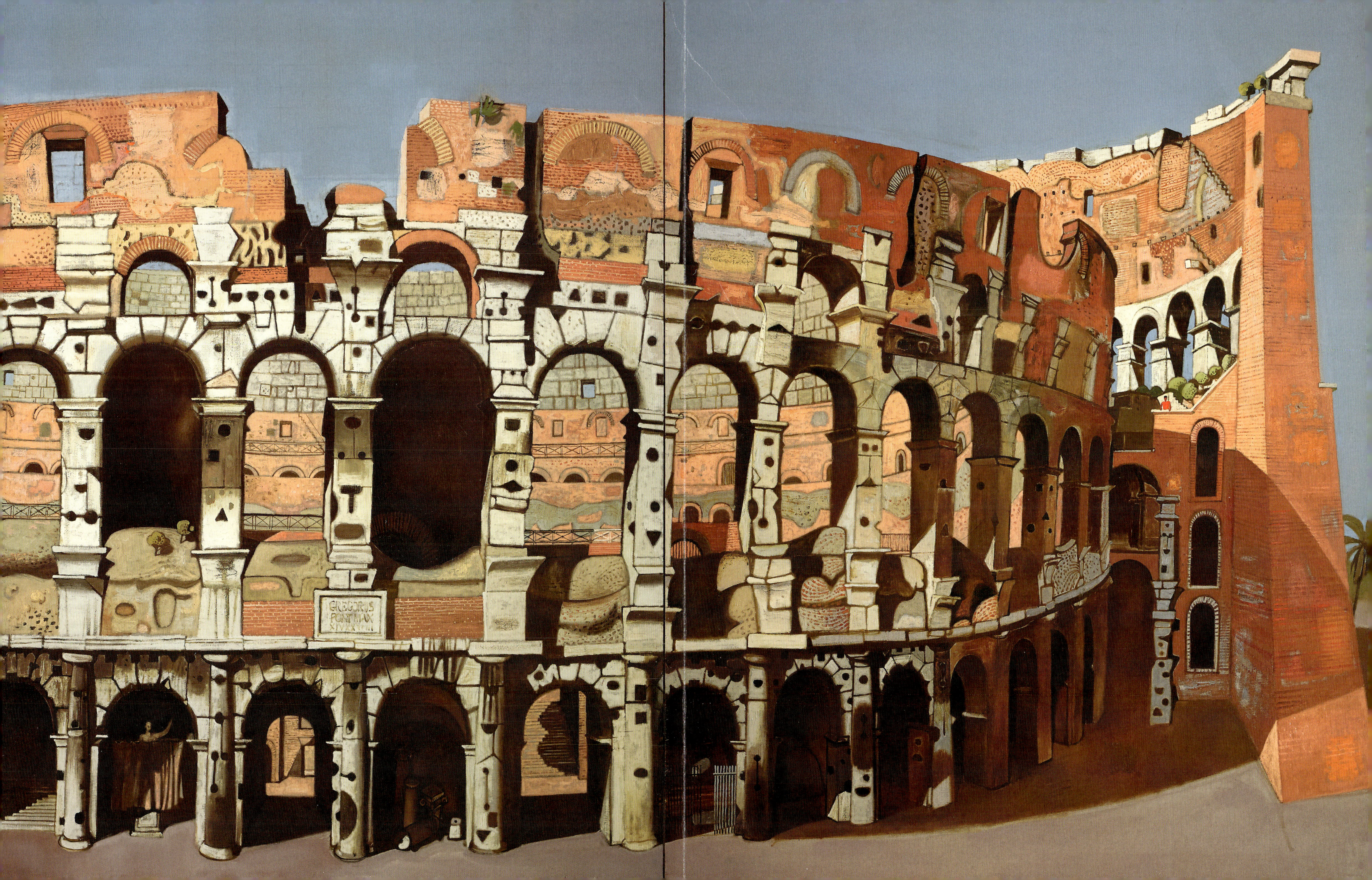
GREGORIUS
PONT MAX

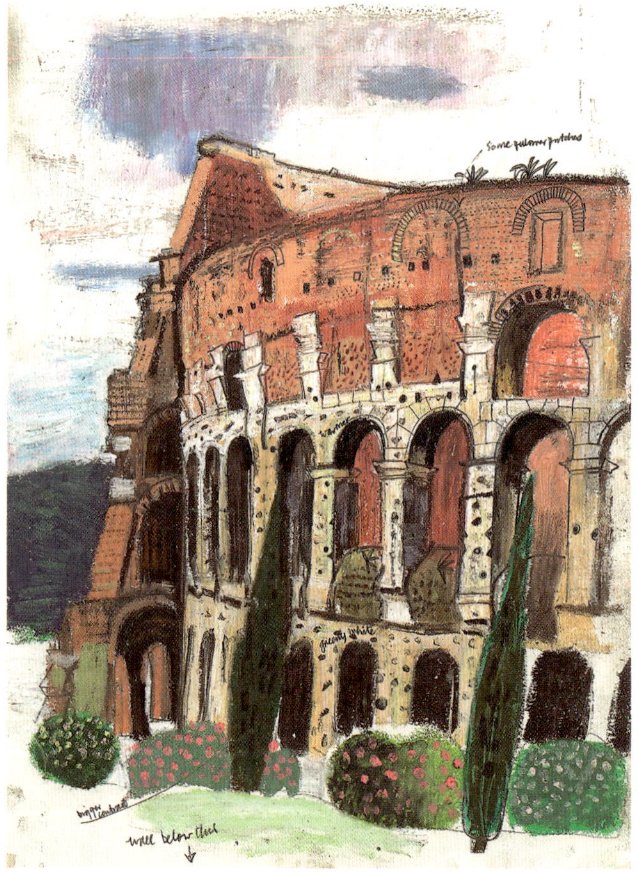
Some yellower patches
warmer
greeny white
bigger contrast
wall below this

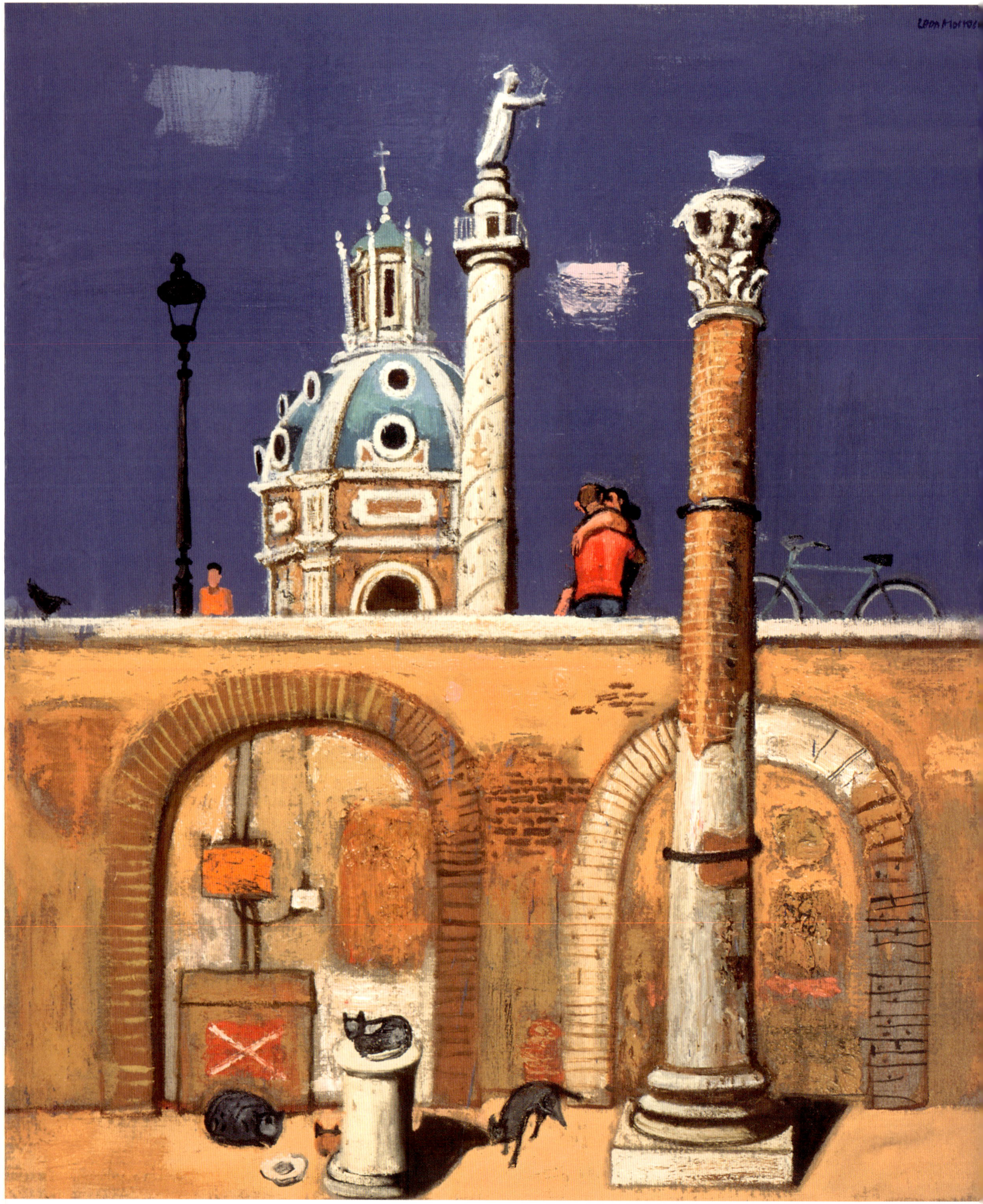

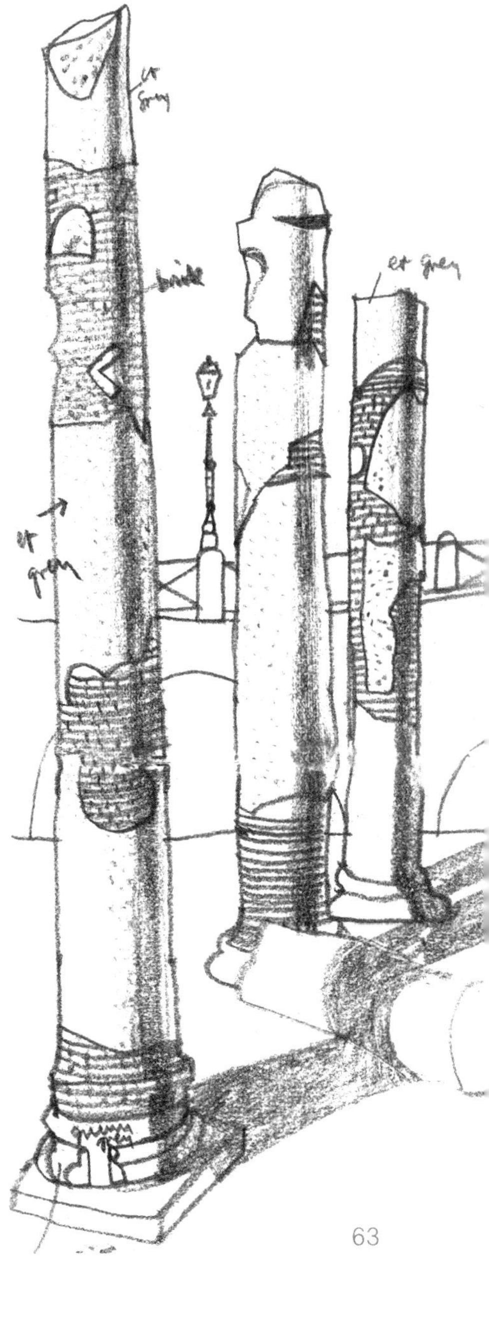
brick

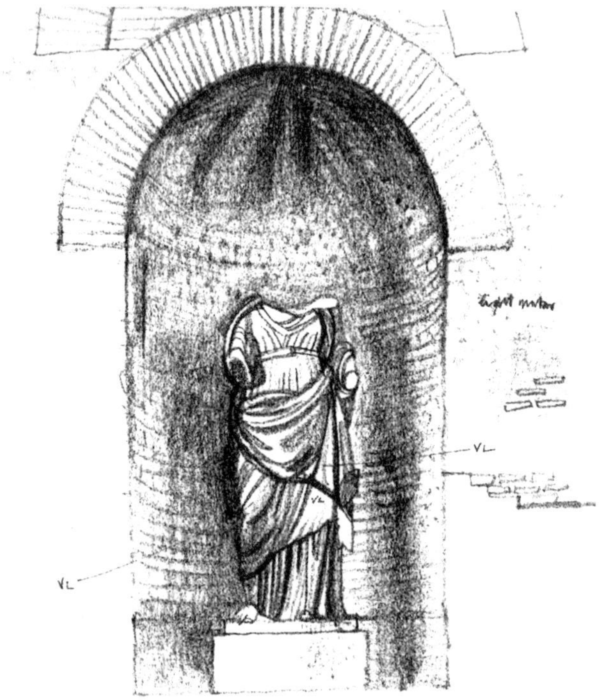
light mortar
VL
VL
VL

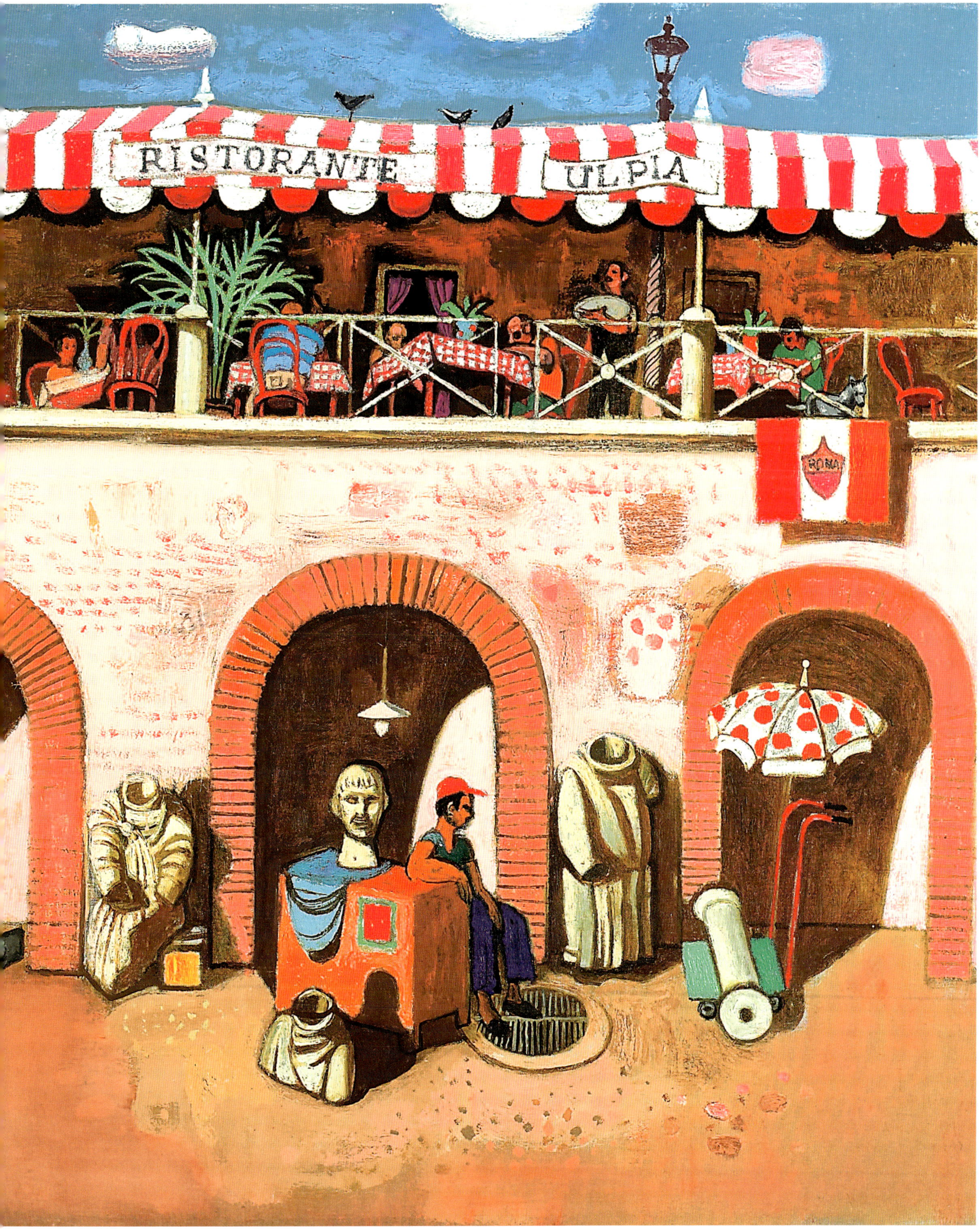

RISTORANTE
ULPIA
ROMA

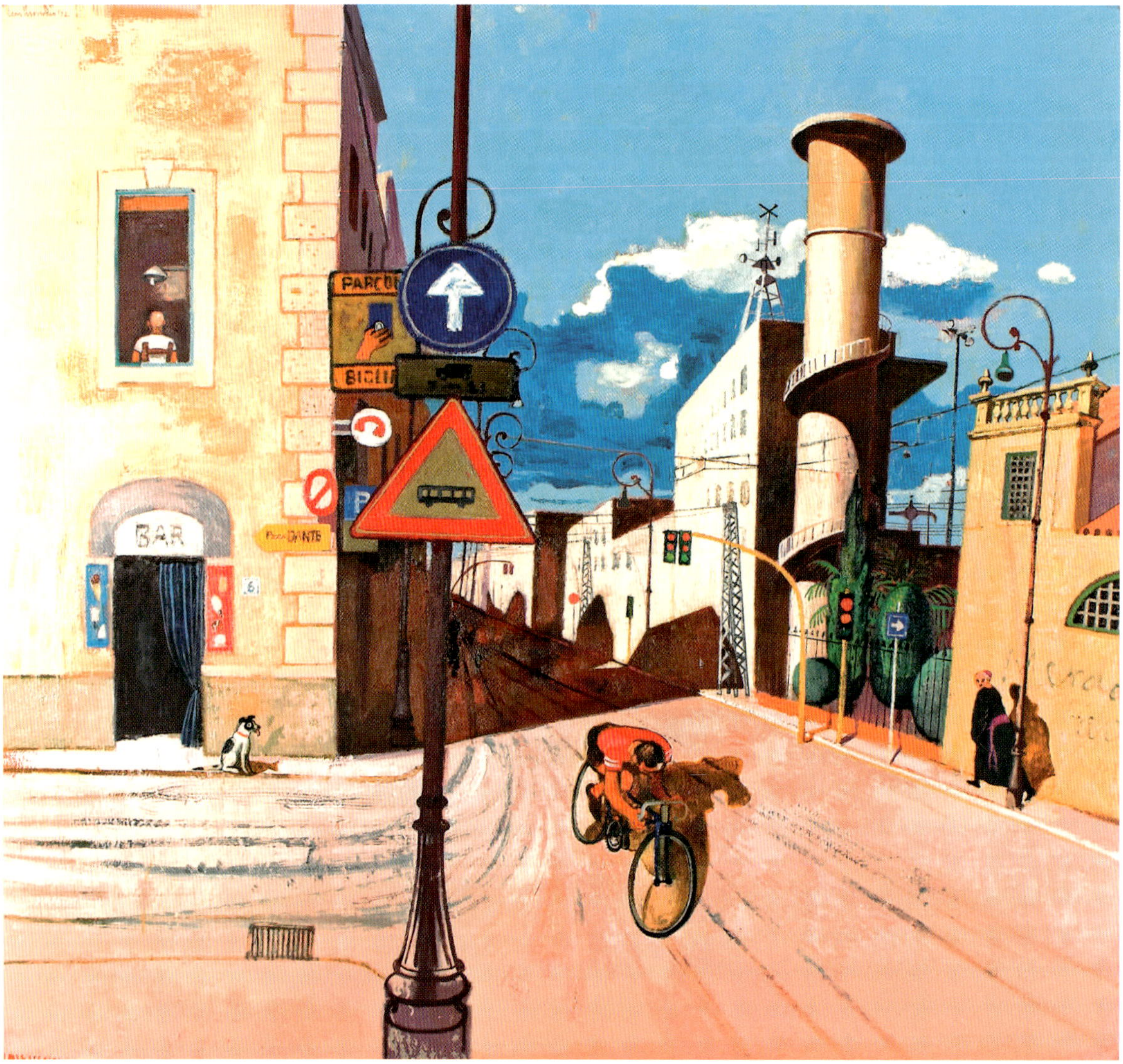
BAR

Page 60: **The Colosseum 2003** oil on canvas 213.5 x 548.5 cm
Page 63: **Section of the Colosseum 2005** pencil & oil pastel 41 x 29 cm
Page 64: **Love in the Forum 2003** oil on canvas 81 x 76.5 cm
Page 66: **The Cyclist, Via Giolitti 2003** oil on canvas 152.5 x 167.5 cm
Page 69: **Motorini Below a High Wall 2004** oil on canvas 101.5 x 122 cm

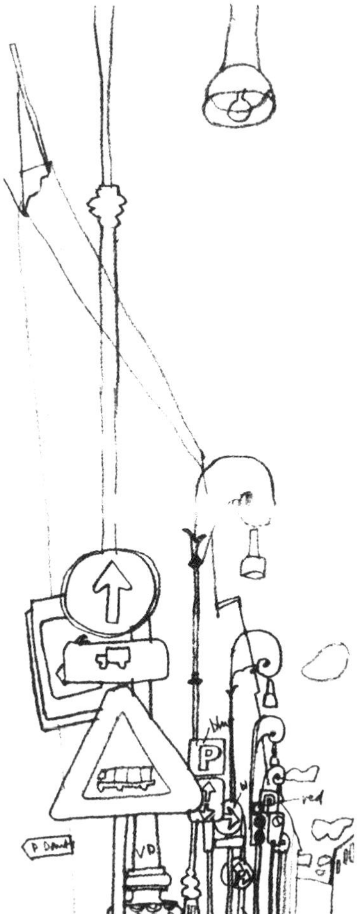

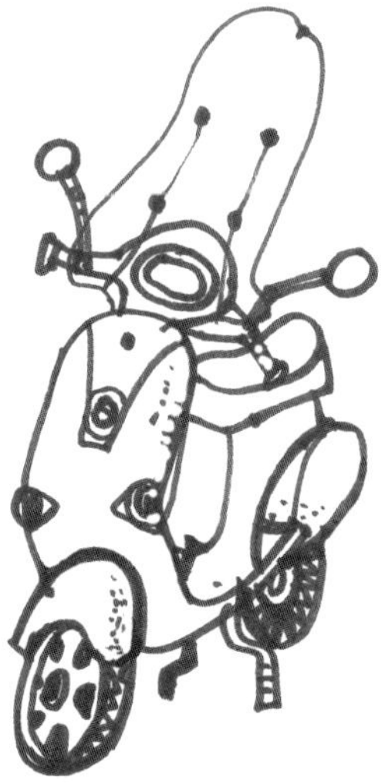

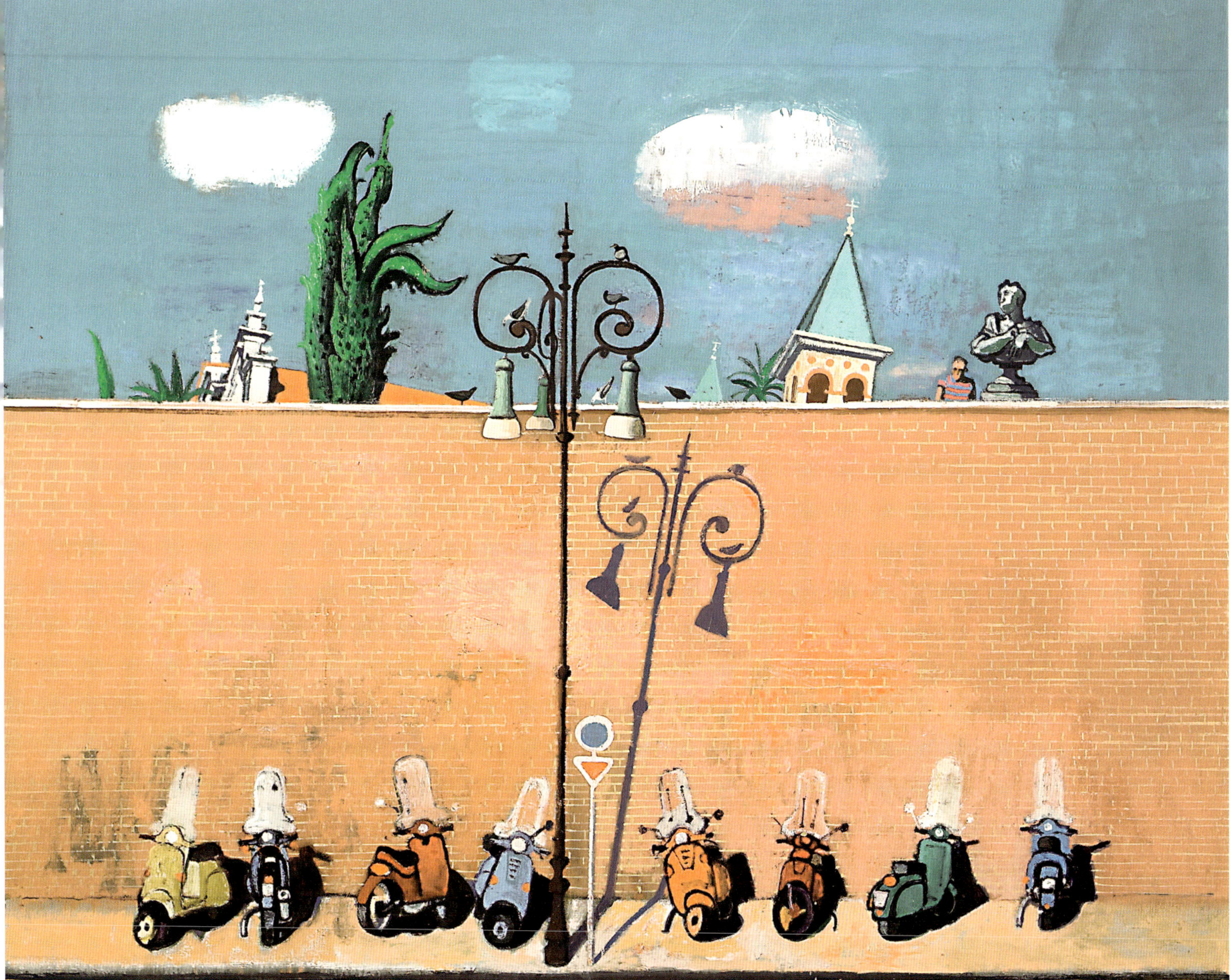

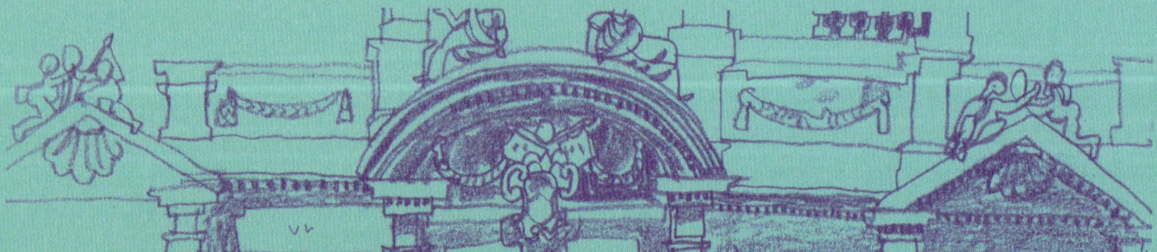

MEDITERRANEAN

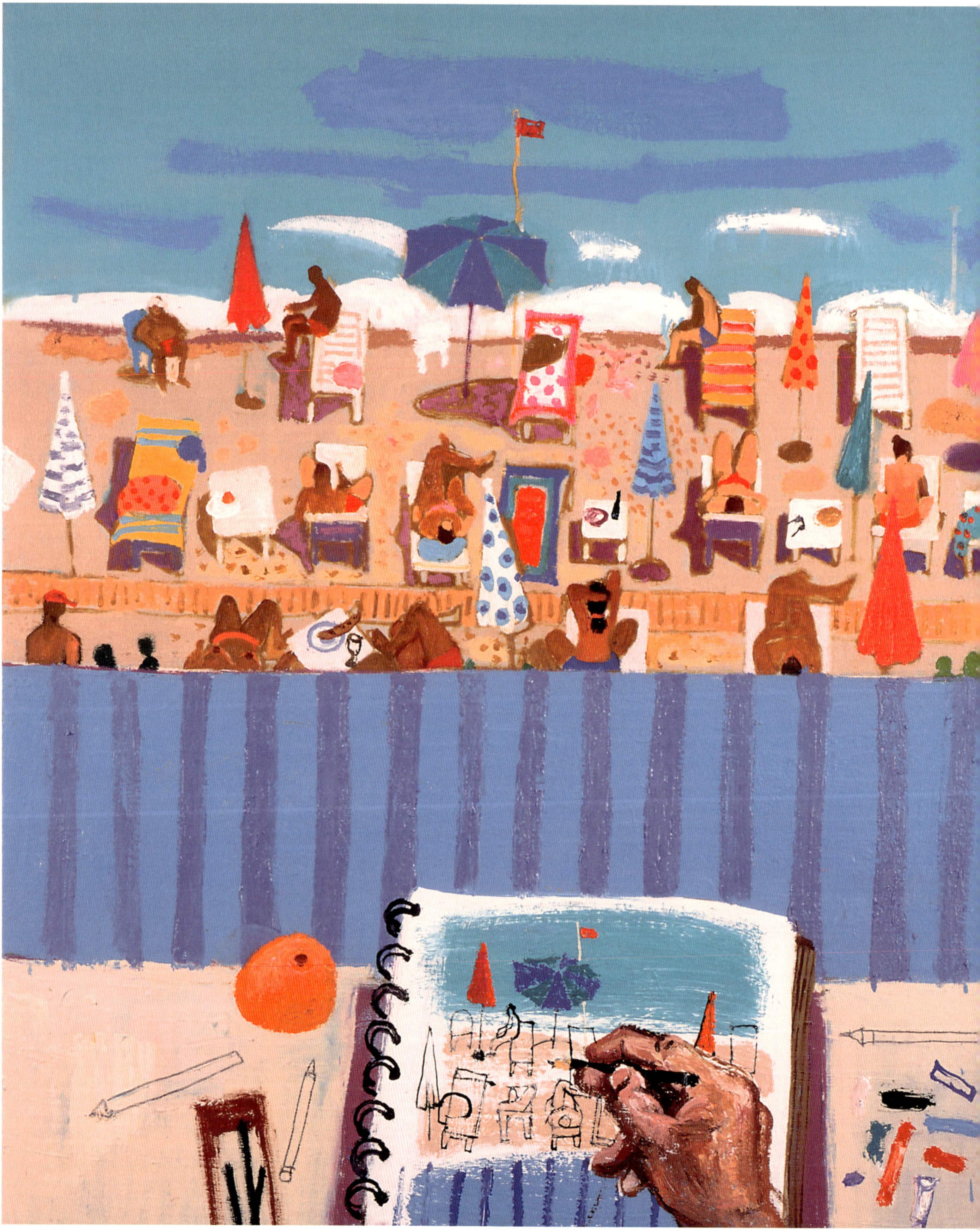

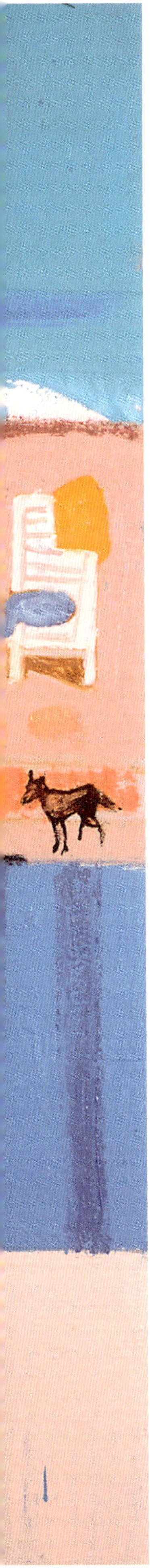

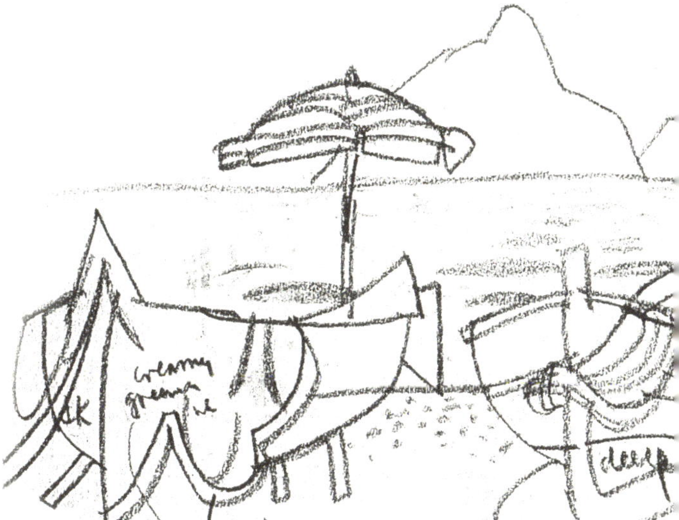
creamy
pink

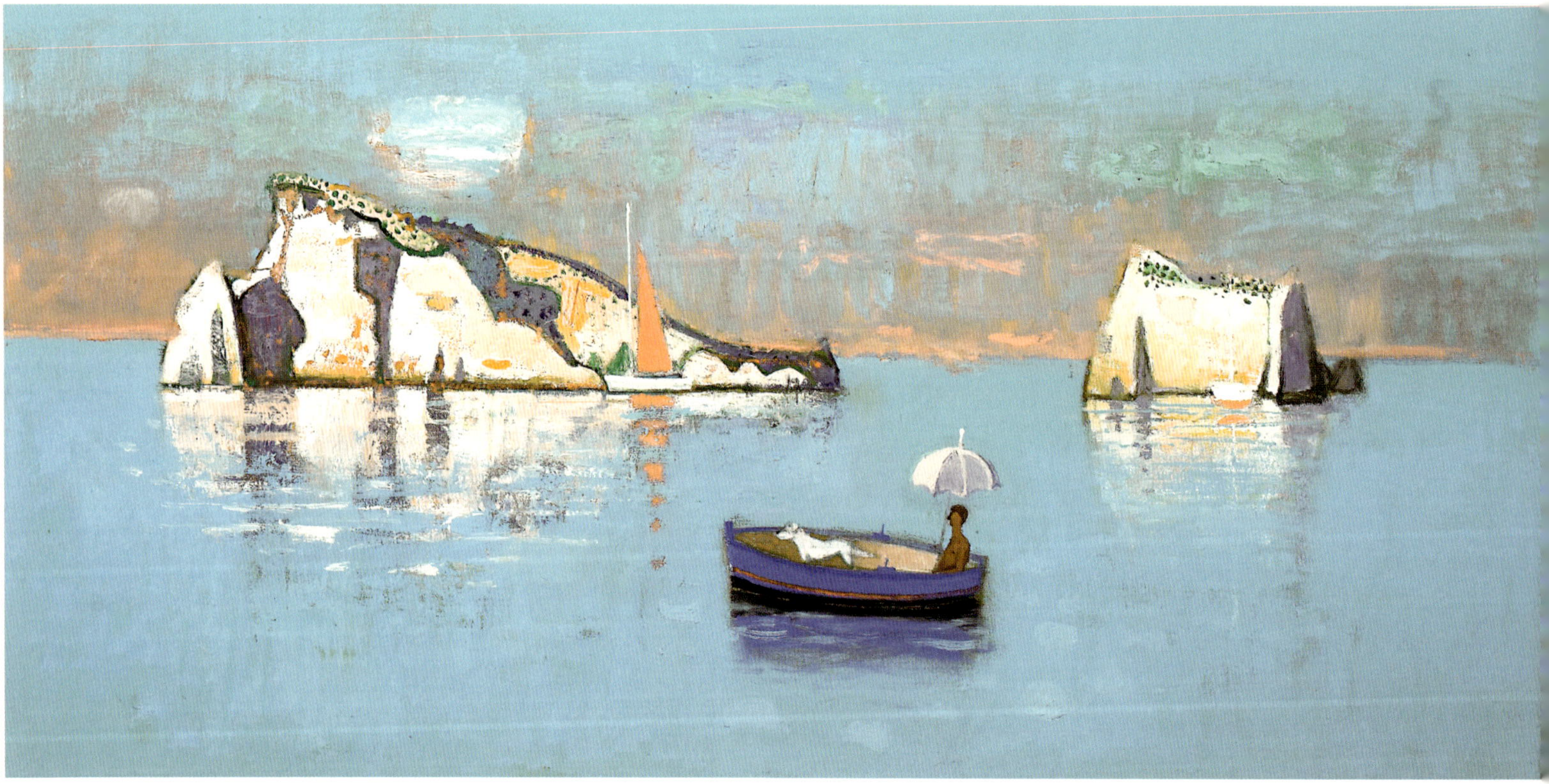

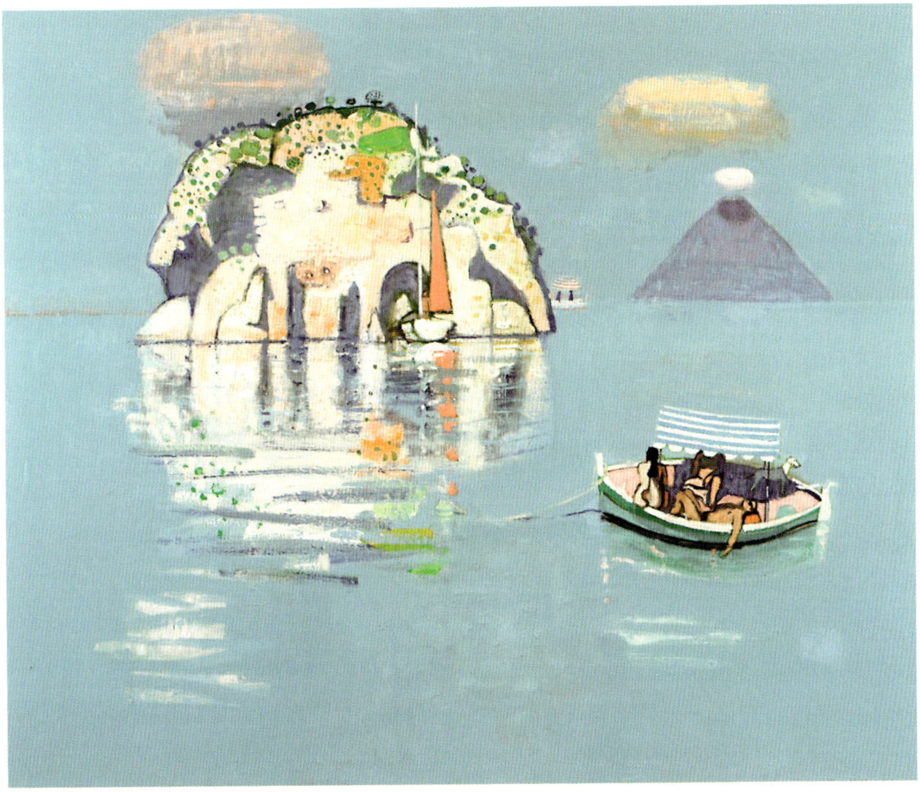

Page 72: **Drawing from the Promenade Des Anglais 2000** oil on canvas 81 x 76 cm
Page 74: **Drifting Past Baziluzzo 2004** oil on canvas 76 x 152 cm
Page 75: **Siesta off Pietranave 2004** oil on canvas 152 x 183 cm
Page 76: **Sketching the Rock, Baziluzzo 2015** oil on board 38 x 38 cm
Page 77: **Jean Writing a Letter (A Quiet Moment), Soller, Mallorca 1998/2015** oil on canvas 60 x 74 cm
Page 78: **Study of Boats, Pietranave 2004** pencil on paper 51 x 25.5 cm

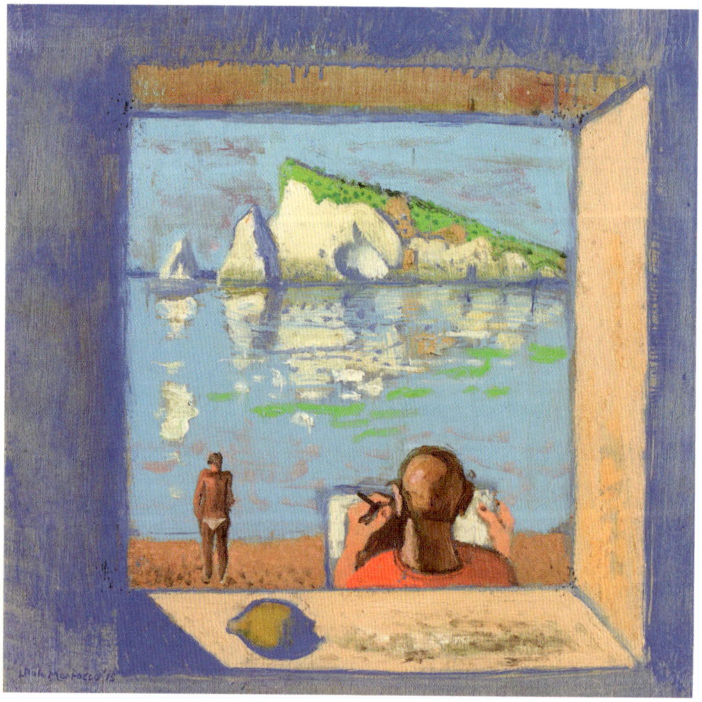

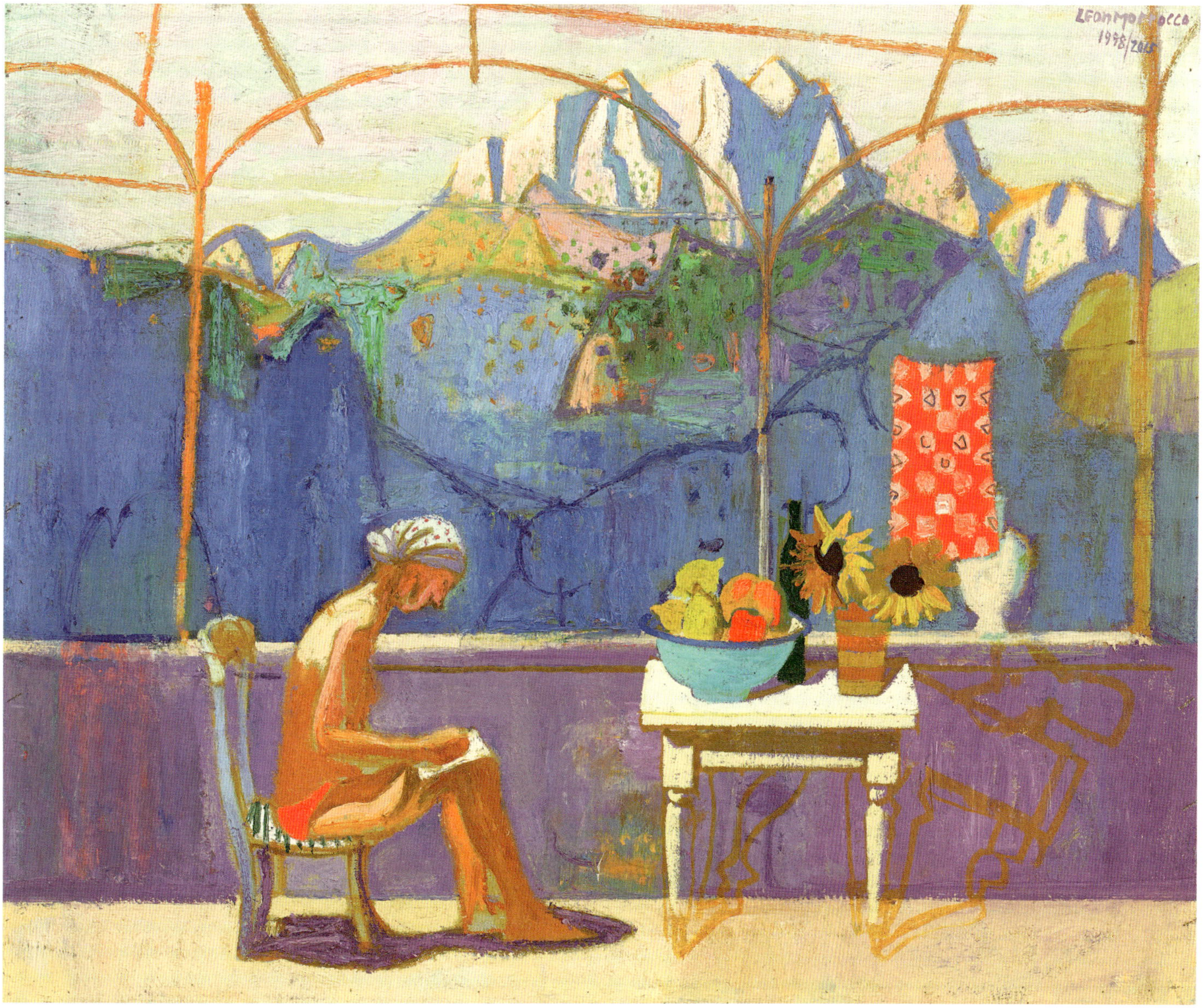

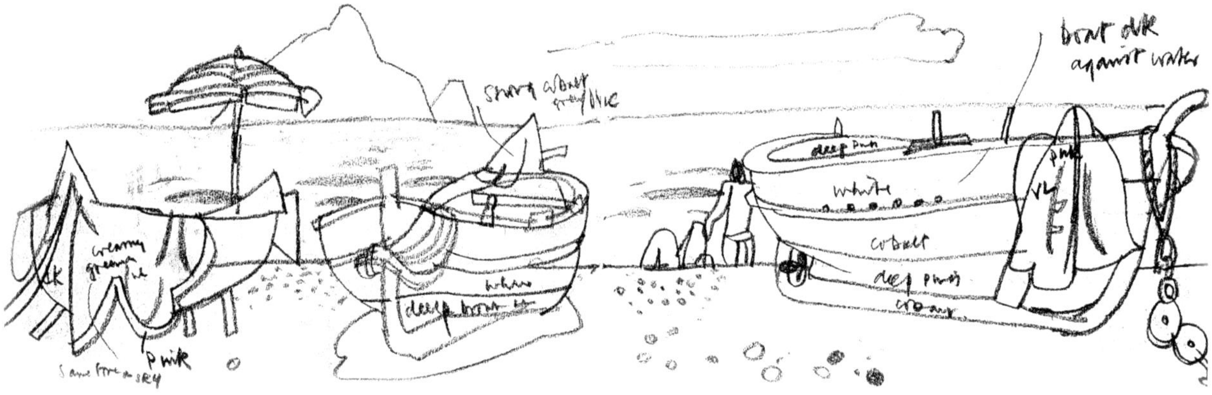
boat dk
against water
white
cobalt
deep pink
Pink

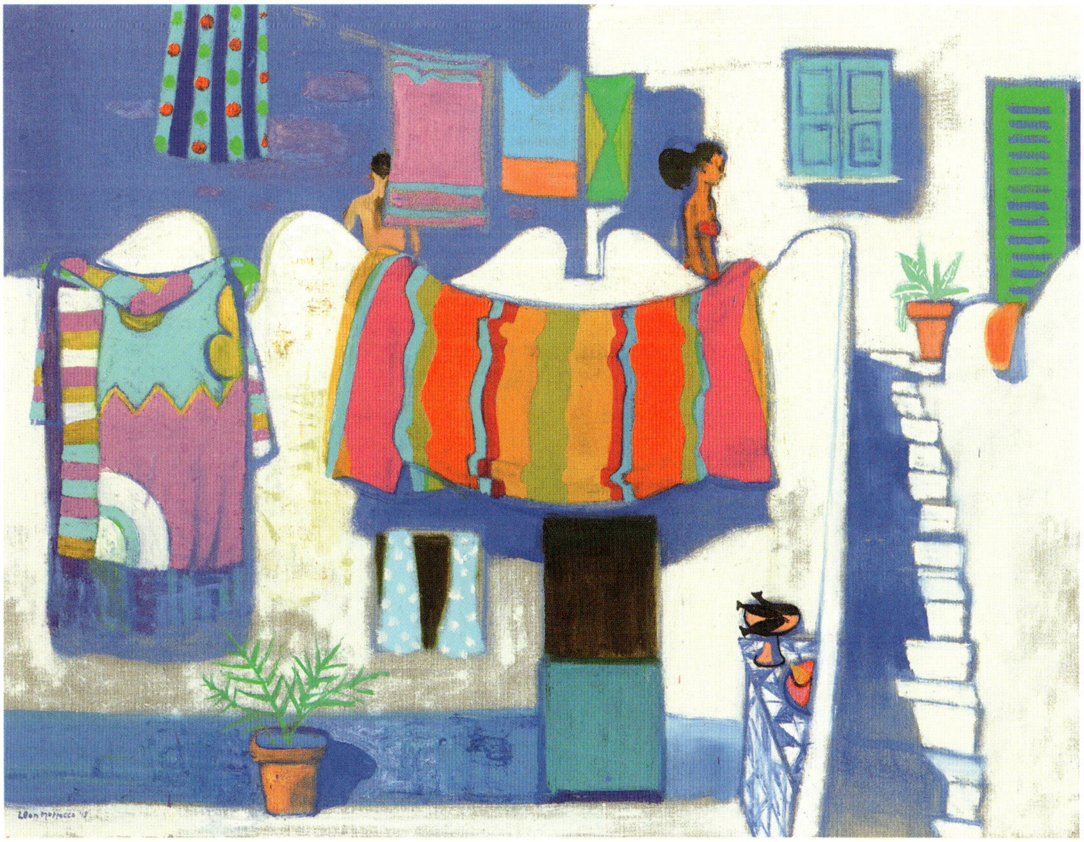

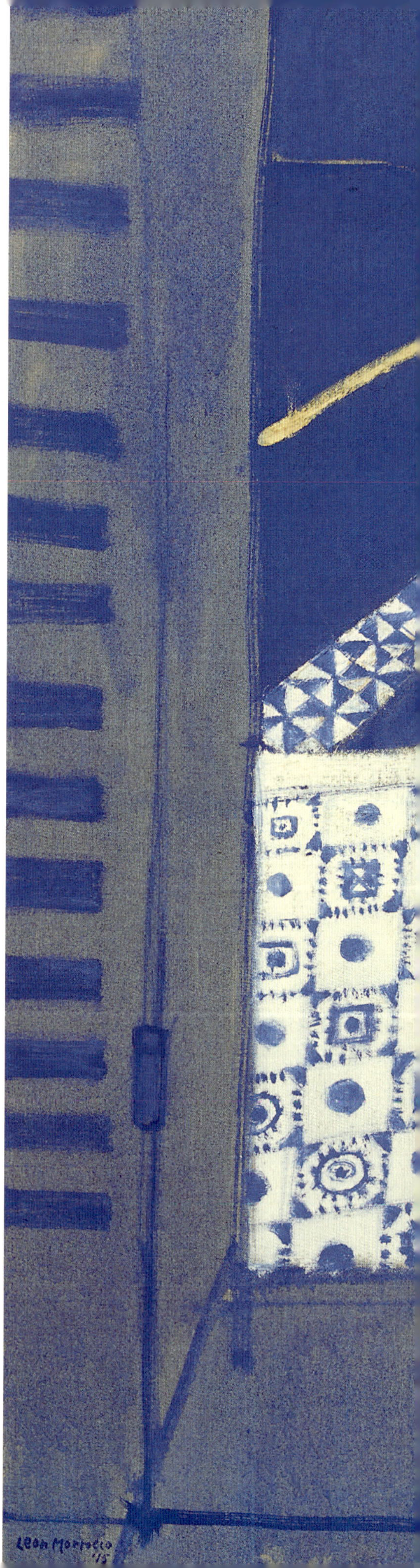
LEON MORROCCO
'15

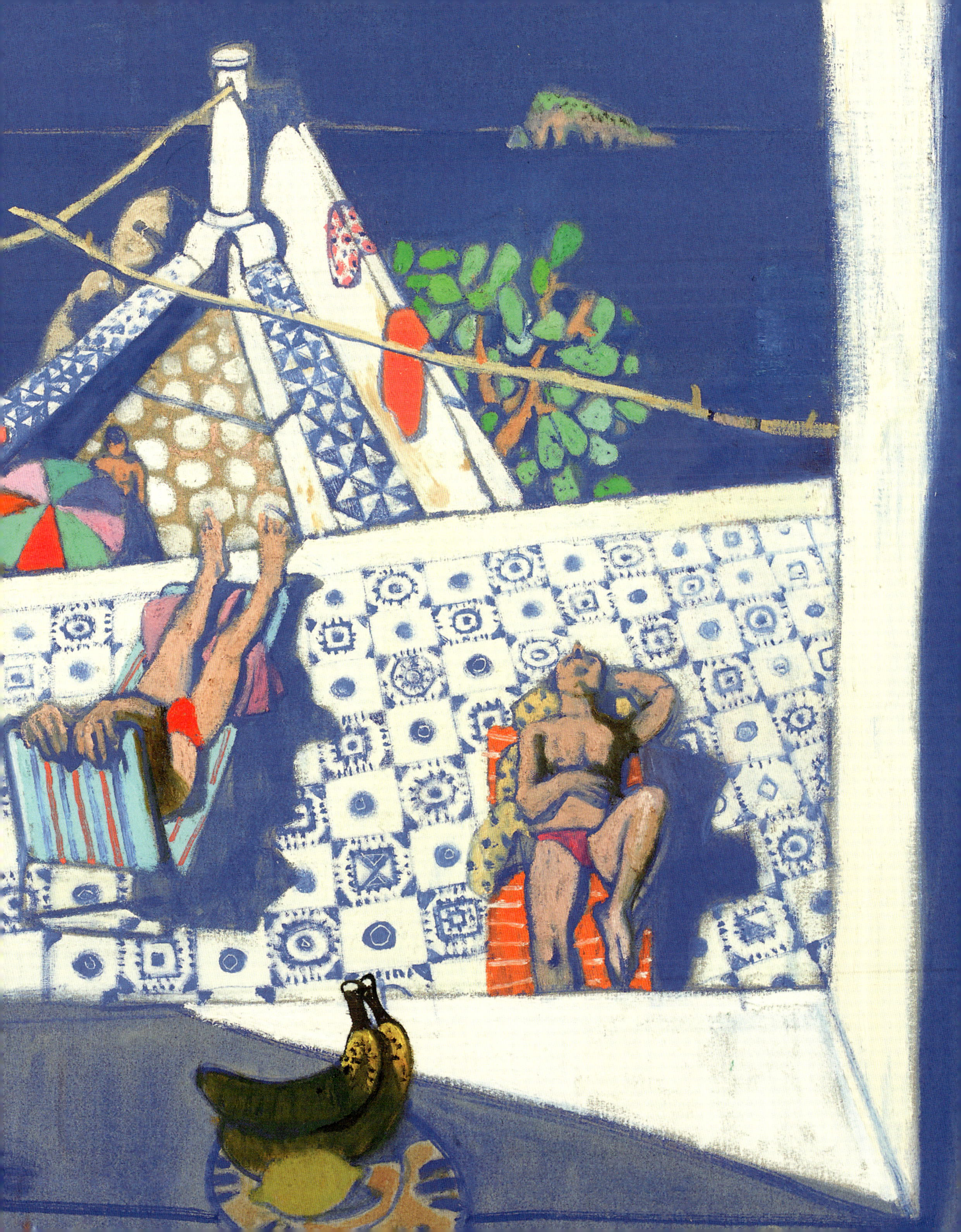

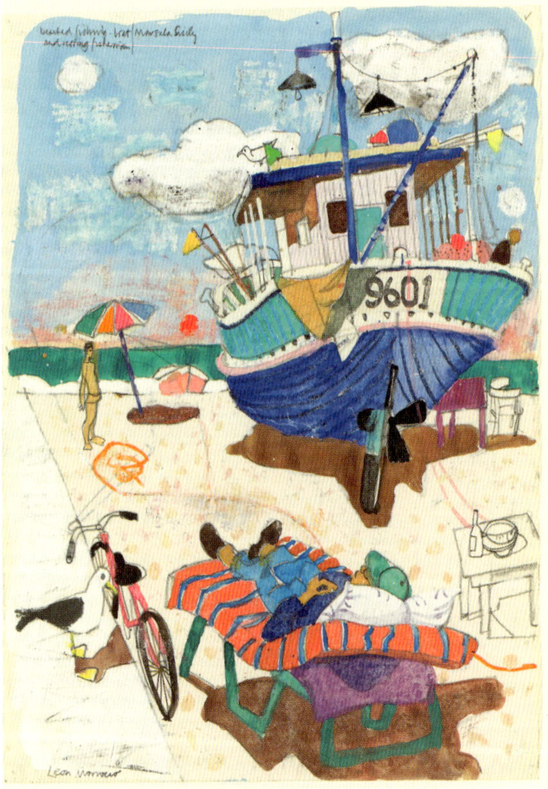

Page 79: **The Striped Towel, Panarea 2015** oil on canvas 75 x 100 cm
Page 80: **Mosaic Patio, Panarea 2015** oil on canvas 90 x 100 cm
Page 82: **Beached Fishingboat and Resting Fisherman, Marsala, Sicily 2012** mixed media 40 x 29 cm
Page 83: **Sketch for Fishingboat and Resting Fisherman 2012** pencil on paper 20 x 25.5 cm
Page 85: **Gardener Asleep in Monastery Garden, Lipari 2012** mixed media 35 x 54 cm
Page 86: **Fishmarket, Palermo 2004** mixed media 30 x 54 cm

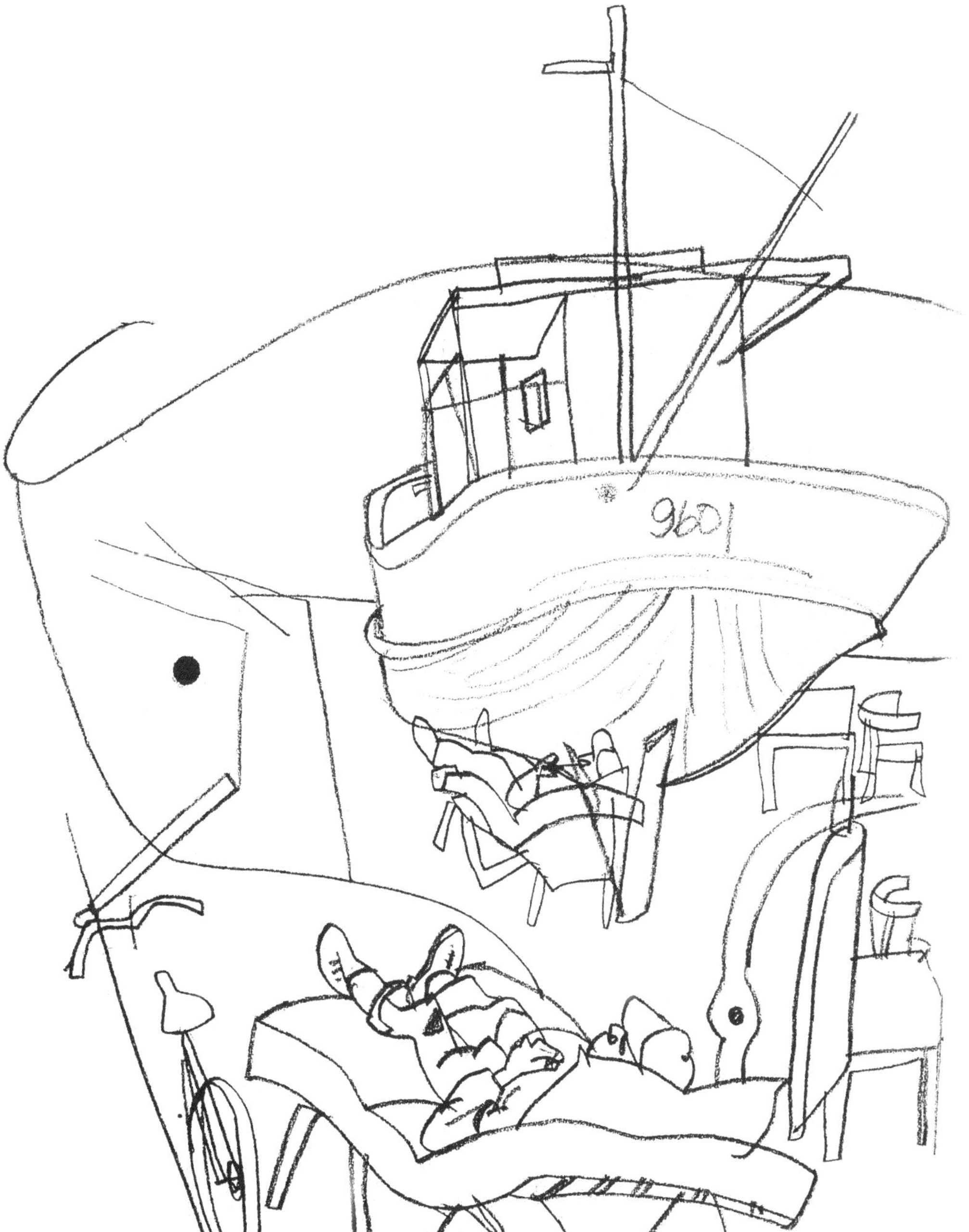
960

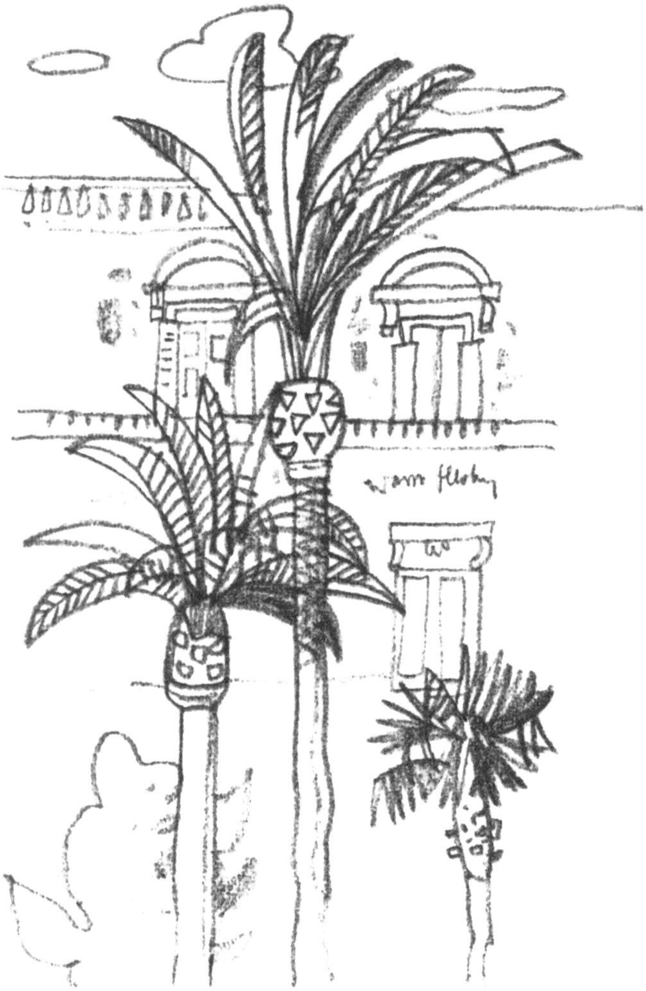

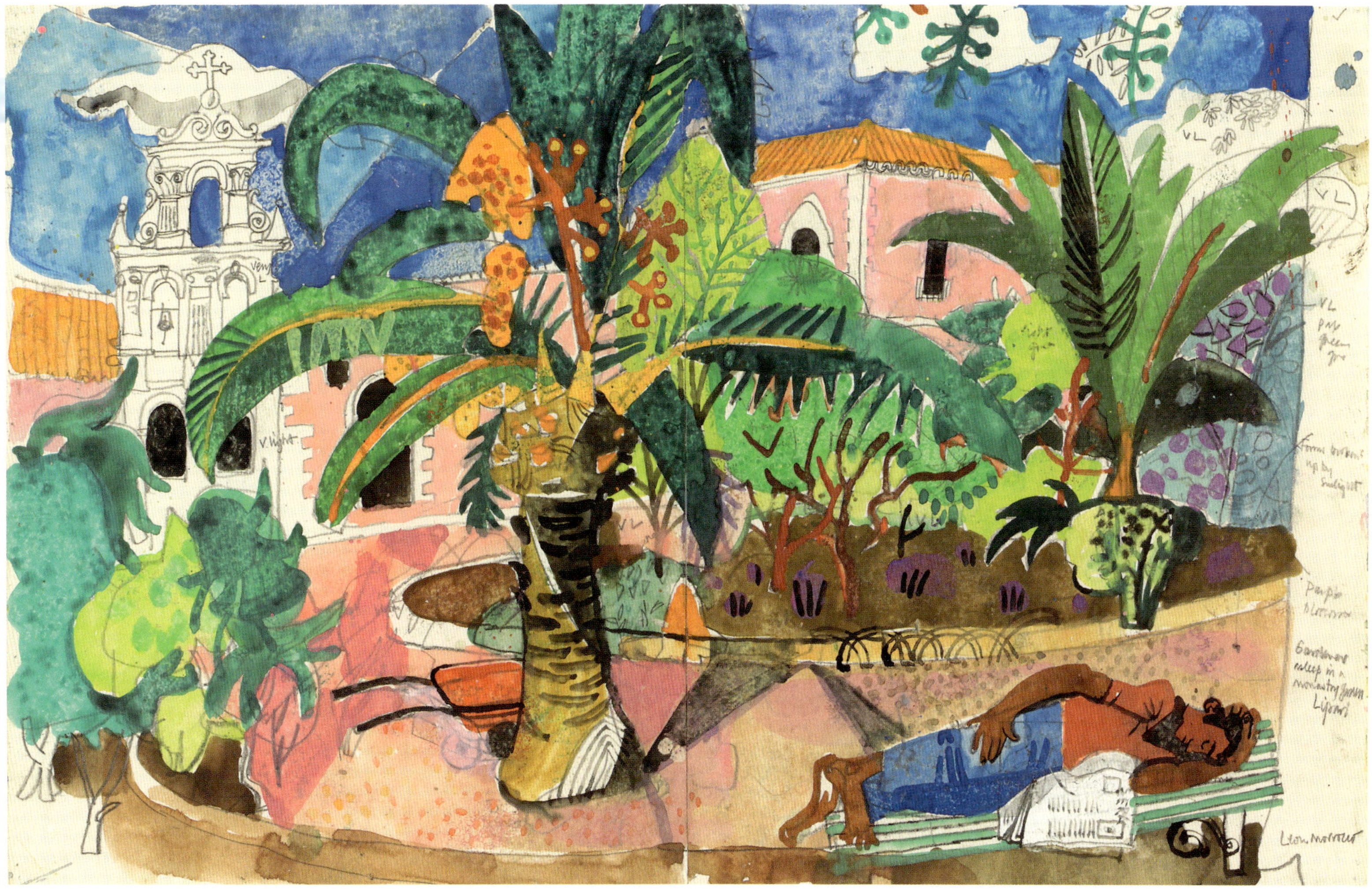

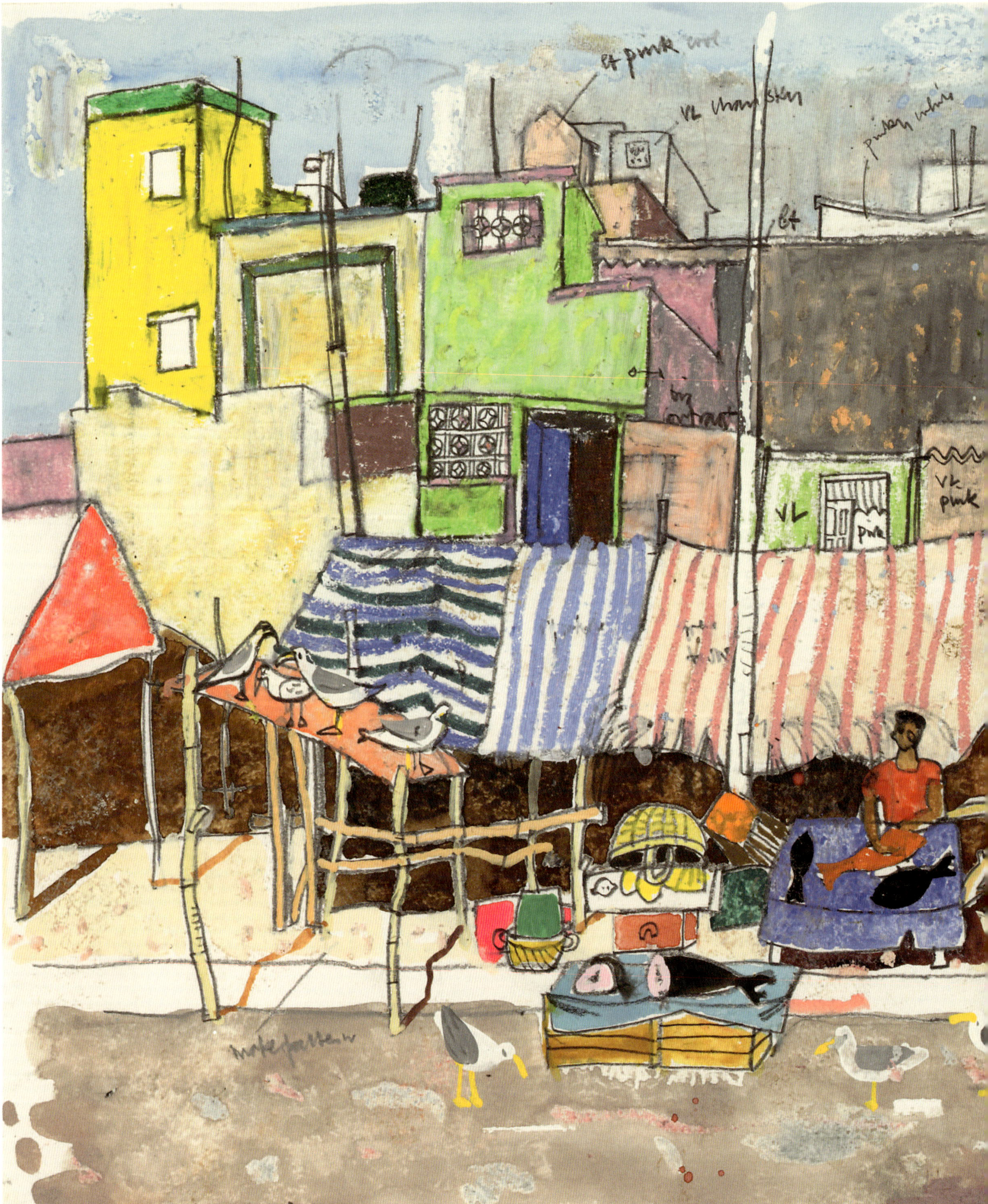

Fishmarket, Palermo

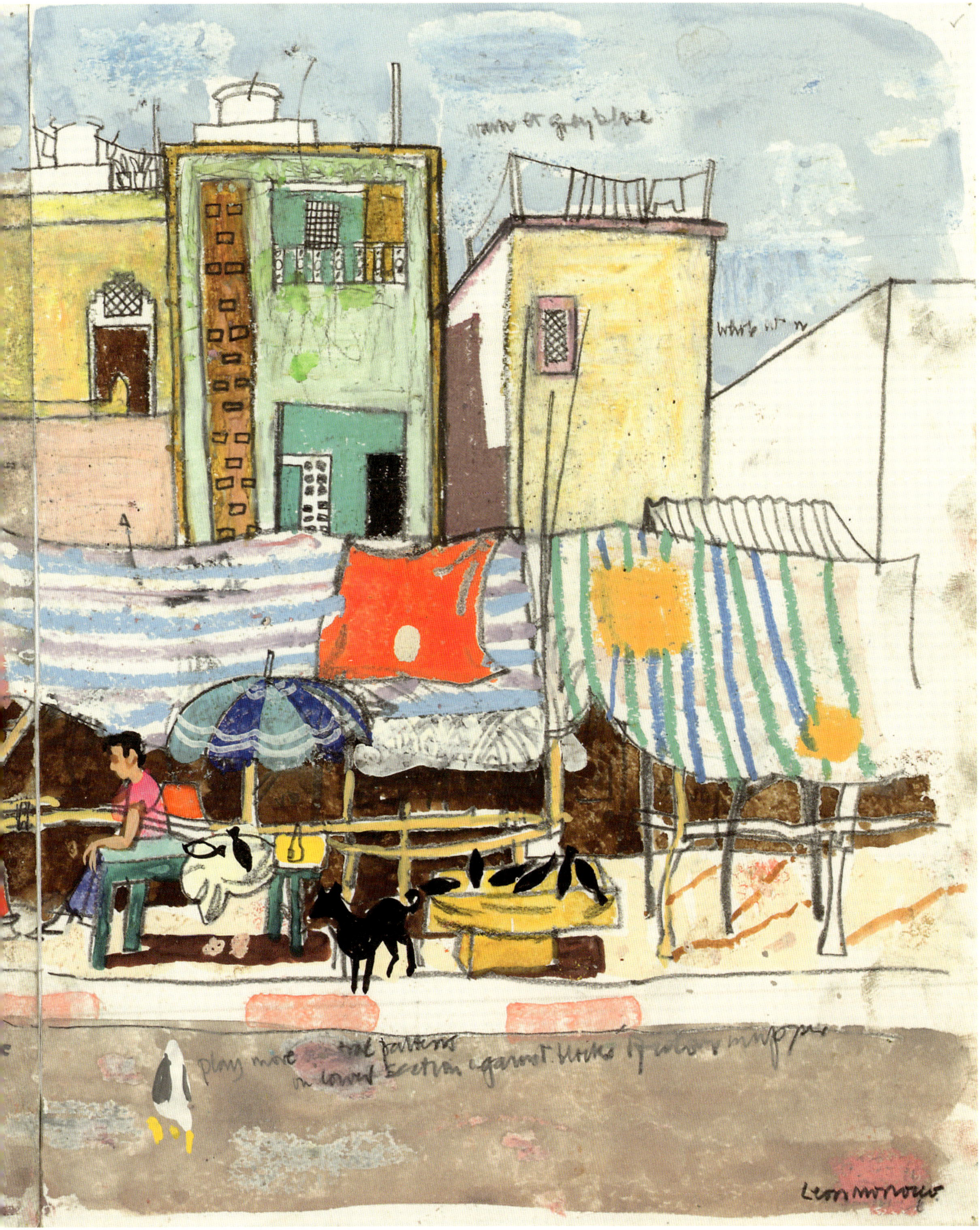
warm or grey blue
Leon Morrocco

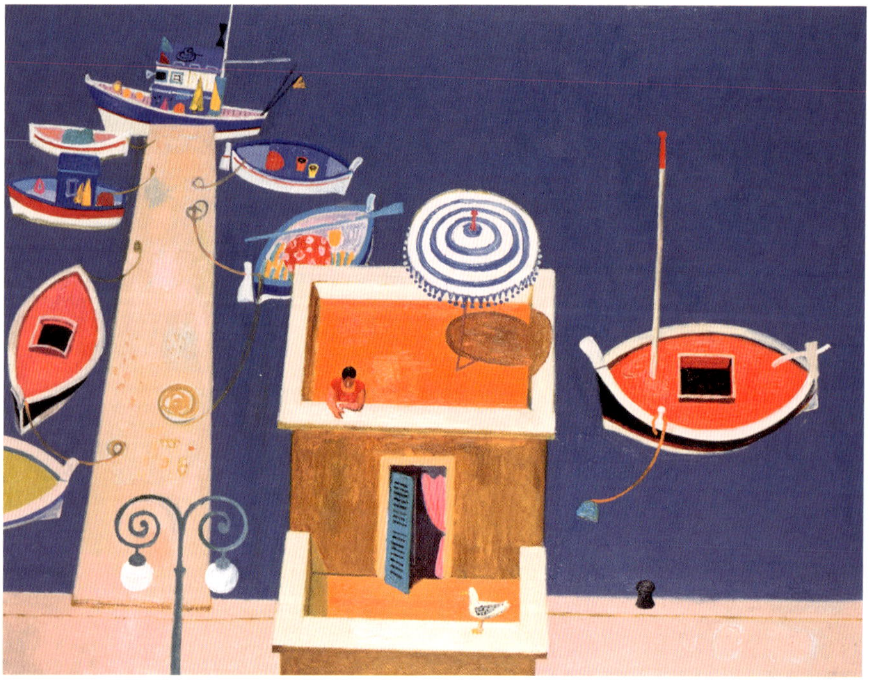

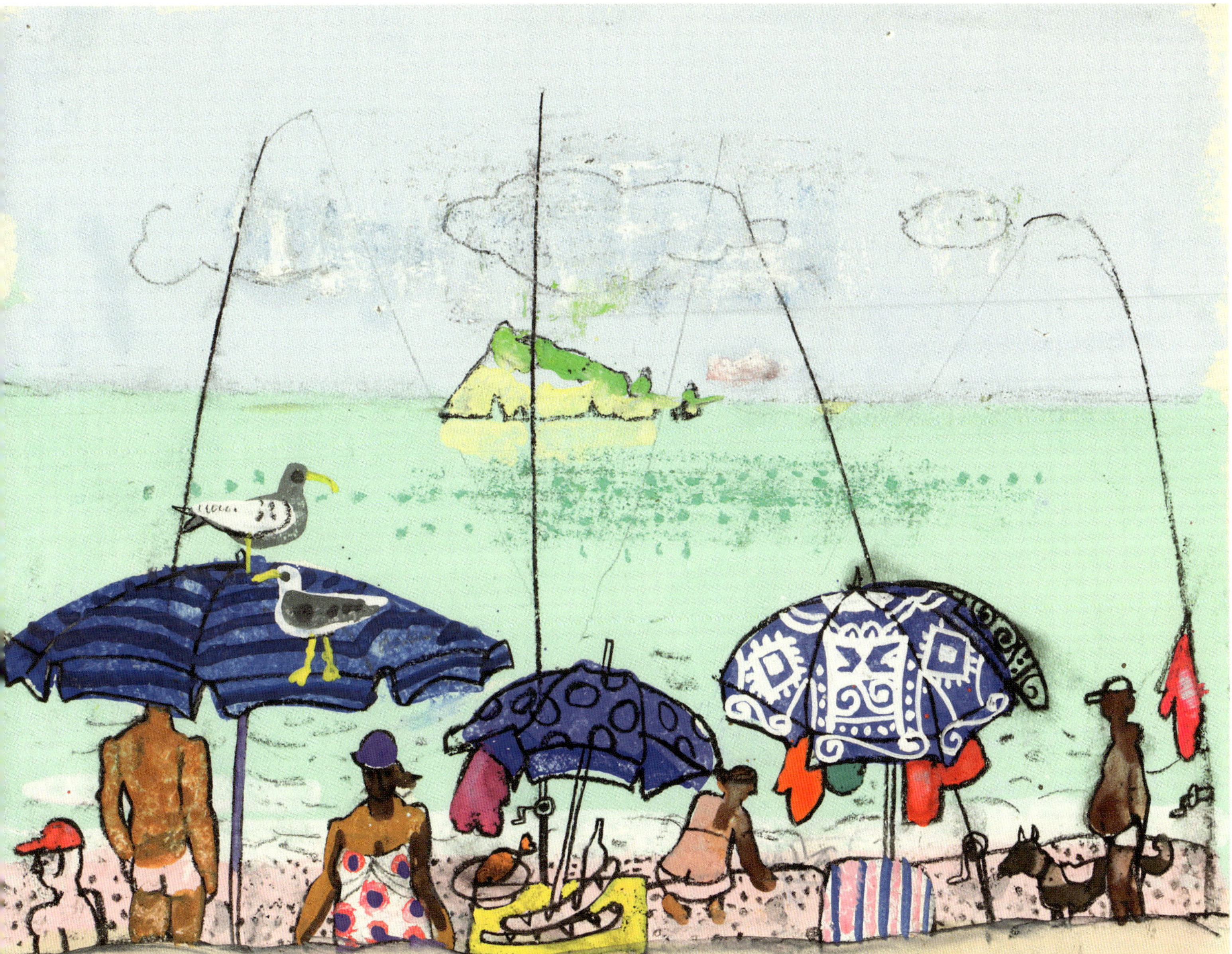
Fishing on the beach, Antibes
Leon Morrocco.

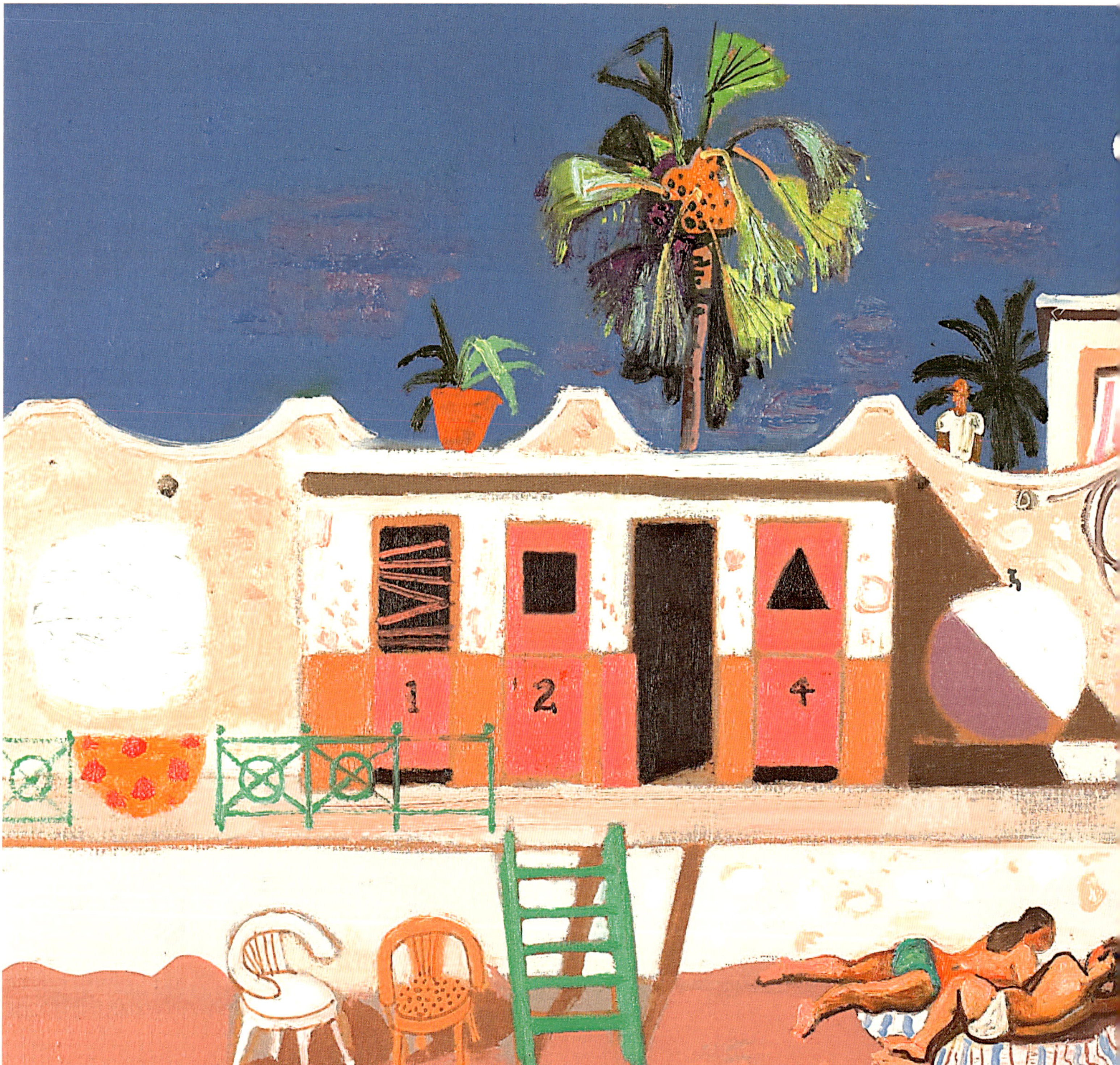
1
2
4

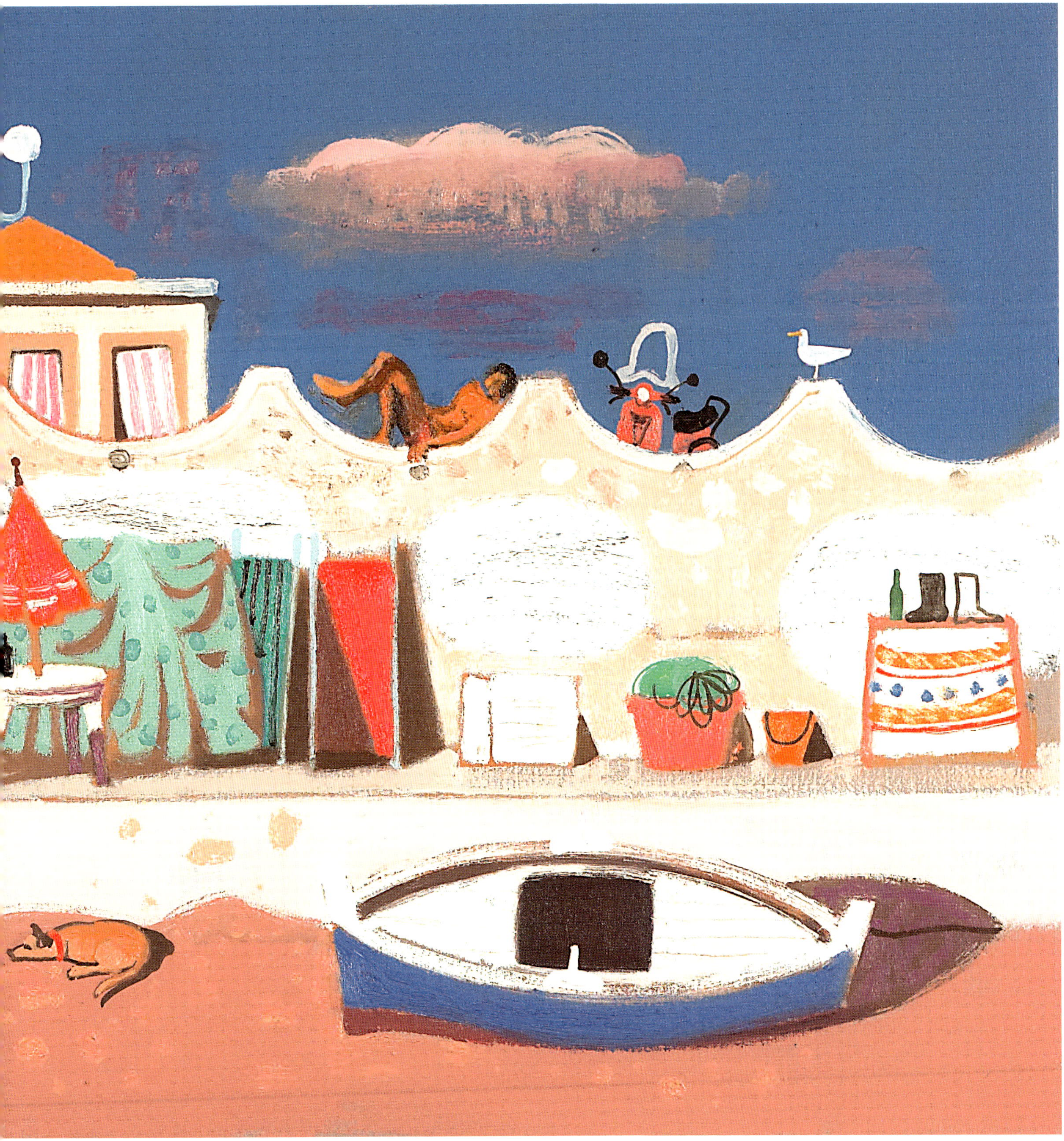

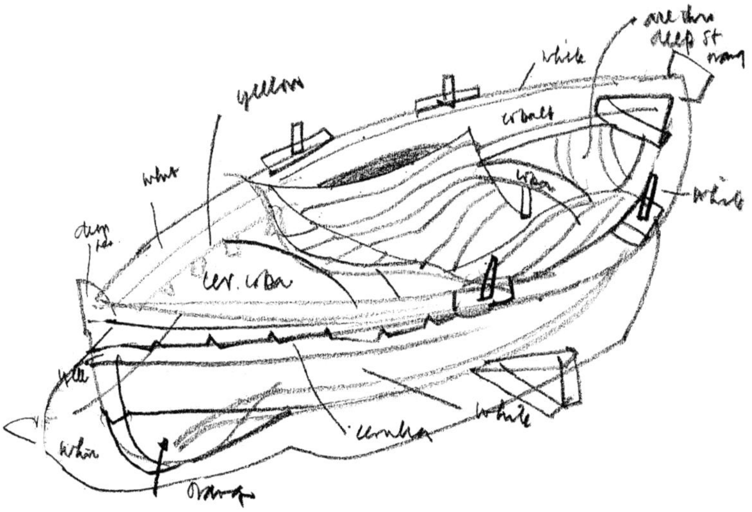
yellow
white
cobalt
white
white
orange

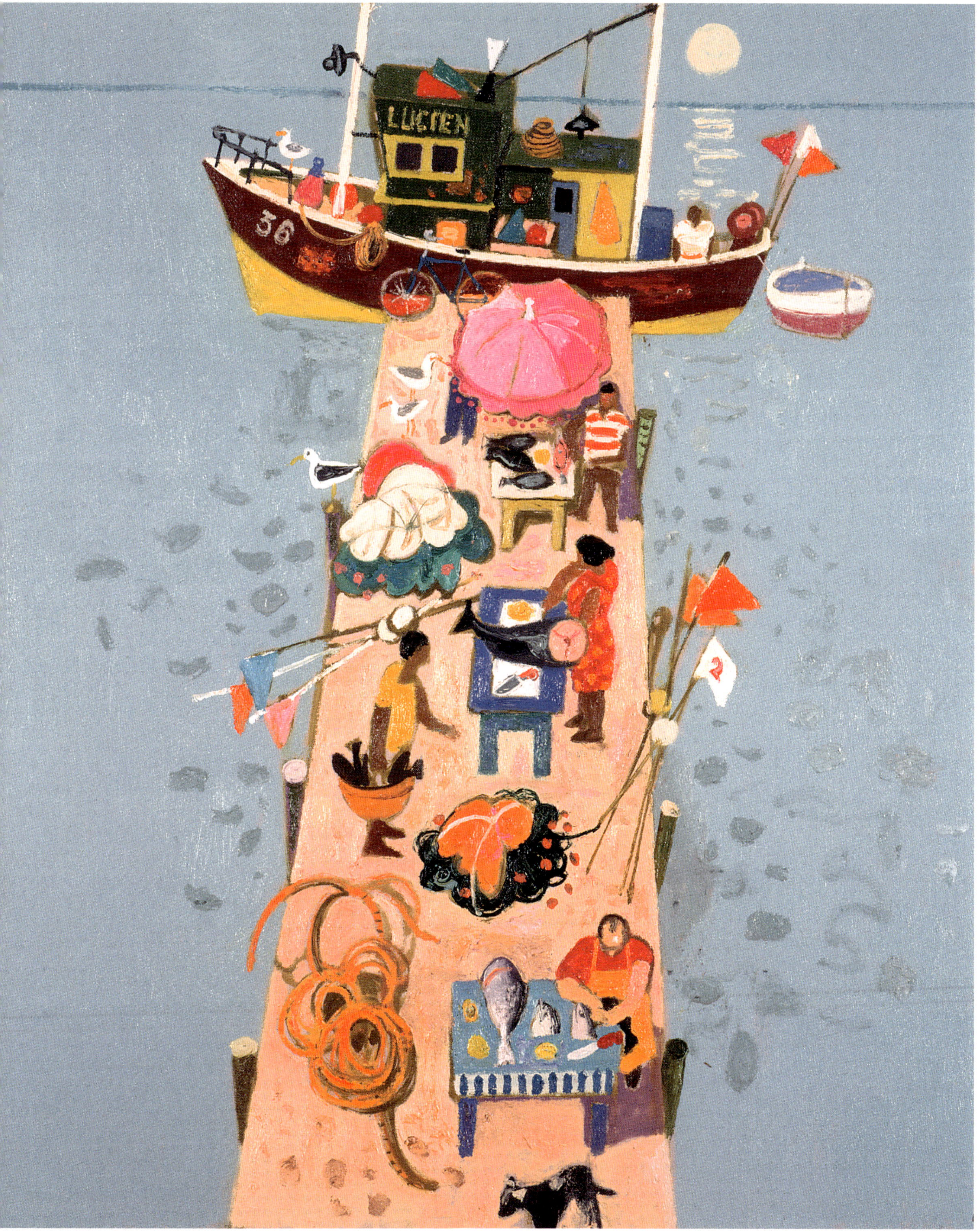
LUCIEN
36

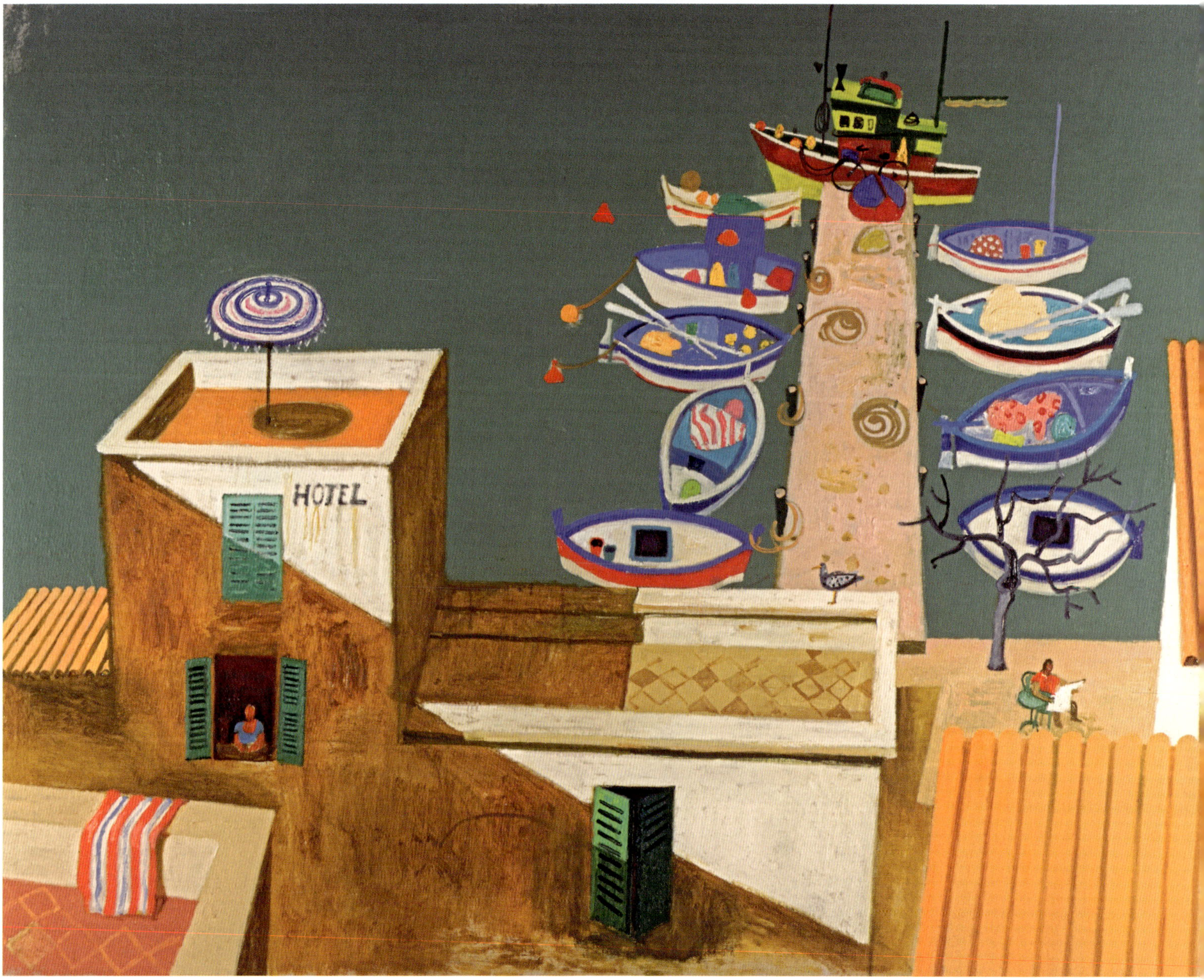
HOTEL

Page 88: **The Red Boat 2000** oil on canvas 91.5 x 122 cm
Page 89: **Fishing on the Beach, Antibes 1999** mixed media 31 x 31 cm
Page 90: **Beachwall and Sunbathers, Naples 2005** oil on canvas 61 x 122 cm
Page 93: **Fisherman's Jetty 1999** oil on canvas 76 x 71 cm
Page 94: **Harbour Hotel, Corsica 2000** oil on canvas 86 x 112 cm
Page 95: **Jour et Nuit, Nice 2002** oil on board 76 x 81 cm

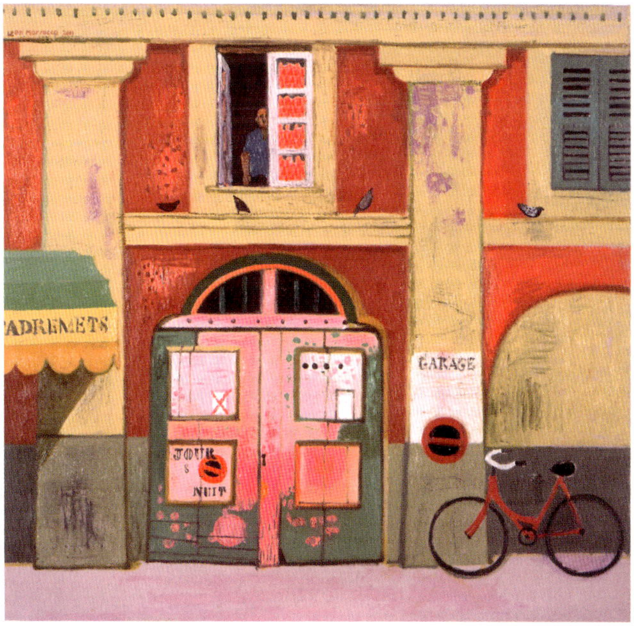

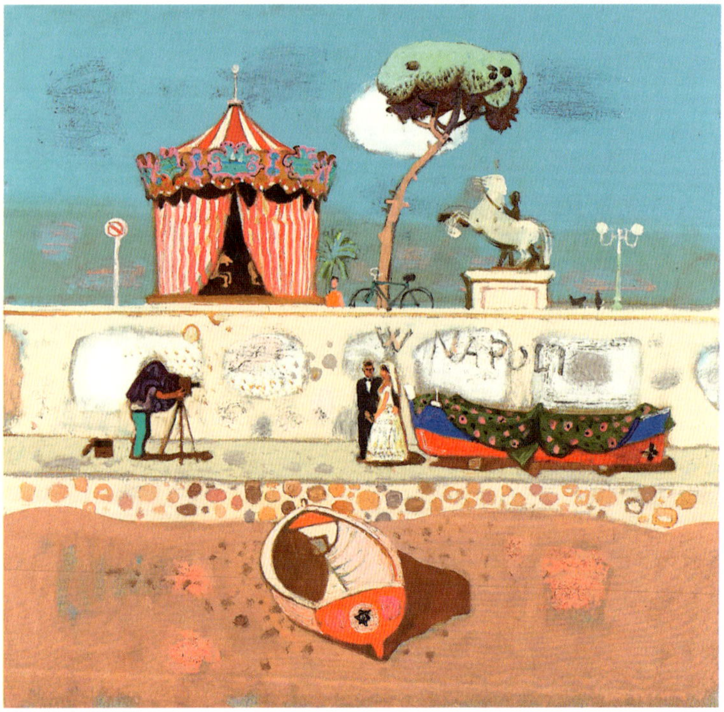

Page 96: **Wedding Photographs, Naples 2003**
oil on canvas 96 x 102 cm
Page 97: **Pink Church at Civitavecchia, with Merry Go Round and Wedding Photographs 2003**
oil on canvas 96 x 71 cm

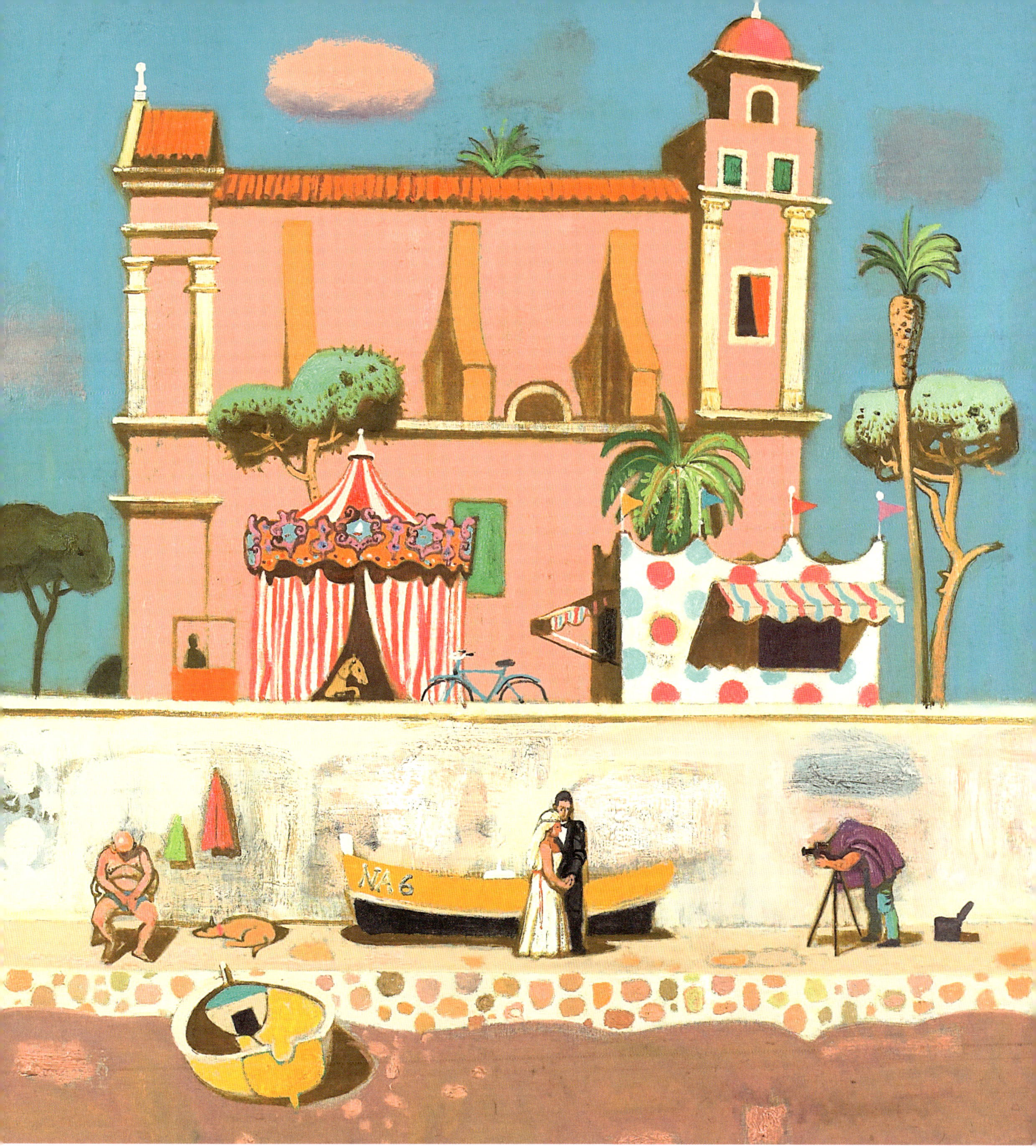
NA 6

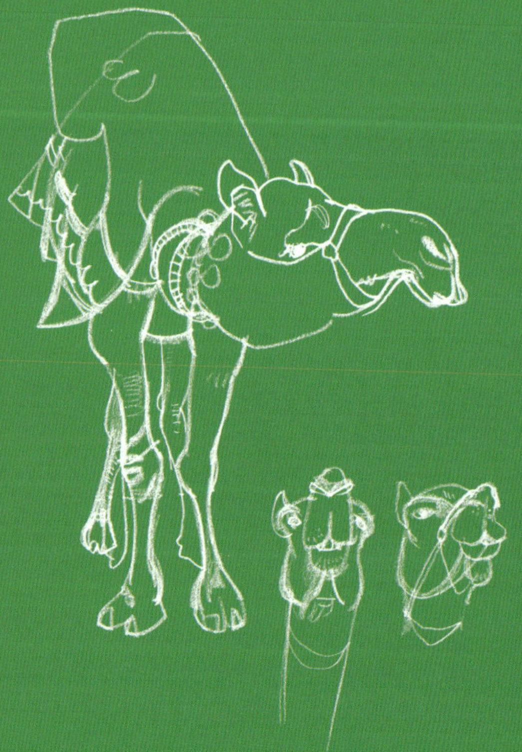

MOROCCO

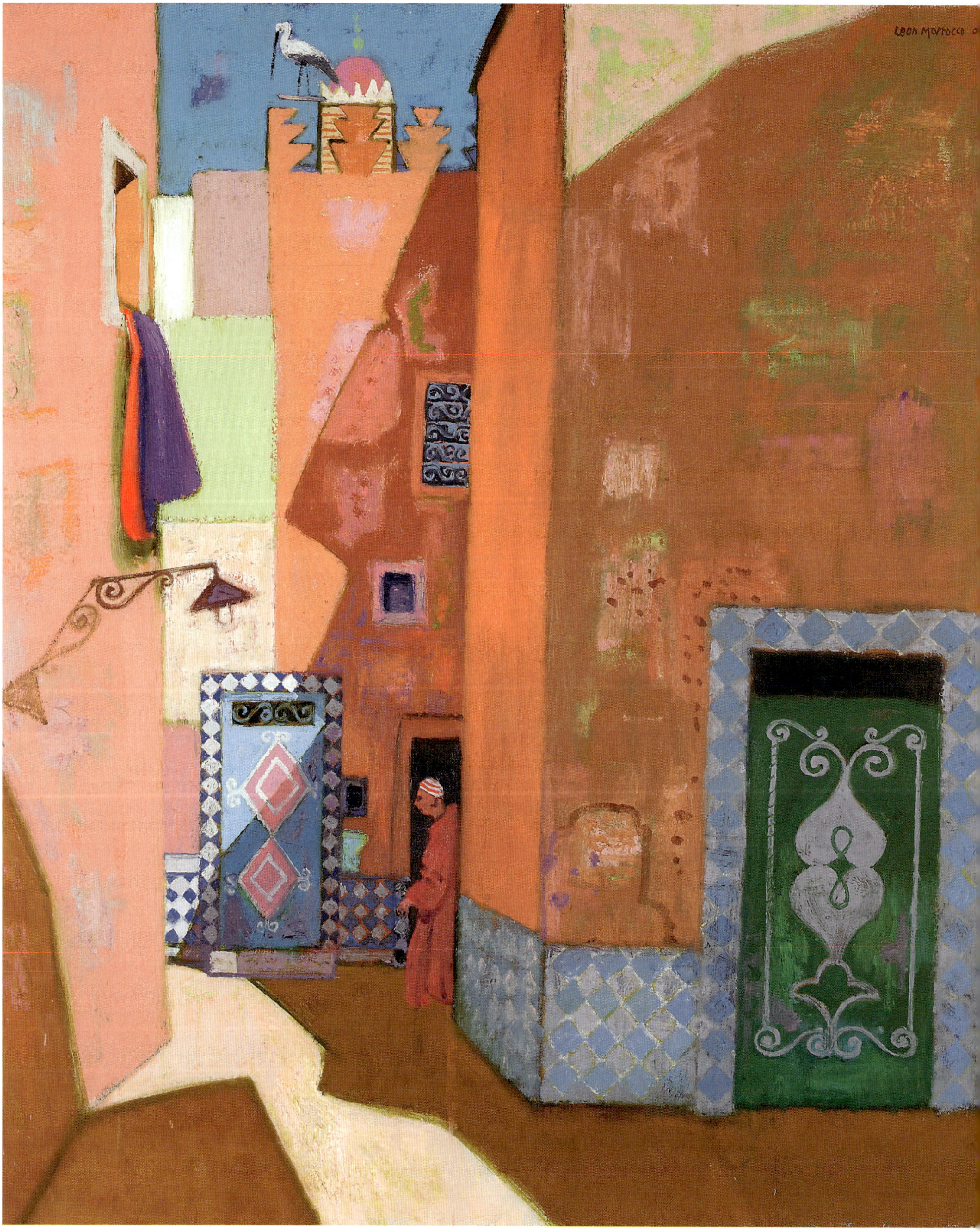
Leon Morrocco

I WAS DRAWING A MOSQUE ONE SCORCHING HOT DAY AT A BUSY INTERSECTION OF four roads on the outskirts of the Medina. In front of me was a slow moving mass of people, animals and motor vehicles. Dust and petrol fumes hung heavily in the humidity and the noise level was high.

Above the din, I was suddenly aware of raised voices, of shouting and screaming and I could see a man a woman, about 20 yards to my right, engaged in a heated argument. The man was raising his arm and threatening to hit the woman who was screaming and in a hysterical state. A crowd quickly formed around this drama, forcing the already painfully slow traffic to a complete standstill and resulting in an escalation of the general bedlam.

Suddenly the midday prayers began to blare out from the mosques, loudspeakers, making the cacophony of sound almost unbearable. From my slightly elevated position on some steps I saw to my left a small door at the side of the mosque being opened and a coffin, supported at head height, being precariously manoeuvred through this aperture out into the street. This was followed by a large group of mourners, and the whole cortege absorbed into the general chaos. Directly in front of me and marooned in this sea of humanity was a taxi containing two elderly American tourists, wide-eyed, bewildered and obviously frightened. The unfolding of the many elements of this scenario was totally mesmerising and, in its random theatricality, reminded me of a Fellini film. Overwhelmed by the bizarre conditions, I was reluctantly forced to abandon my drawing which was in fact never finished.

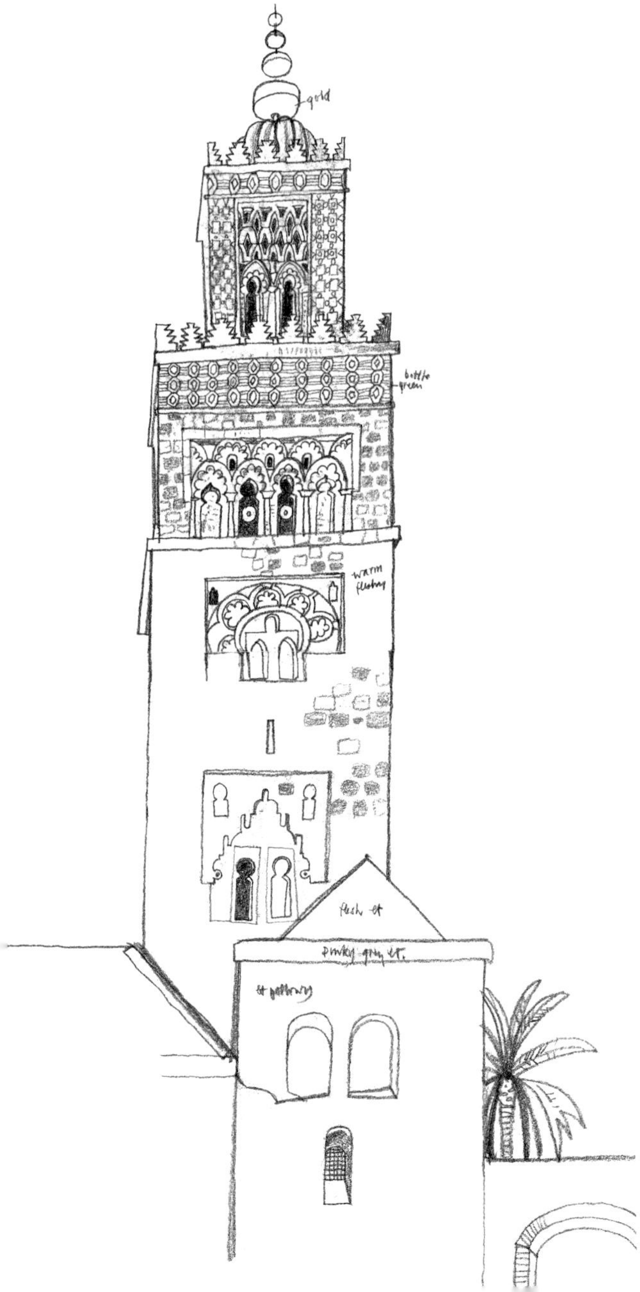

Page 100: **Shadows in a Narrow Back Street, Old Town Marrakech 2007** oil on canvas 86.5 x 91.5 cm

Page 102: **Looking Through to the Mosque Pencil Study, Marrakech 2007** pencil on paper 20 x 20 cm

Page 103: **Midday, Looking Through to the Mosque 2007** oil on canvas 81 x 101.5 cm

Page 104: **Wall in Marrakech 2007** pencil & oil pastel on paper 25.5 x 51 cm

Page 106: **Minaret & Door 2007** pencil on paper 20 x 20 cm

Page 107: **Market with Rugs 2007** pencil on paper 25.5 x 51 cm

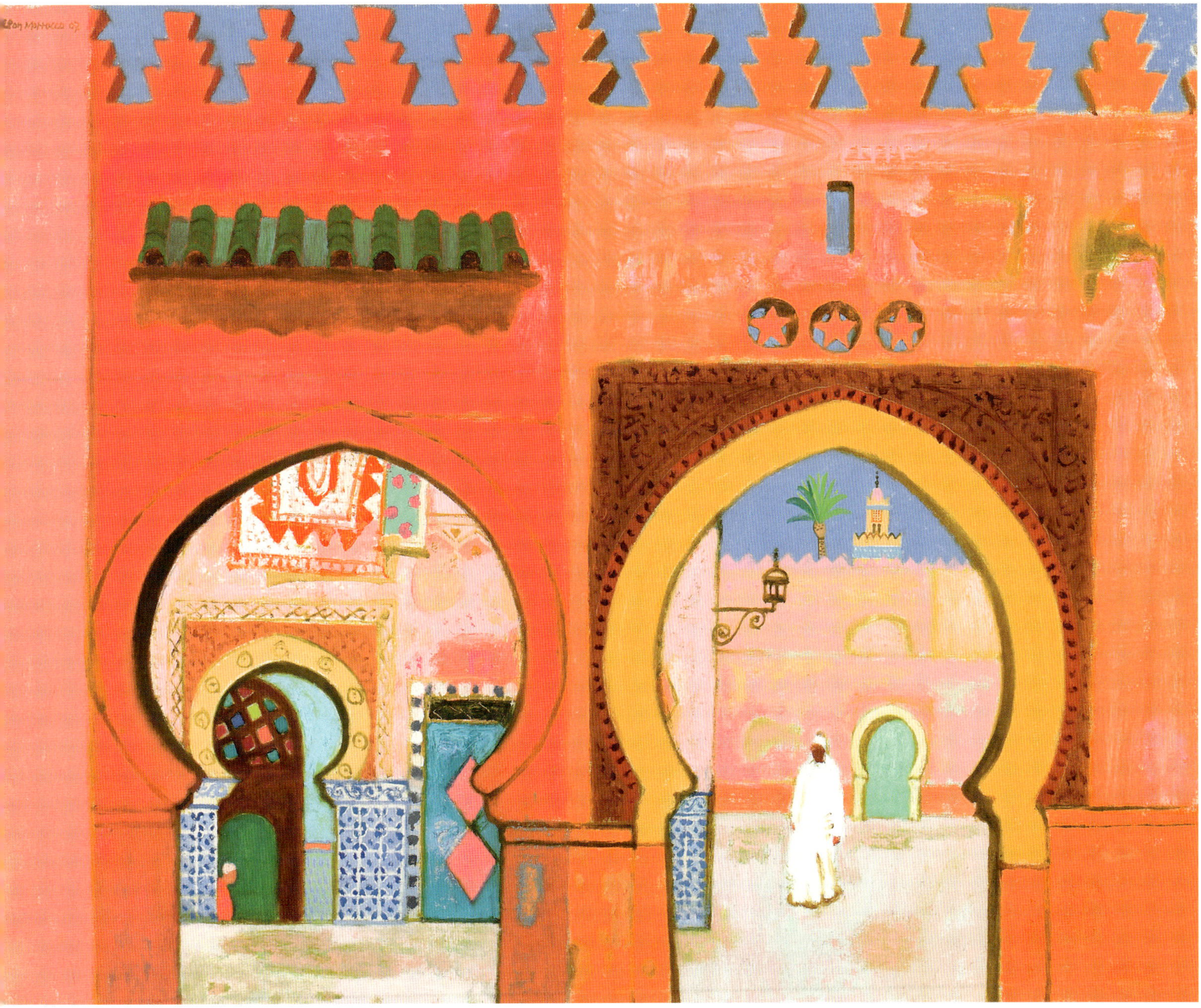

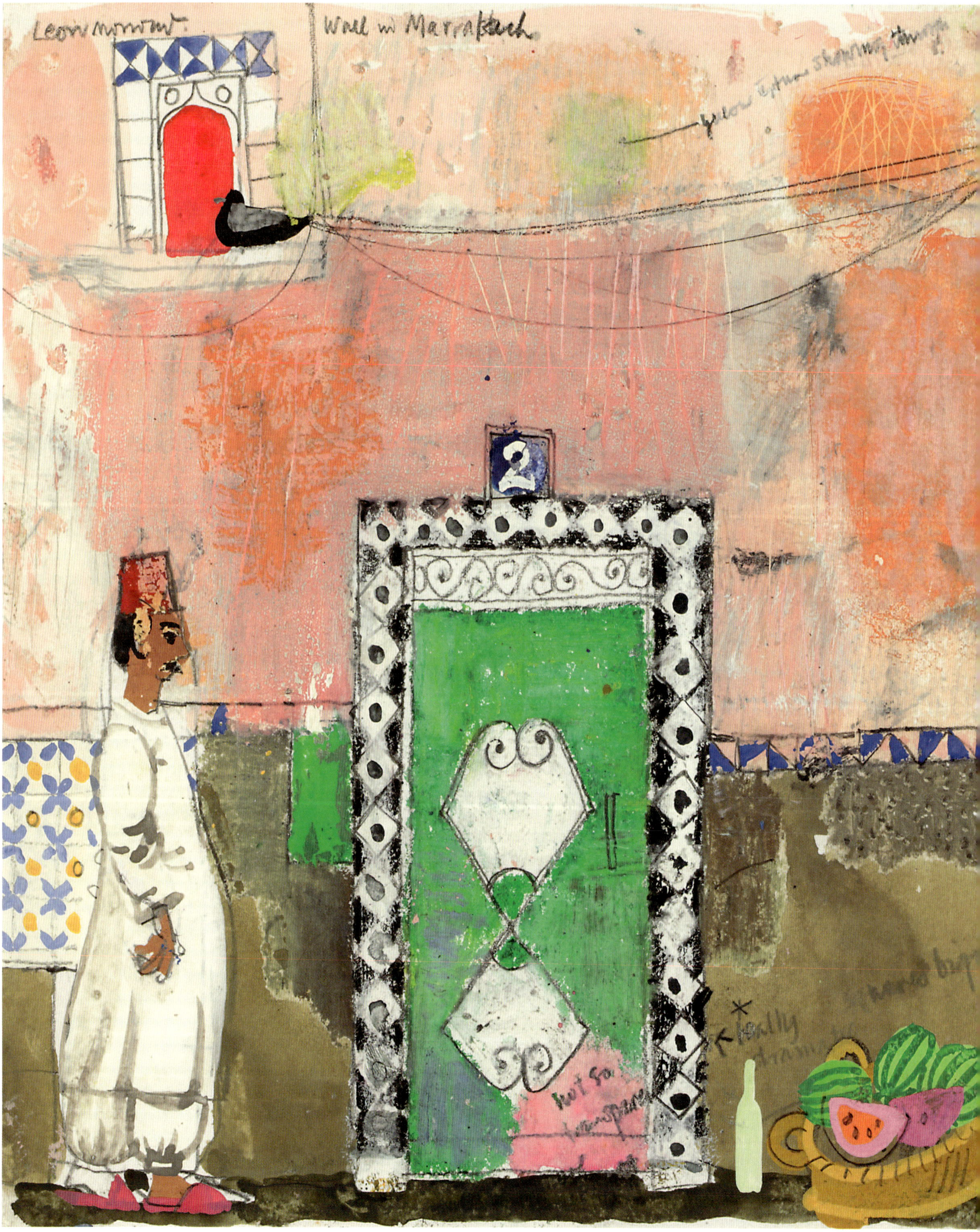
Wall in Marrakech

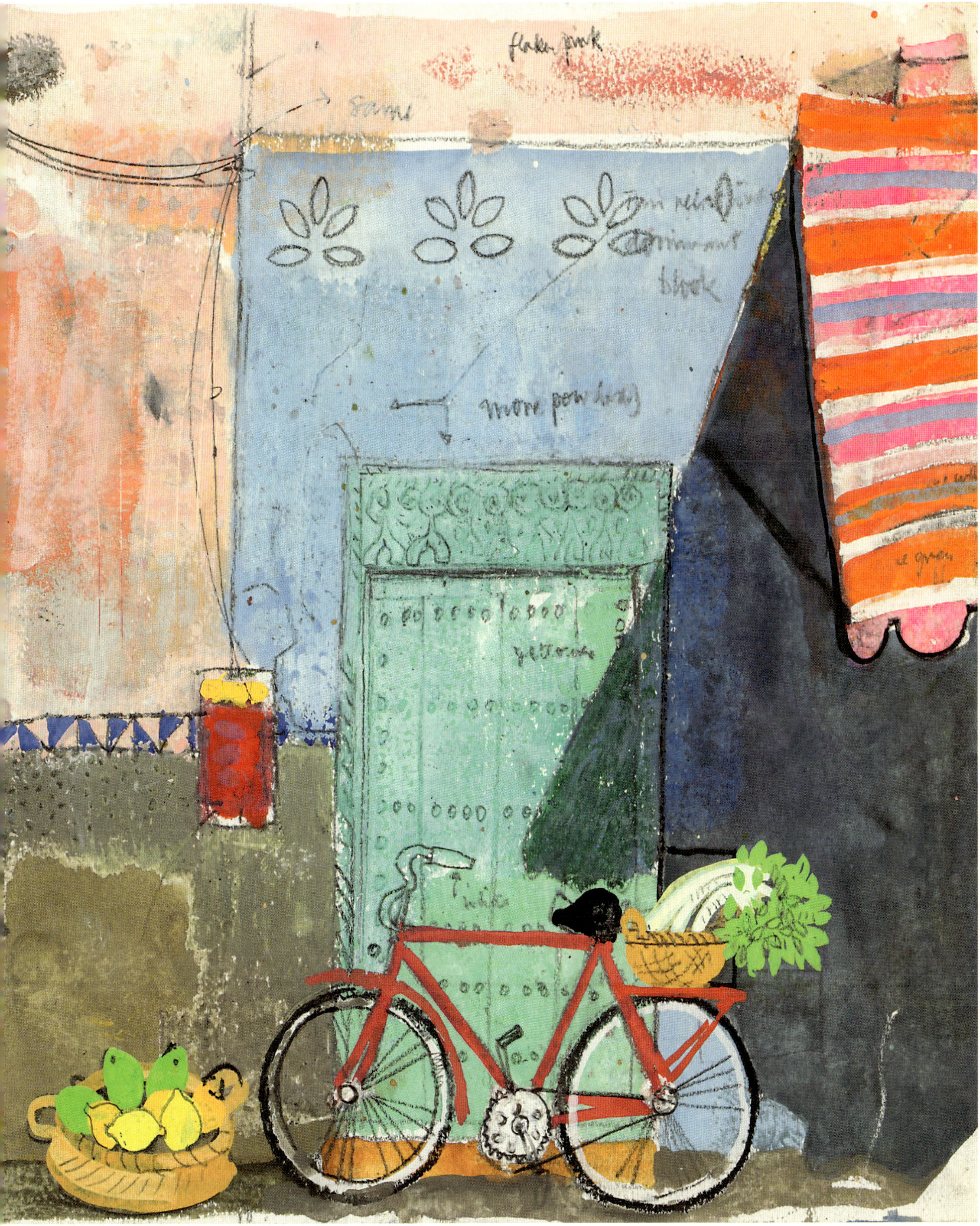
flake pink
same
block

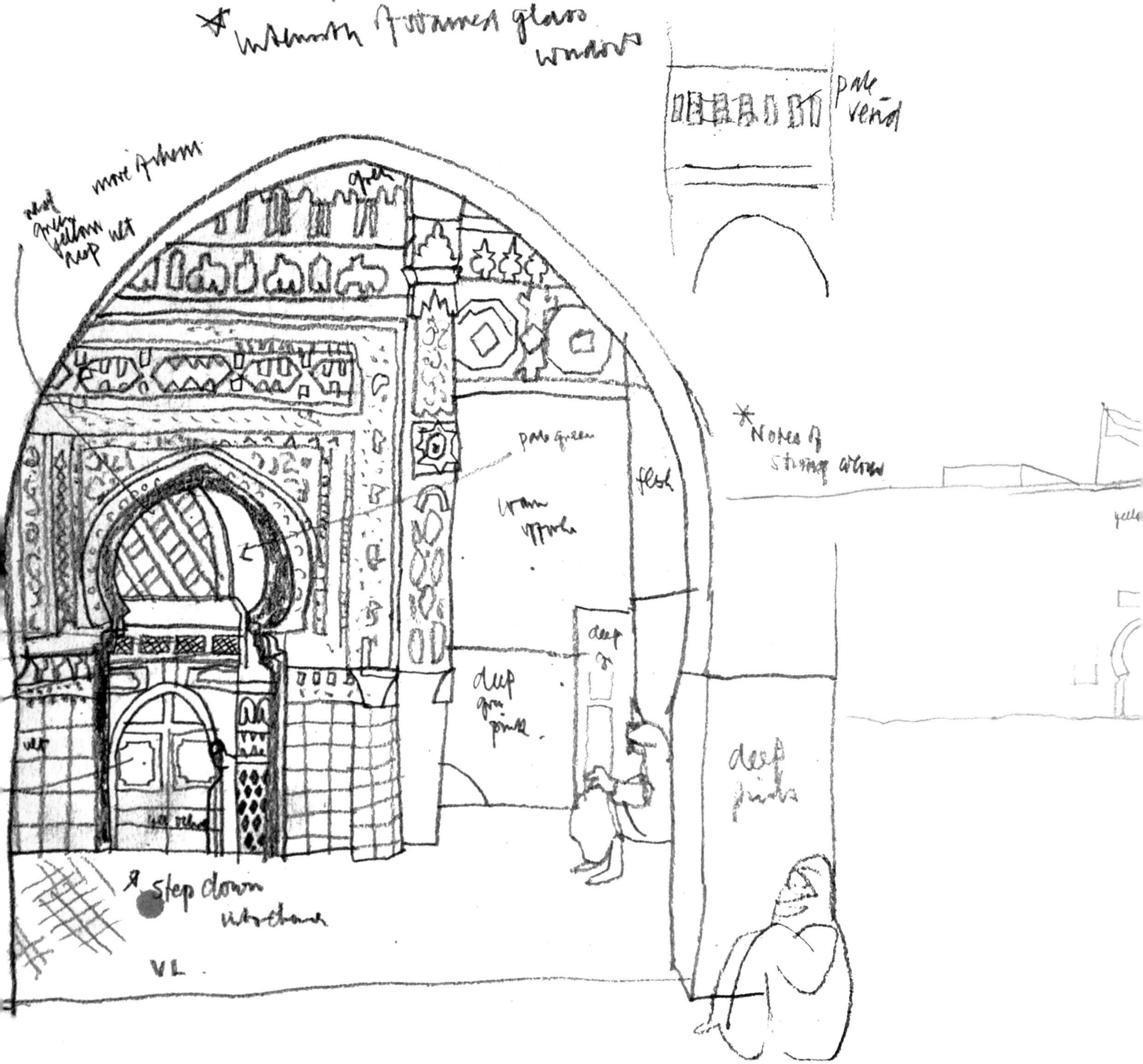
pale green
deep pinks
step down
VL

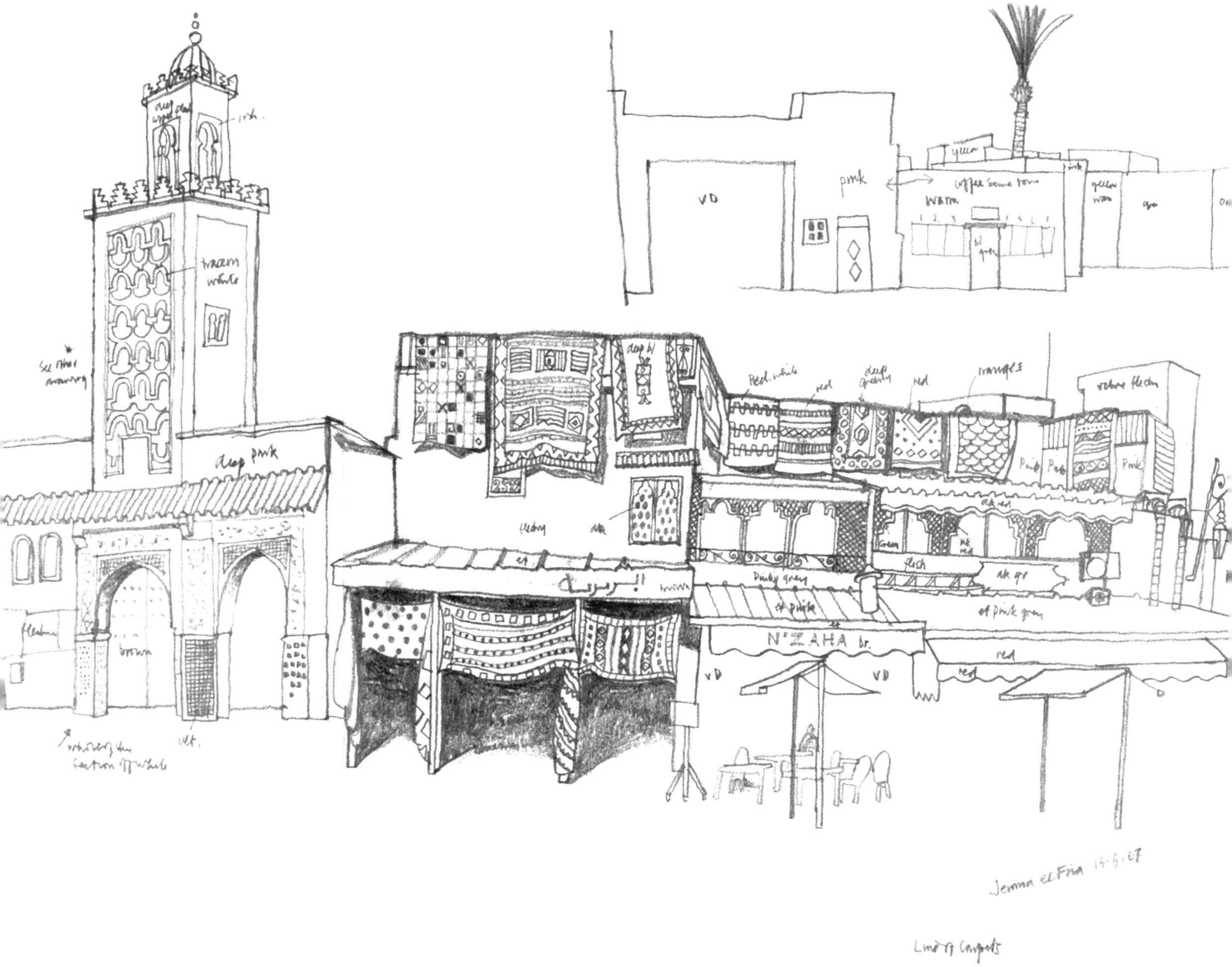
deep pink
brown
pink
VD
warm
red
N'ZAHA
Jemma el Fna
Line of Carpets

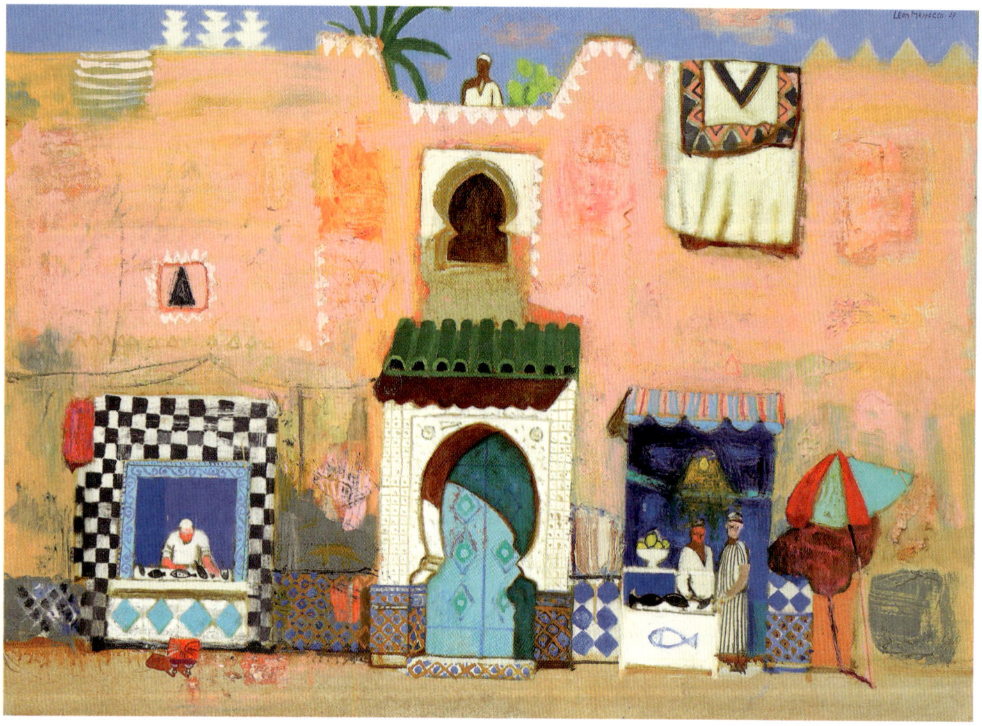

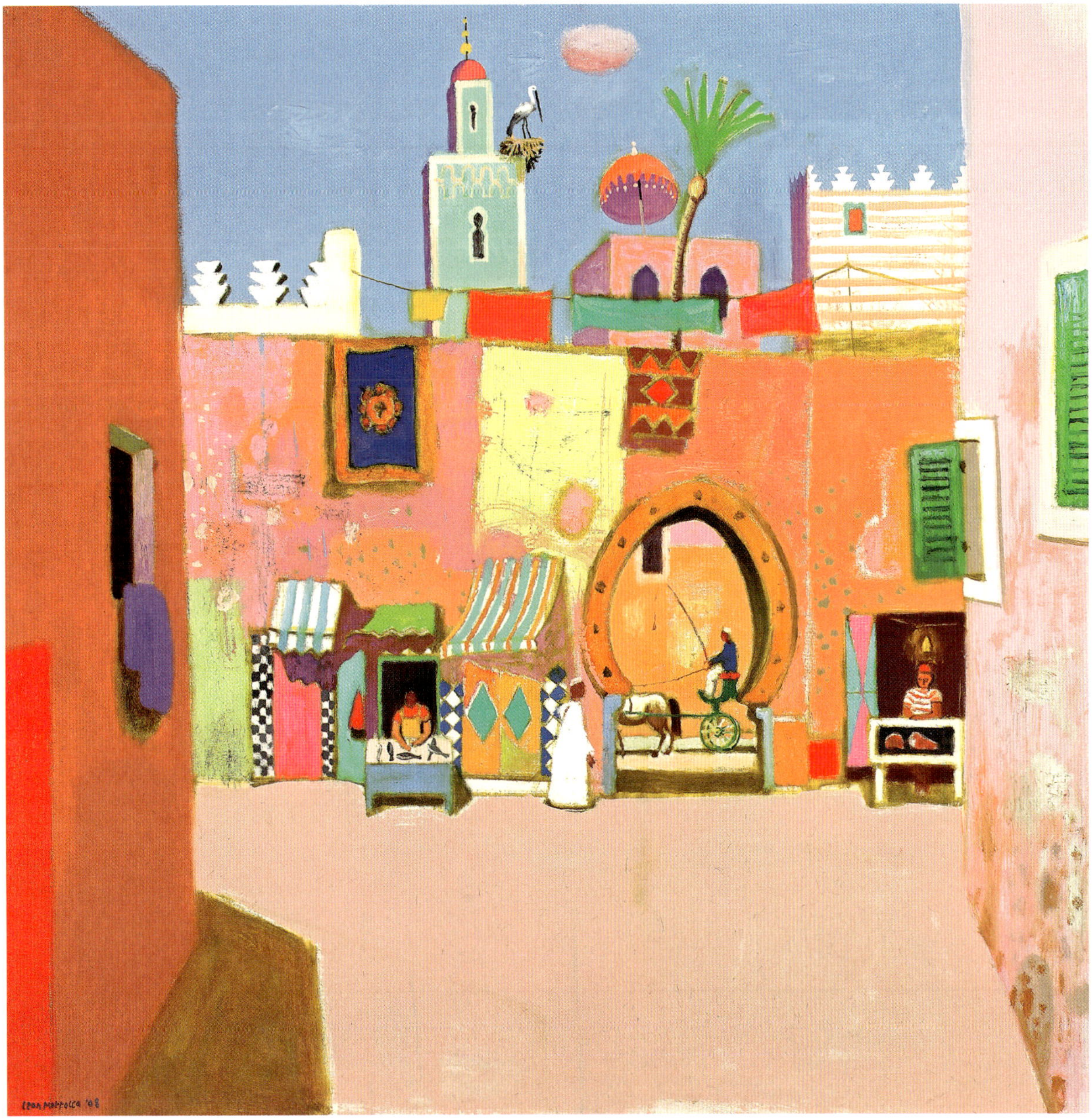

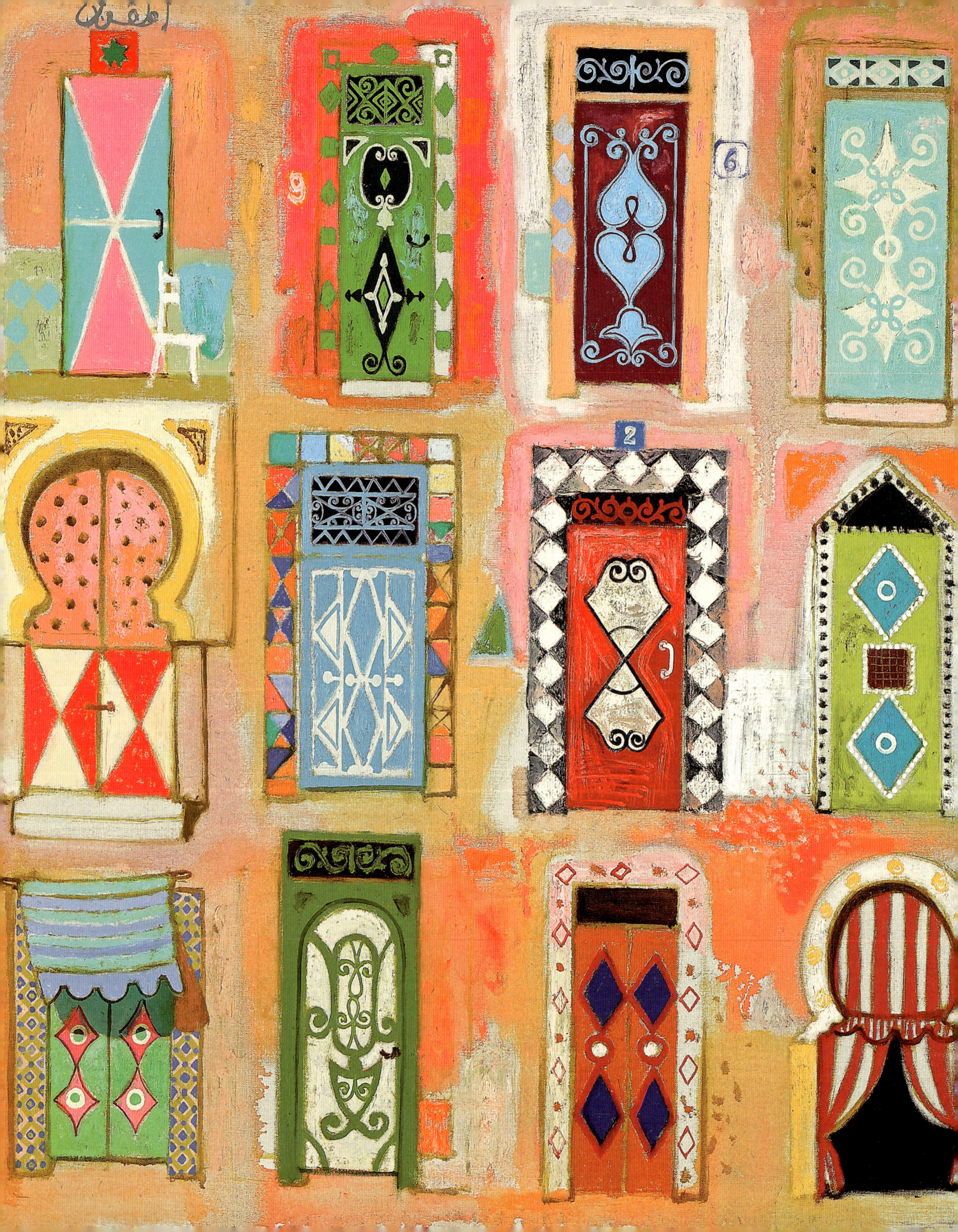

Page 108: **Fish Market by thc Mosque 2007** oil on canvas 76 x 106.5 cm
Page 109: **Looking Through to the Market 2007** oil on canvas 86.5 x 101.5 cm
Page 110: **Twelve Doorways 2007** oil on canvas 86.5 x 101.5 cm
Page 111: **Decorative Door next to Mosque 2007** oil on canvas 76 x 101.5 cm

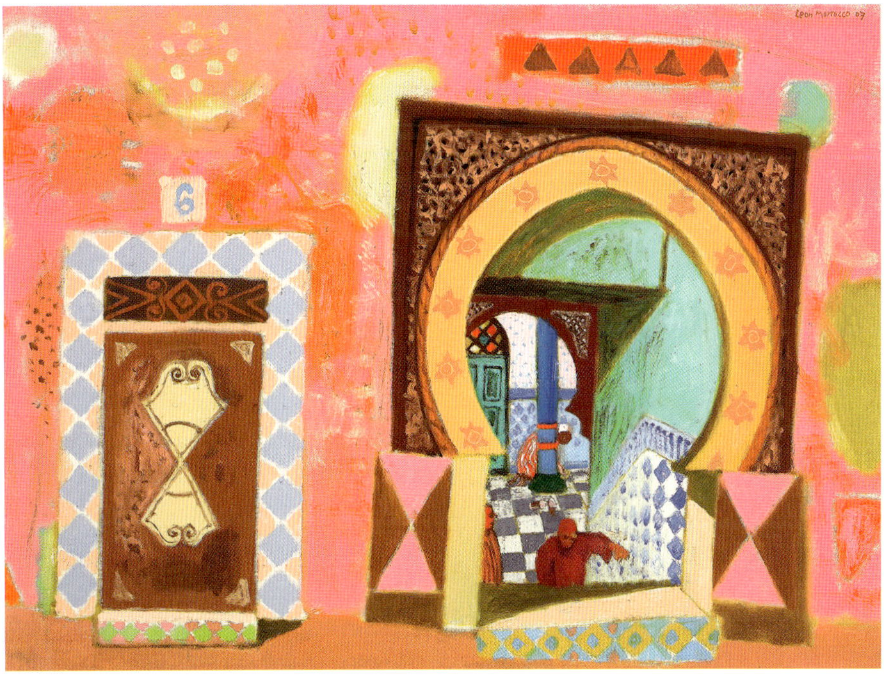

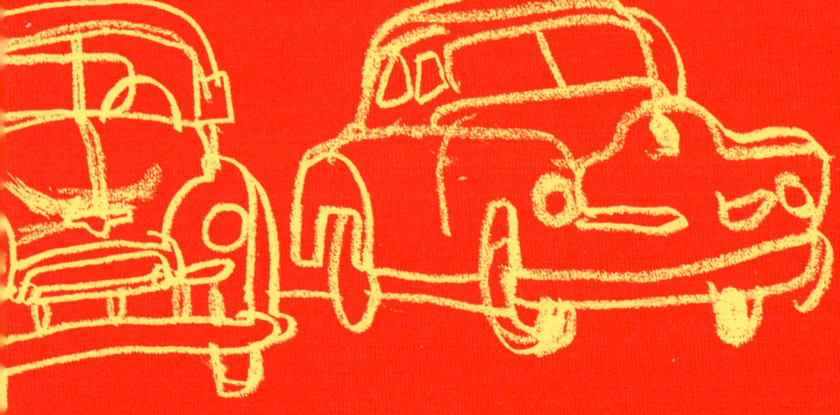

HAVANA

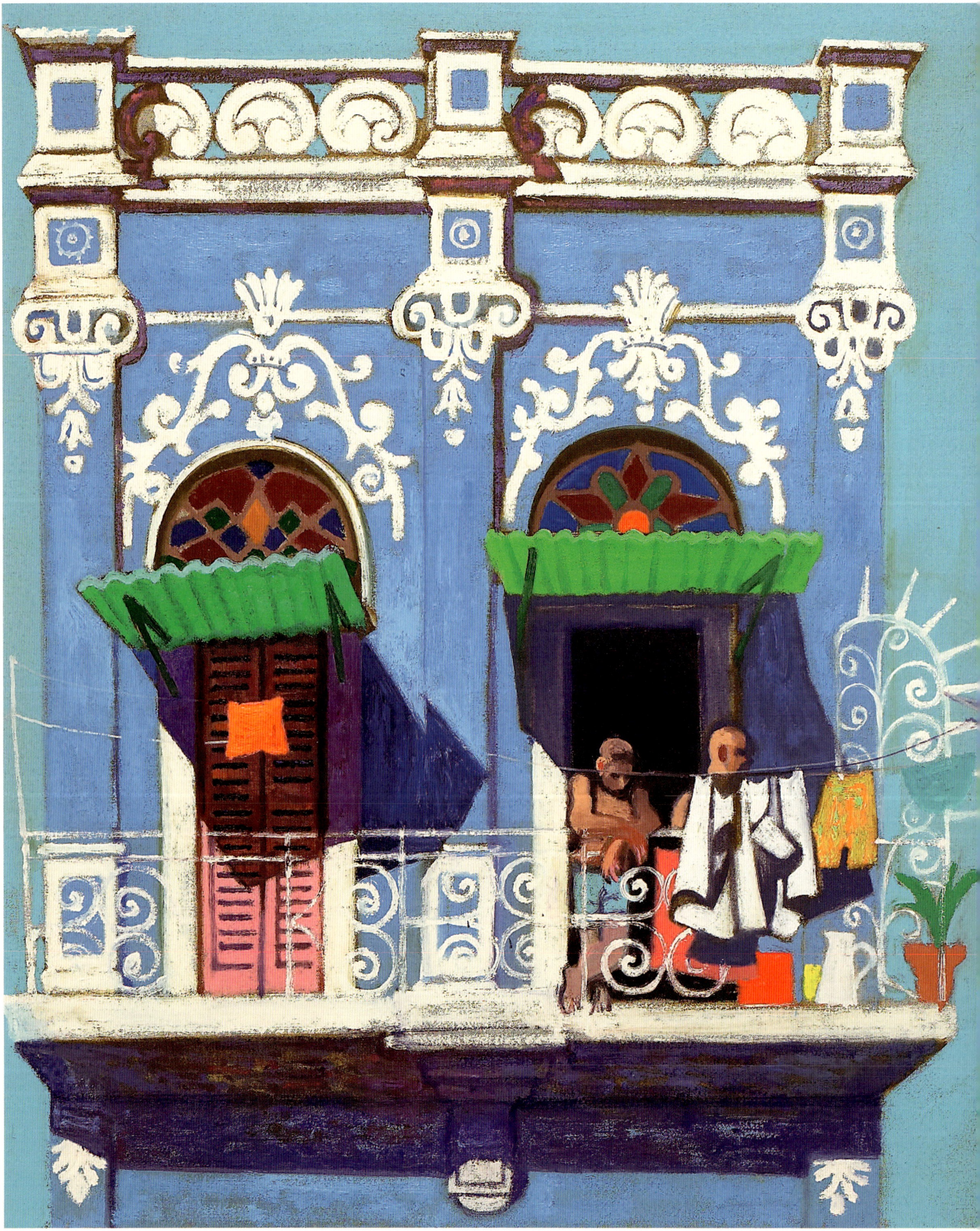

THIS WAS ONE OF THE BEST DRAWING TRIPS THAT I HAVE BEEN ON. MY WIFE, Jean, accompanied me and we were fortunate to have the help and guidance of a well-known Havana painter, Jose Antonio Hechavarria. We were introduced to many painters, sculptors, ceramicists, printmakers and film-makers. We were also taken to the National Art School in Havana and met students and staff as well as seeing a survey of student work, some of which was impressive. Sitting in on rehearsals at the Cuban National Ballet was a highlight.

What impressed us most was a strong sense of camaraderie amongst artists of all disciplines. There seemed to be a common understanding to support each other in the face of what were often extreme difficulties, not just in the sense of political censorship (certain subject matter was problematic) but also in coping with severe shortages in basic materials. Some painters we met were short of essential colours and one art shop we were taken to had only tubes of sap-green in stock.

Printmakers we met had no metal etching or lithography plates and were resorting to thick cardboard or plastic tiles to scratch into. A large box of printing inks and zinc plates that I sent to a young printmaker never reached him and was confiscated by Cuban Customs and sent back to me in London six months later.

Visually Havana was exciting to respond to: the crumbling buildings of the old town, the decorative verandas, the ever-present lines of washing and life lived essentially outside – all rich pickings for the inquisitive eye of the painter. Days were spent drawing in the back alleys of old-Havana, often accompanied by the sound of live music emanating from some open window.

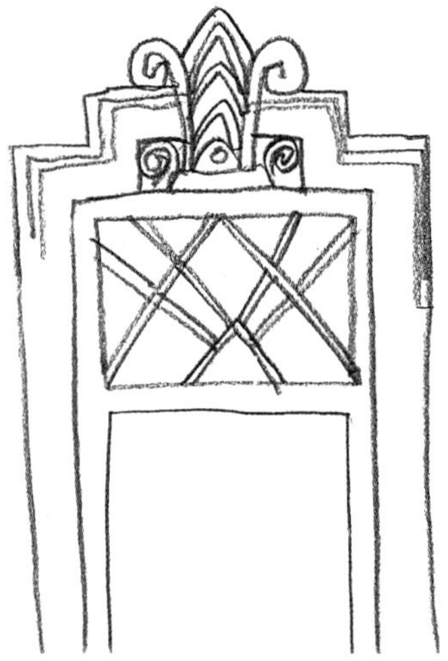

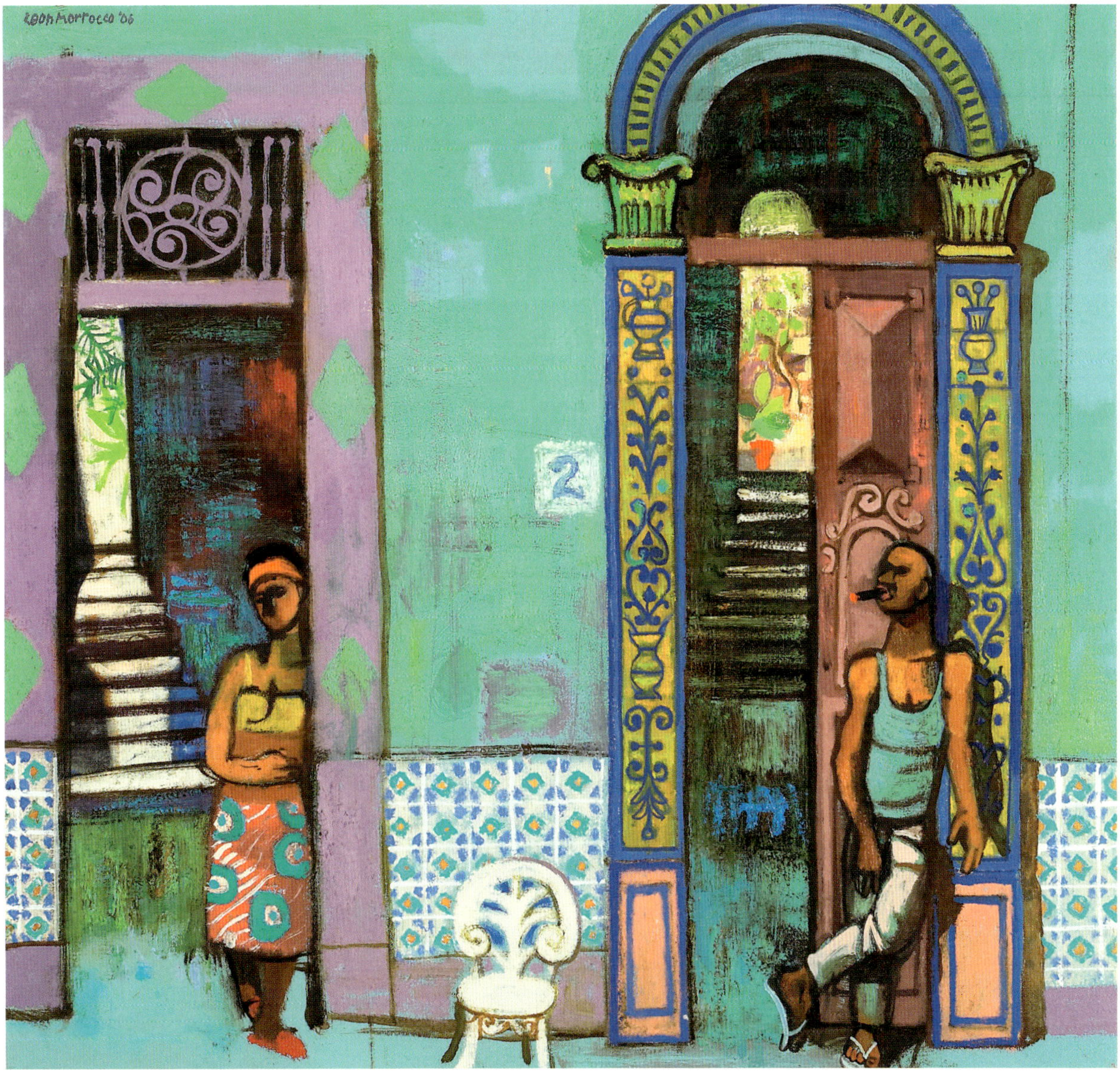
Leon Morrocco '06
2

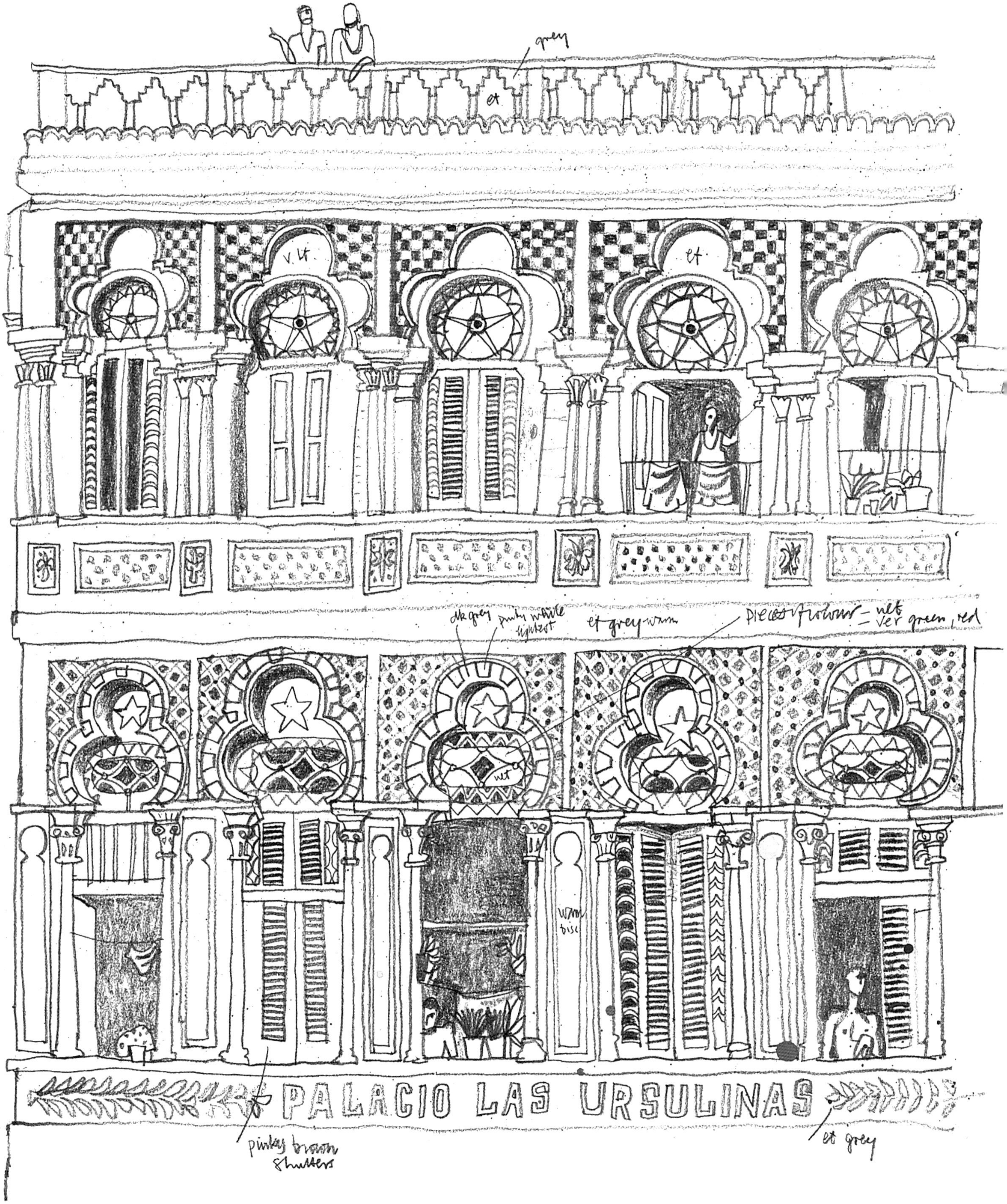
PALACIO LAS URSULINAS
grey
dk grey
pinky white lightest
pinky brown shutters
lt grey

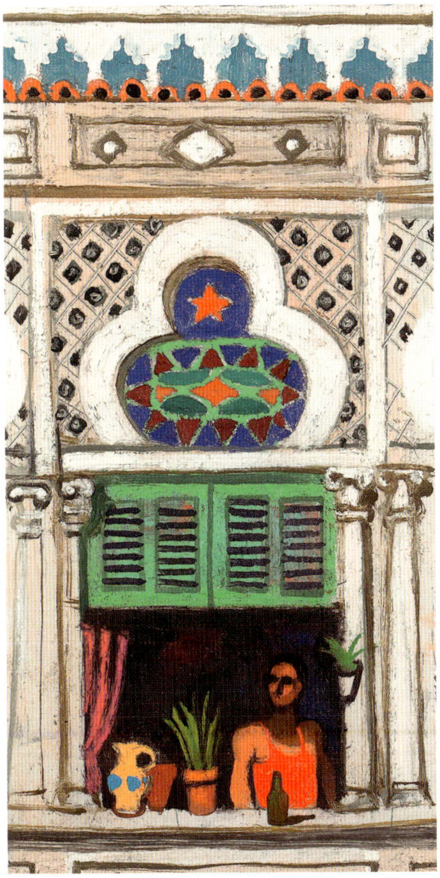

Page 114: **Bright Morning on the Balcony 2006** oil on canvas 76 x 81 cm

Page 117: **Silent Couple 2006** oil on canvas 71 x 76 cm

Page 118: **Palacio Las Ursulinas 2006** pencil on paper 29 x 28 cm

Page 119: **Looking Out from the Kitchen 2006** oil on board 40.5 x 20 cm

Page 120: **Palacio Las Ursulinas with Street Lamp 2006** oil on canvas 101.5 x 106.5 cm

Page 122: **The Egg Seller's Family 2006** oil on canvas 91 x 86 cm

Page 123: **Windows & Balconies 2006** pencil on paper 28 x 30 cm

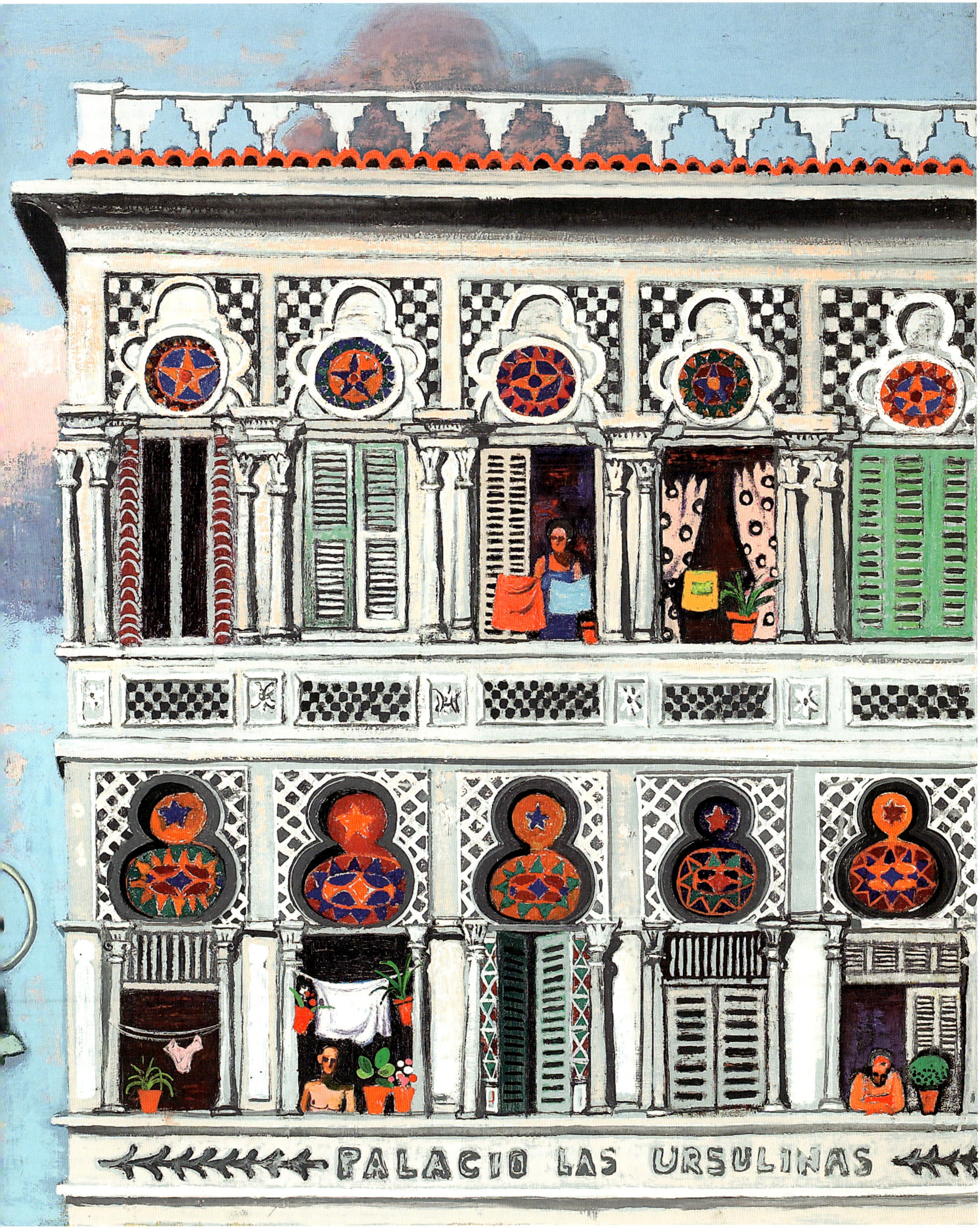
PALACIO LAS URSULINAS

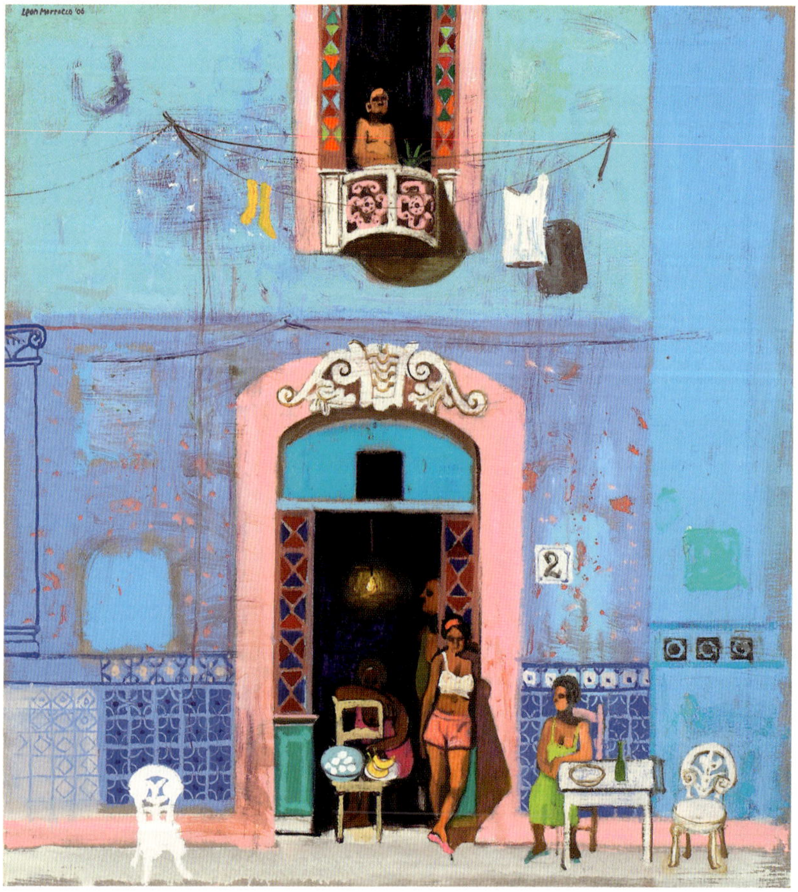
Leon Morrocco '06
2

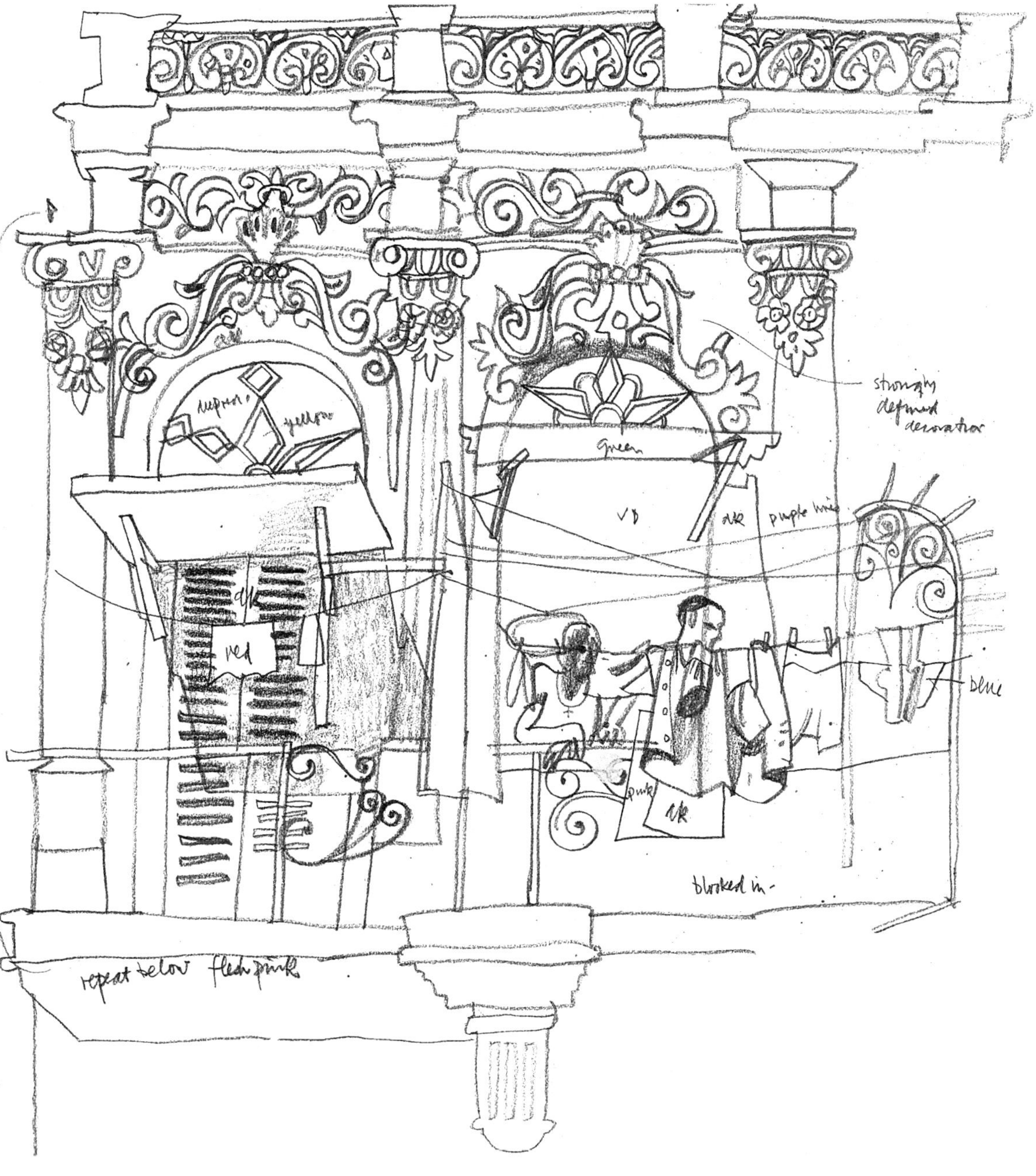
strongly defined decoration
yellow
green
dk purple lines
red
blue
pink
dk
blocked in-
repeat below flesh pink

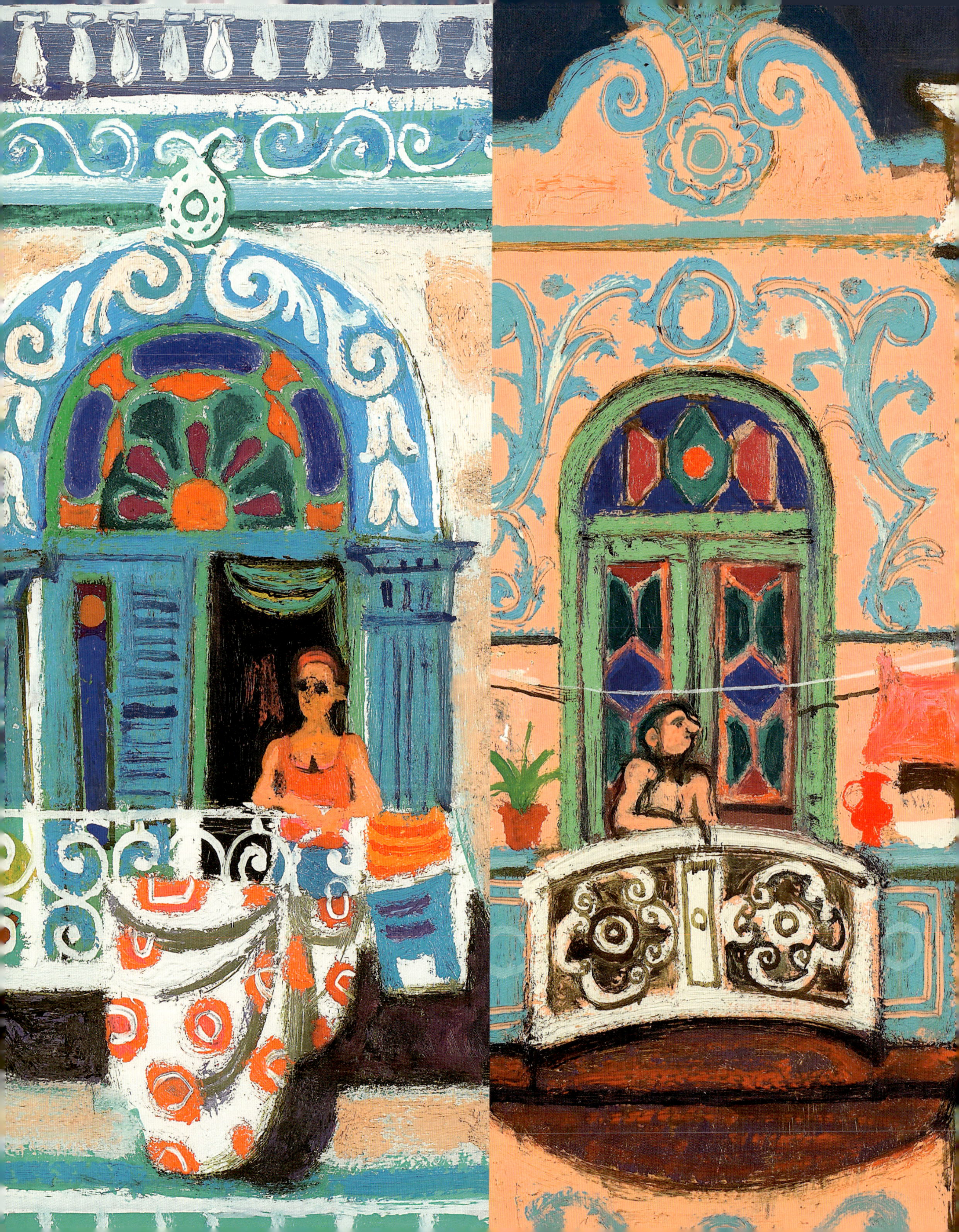

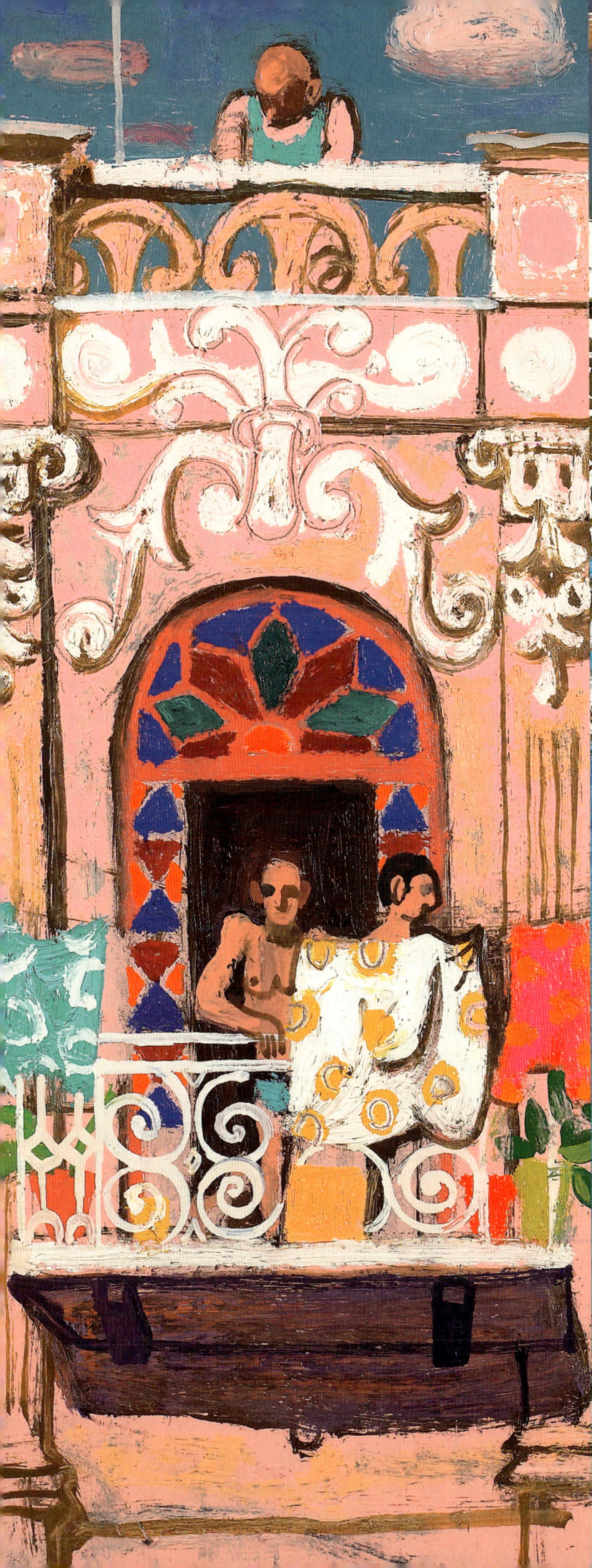

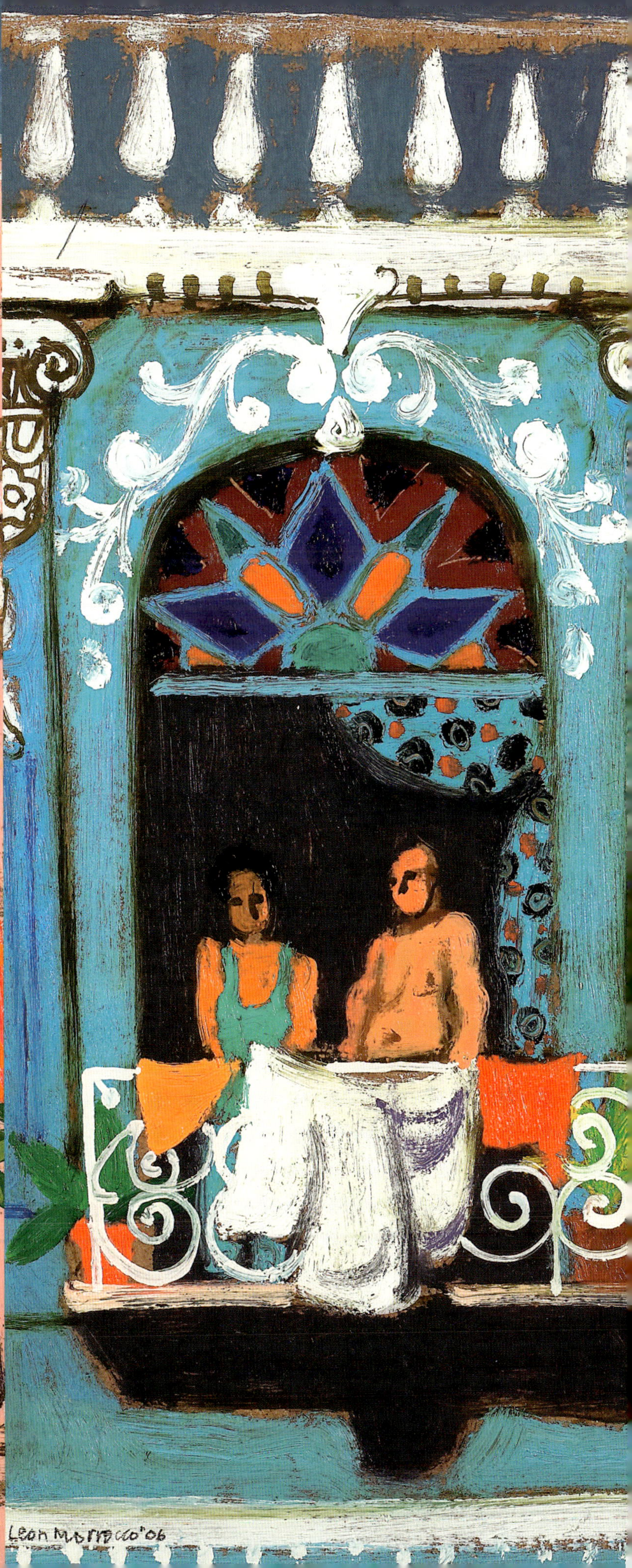
Leon Morrocco '06

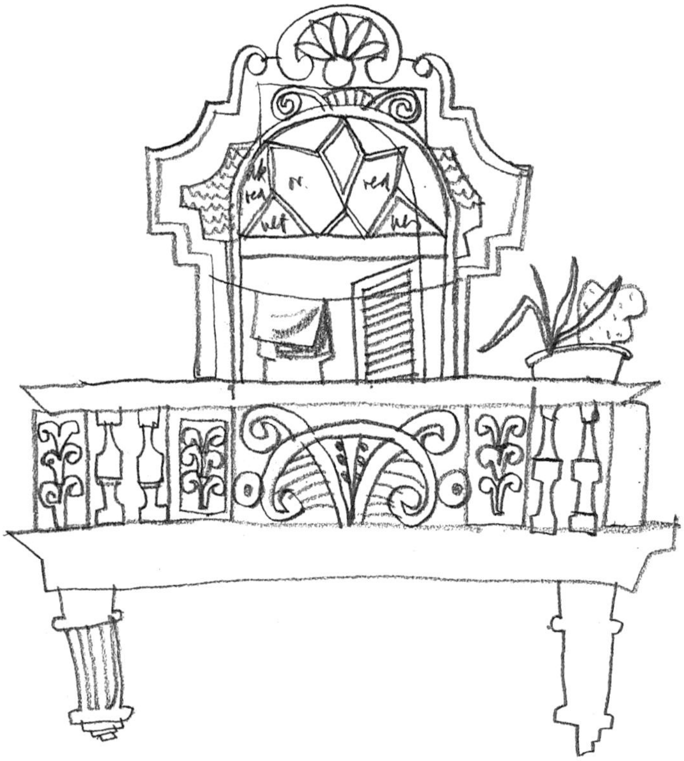

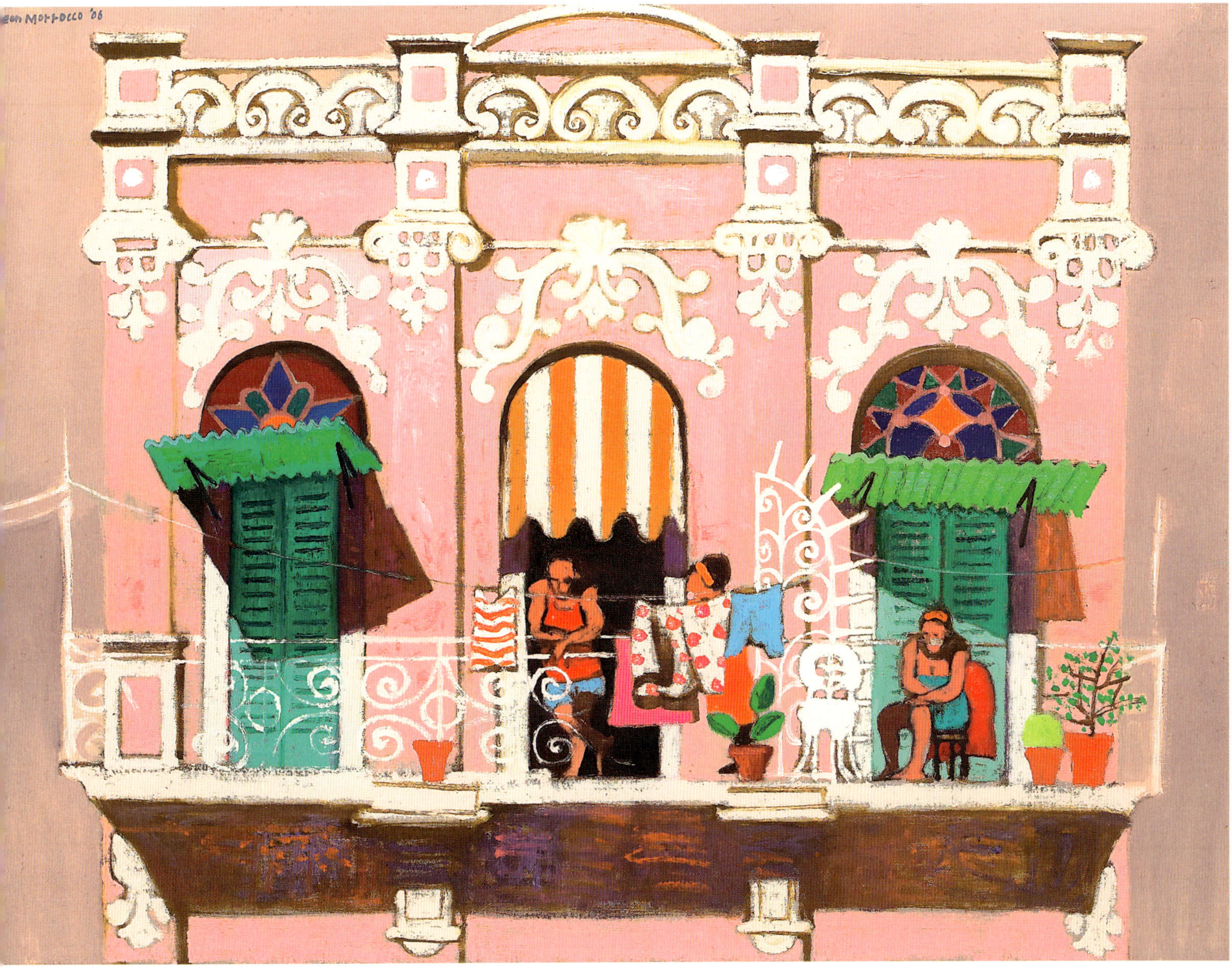

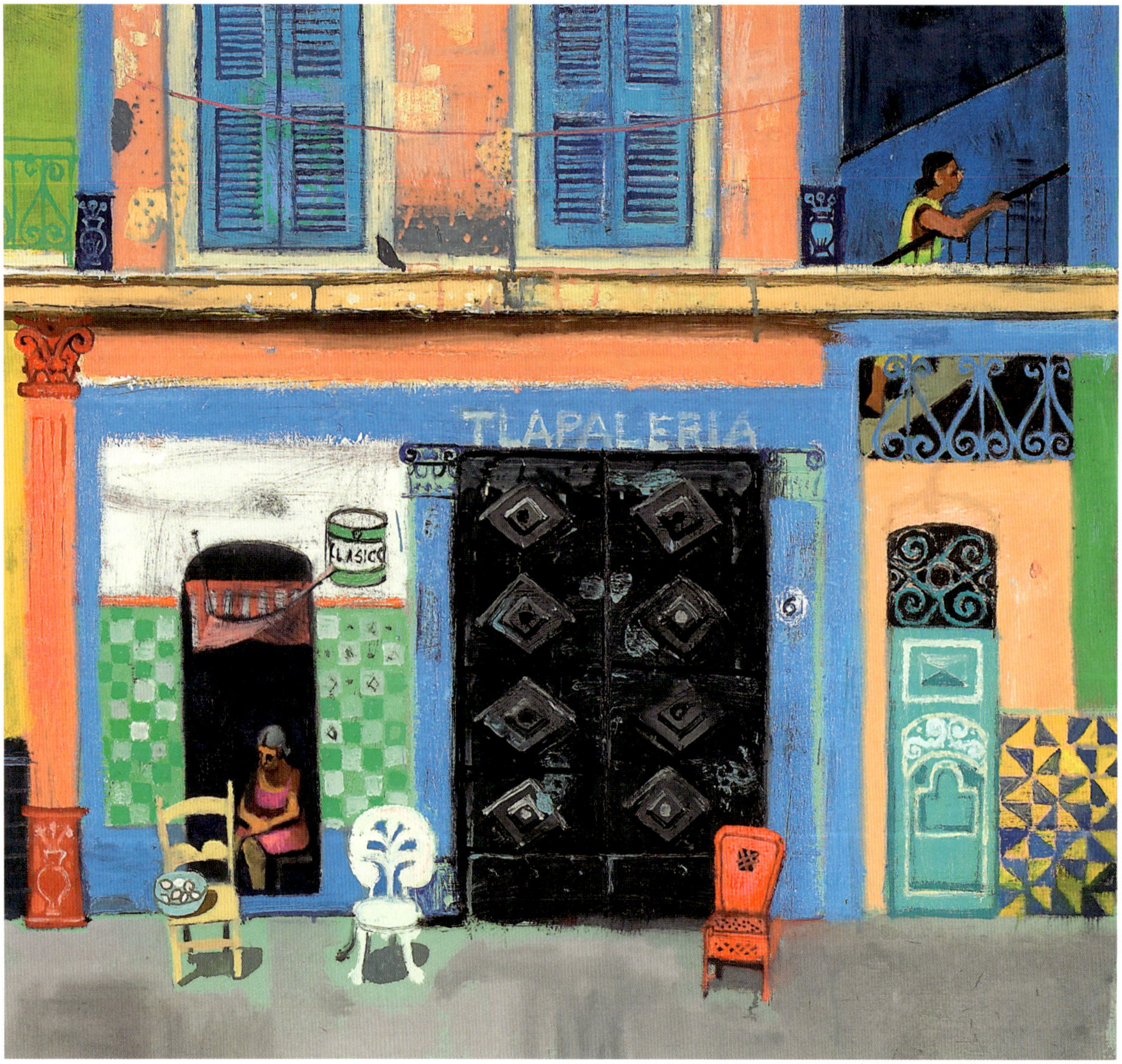
TLAPALERIA
CLASICO
6

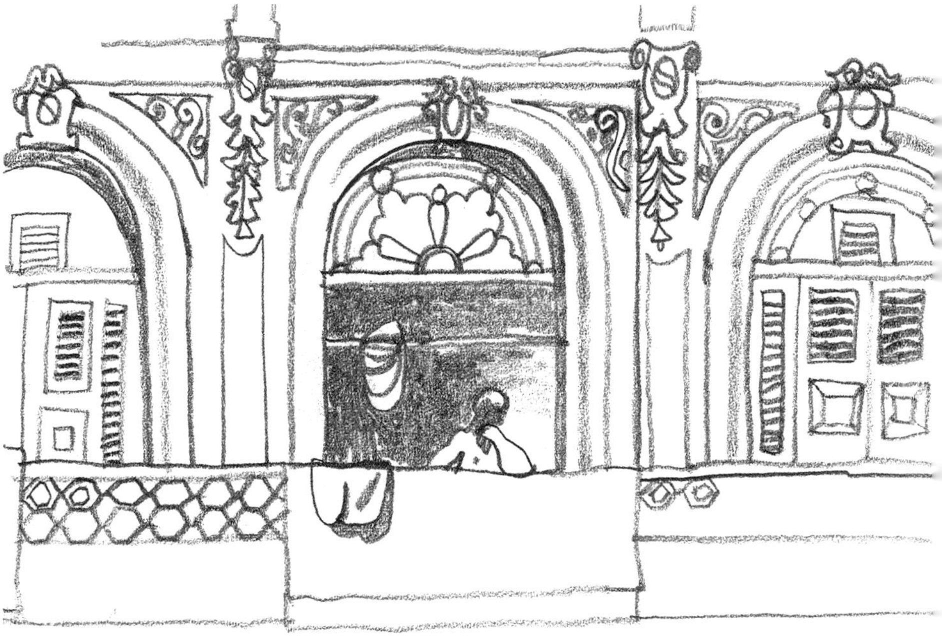

Pages 124-125 *from left*:
Decorative Balcony 2006 oil on board 40.5 x 20 cm
The Red Jug 2006 oil on board 40.5 x 20 cm
Out on the Balcony 2006 oil on board 40.5 x 20 cm
Couple on a Balcony 2006 oil on board 40.5 x 20 cm
Page 127: **Midday on the Balcony 2006** oil on canvas 76 x 95 cm
Page 128: **La Tlapaleria (Paint Shop) 2006** oil on canvas 91.5 x 96.5 cm
Page 130: **The Chess Players 2006** oil on canvas 61 x 76 cm
Page 133: **Three 1948 Ford Plymouths 2006** oil on canvas 81 x 76 cm

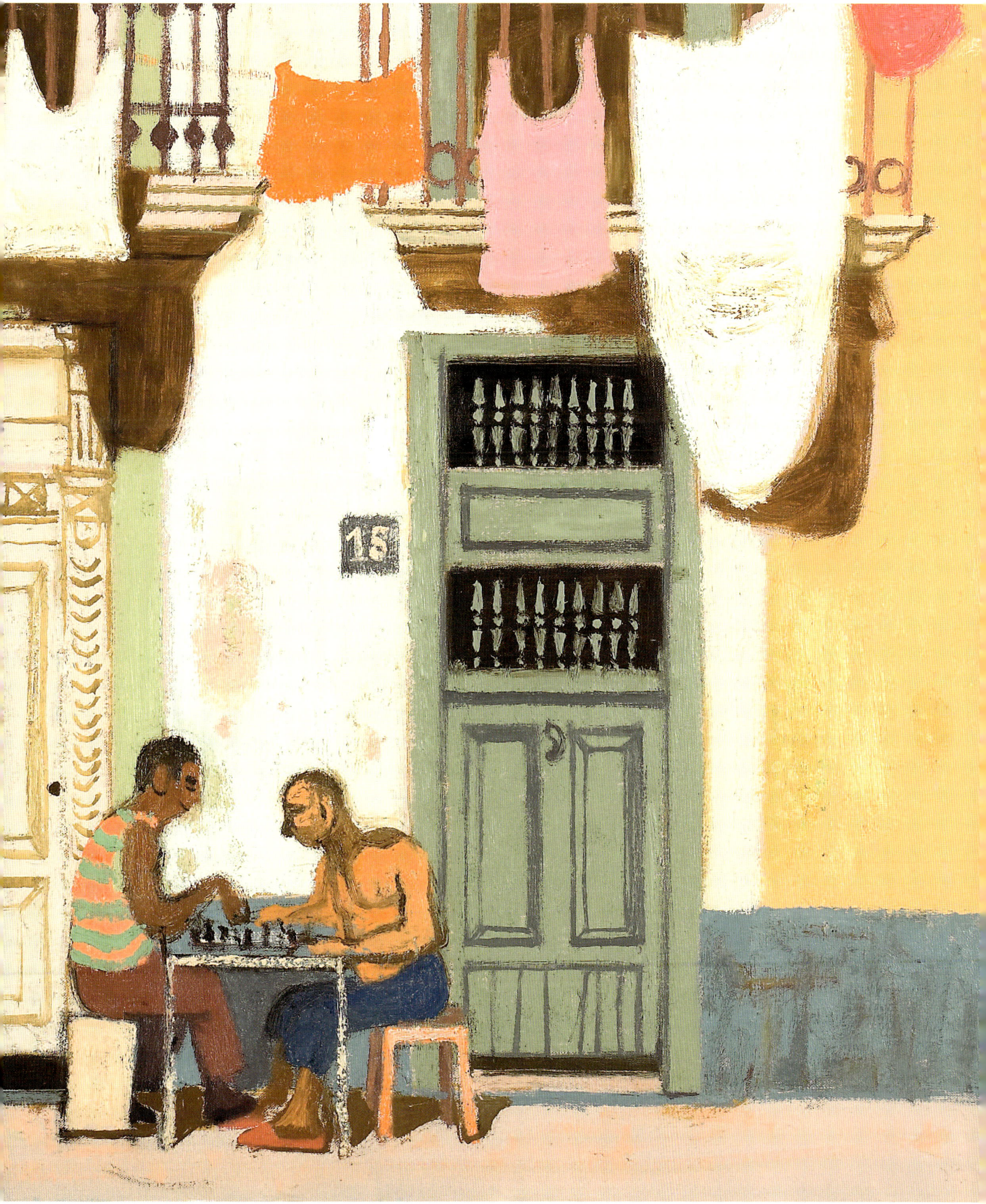
15

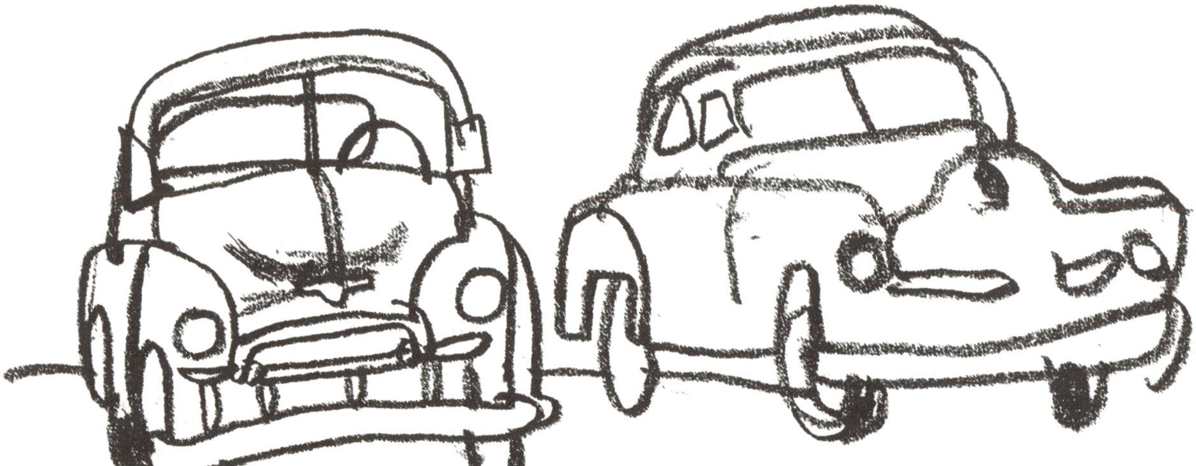

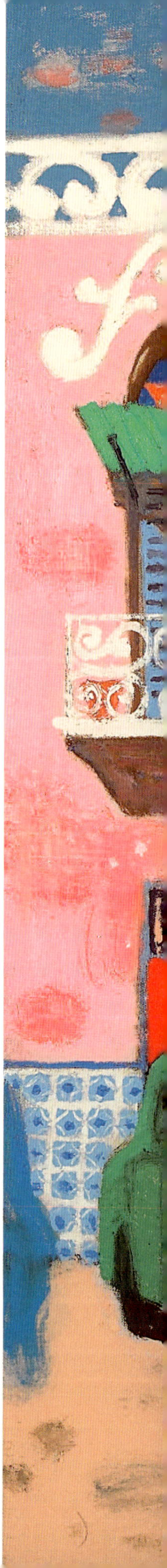

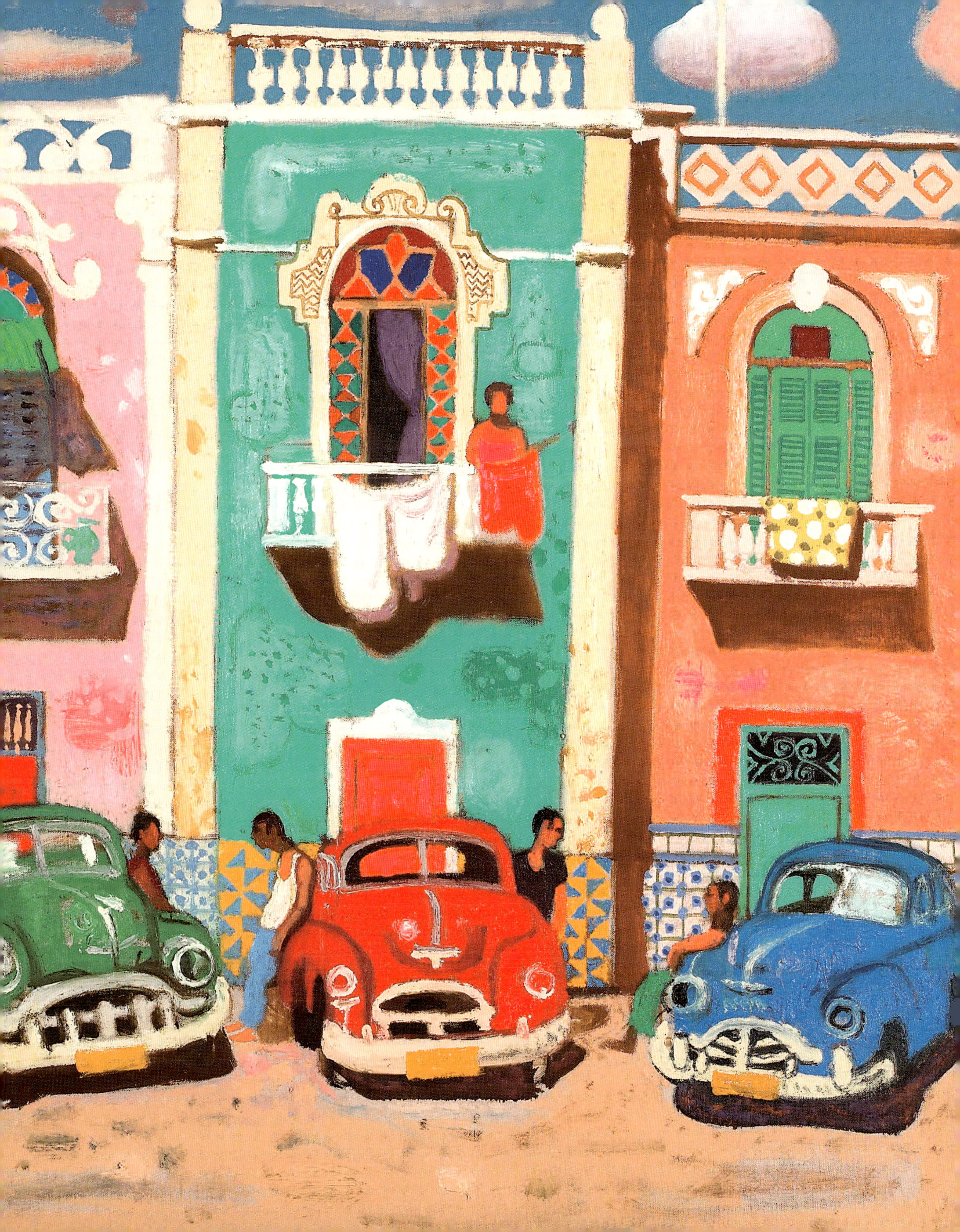

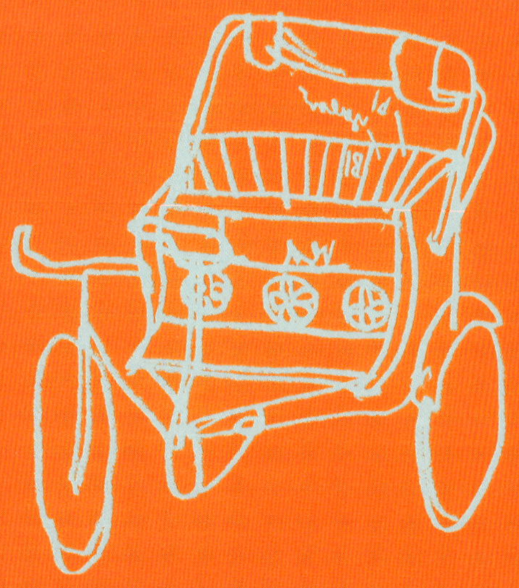

INDIA

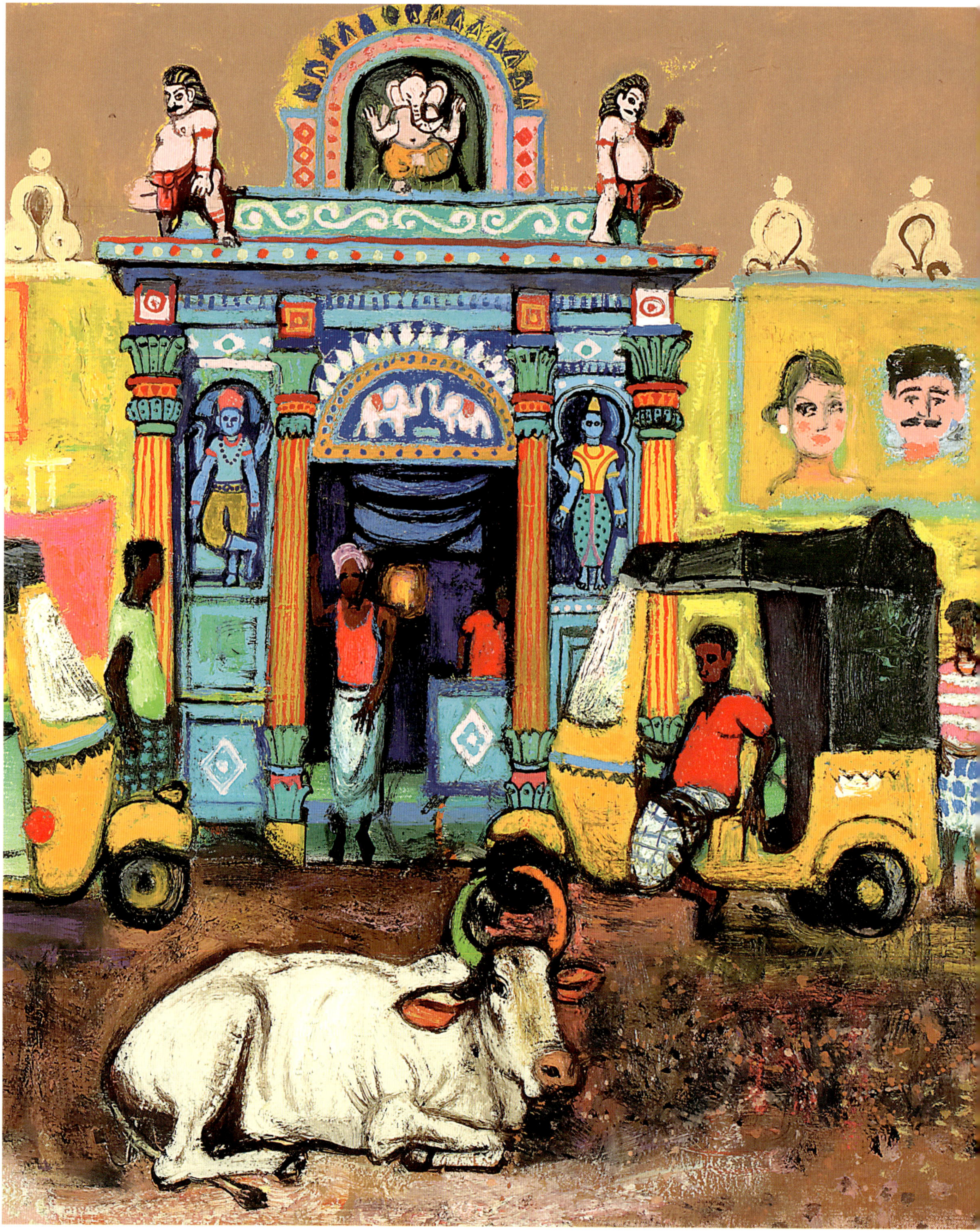

MY FIRST VISIT TO INDIA FRANKLY OVERWHELMED ME. THE ASSAULT on the senses was exhilarating but exhausting. The sheer barrage of sight, sound and smell seemed to paralyse me and I had no idea how – or where – to begin the drawing process. The visit was frustratingly un-productive from a working point of view but India won me over with its vitality and vibrancy, and I was determined to return for a second attempt.

On this next visit I realised that waiting for some obvious starting point was futile and that I should begin drawing anywhere. This approach, recognising as it did that practically everything in India is worth drawing, seemed to work and I had no further problems. Colour is a predominant factor in India and sometimes it is of such intensity that it is breath-taking. A group of market women against an aquamarine wall and saris at the extreme end of the colour spectrum, would be a highly charged visual experience . . . and almost unbelievable.

Kolkata had a profound if disturbing effect on me. The area around the Howrah Bridge and the flower market offered unlimited opportunities for drawing. The streets were literally teeming with life – trading, washing, sleeping, shaving, sewing, all human activity displayed in public.

However, after a few days of frenetic drawing I found the spectacle of abject poverty, on a grand scale, difficult to stomach and

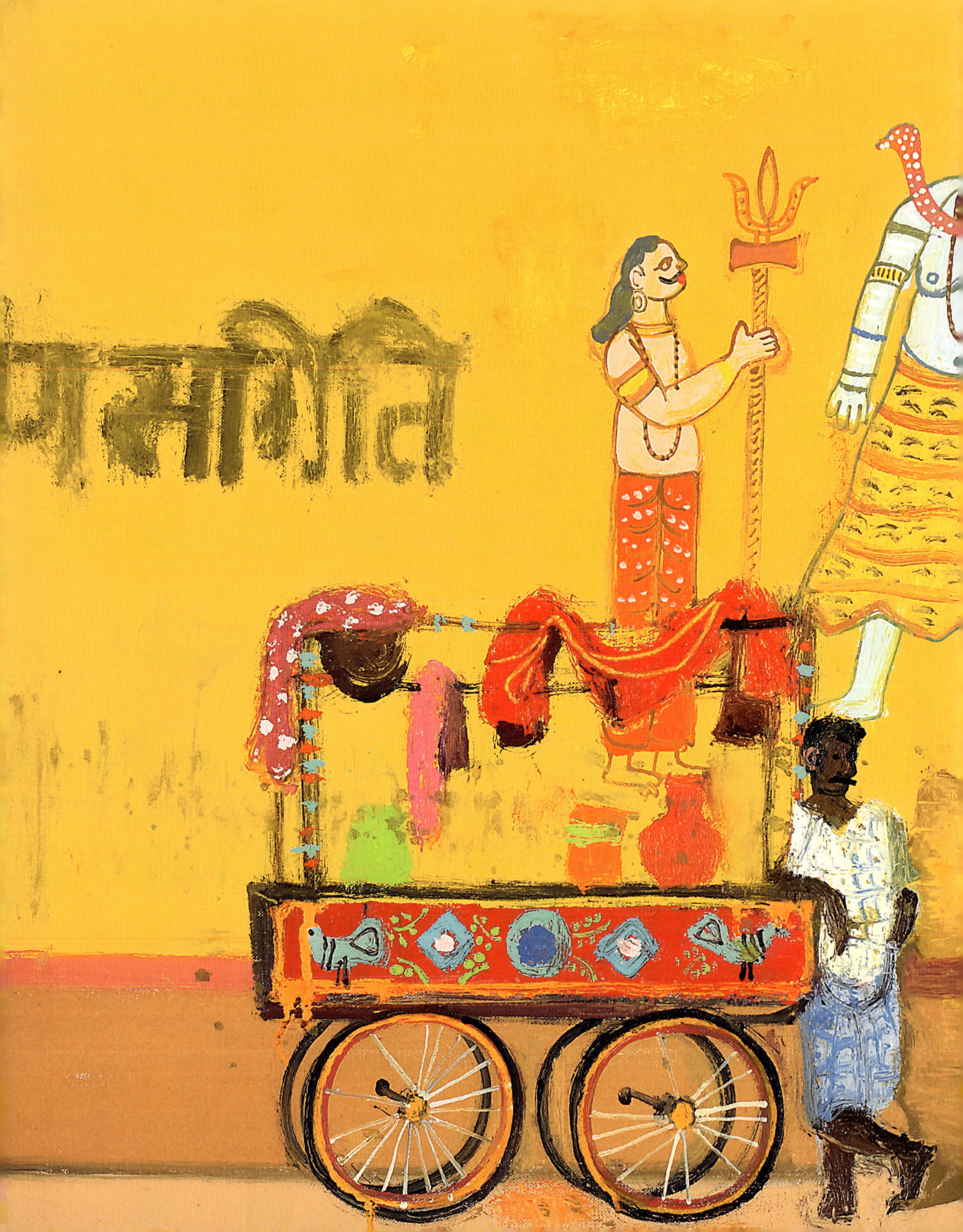

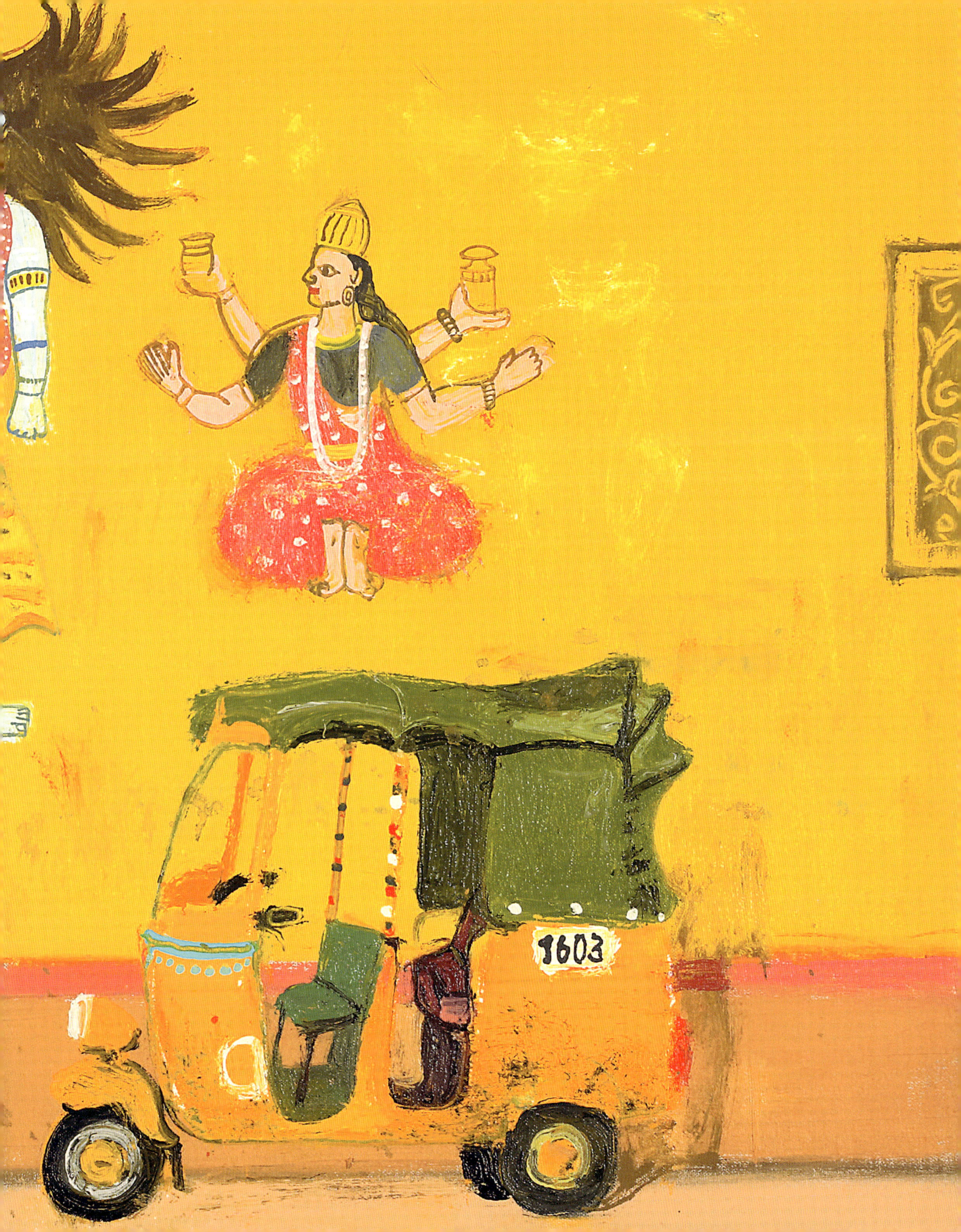
1603

my observations seemed voyeuristic. I saw amazing painting possibilities but was unable to continue and left the city with a sense of relief. Smaller cities, such as Madurai in Tamil Nadu and Jodhpur in Rajasthan, were easier to cope with and the levels of poverty seemed less severe. The streets in these places offered all the tumultuous chaos that so interests me as drawing material, with markets of every denomination, with flower, meat, vegetable and banana – plus the addition of camels, elephants and the ever present holy cows.

I made four working trips to India between 2008 and 2012 and found the experiences amongst the most rewarding of my professional life.

However, in working over that period within a colour range of high intensity I began to tire of that very element. The need to find subject matter that might require me to use colour in a less strident manner became paramount. The London paintings that followed provided the perfect vehicle.

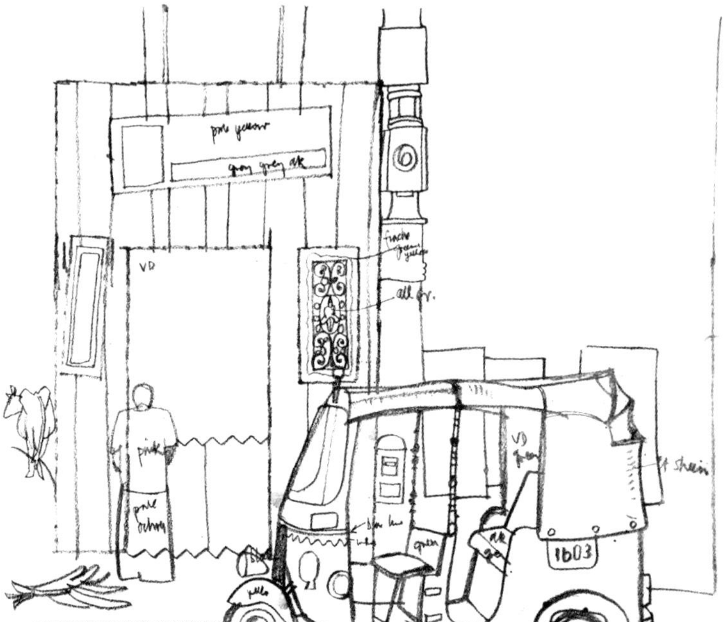

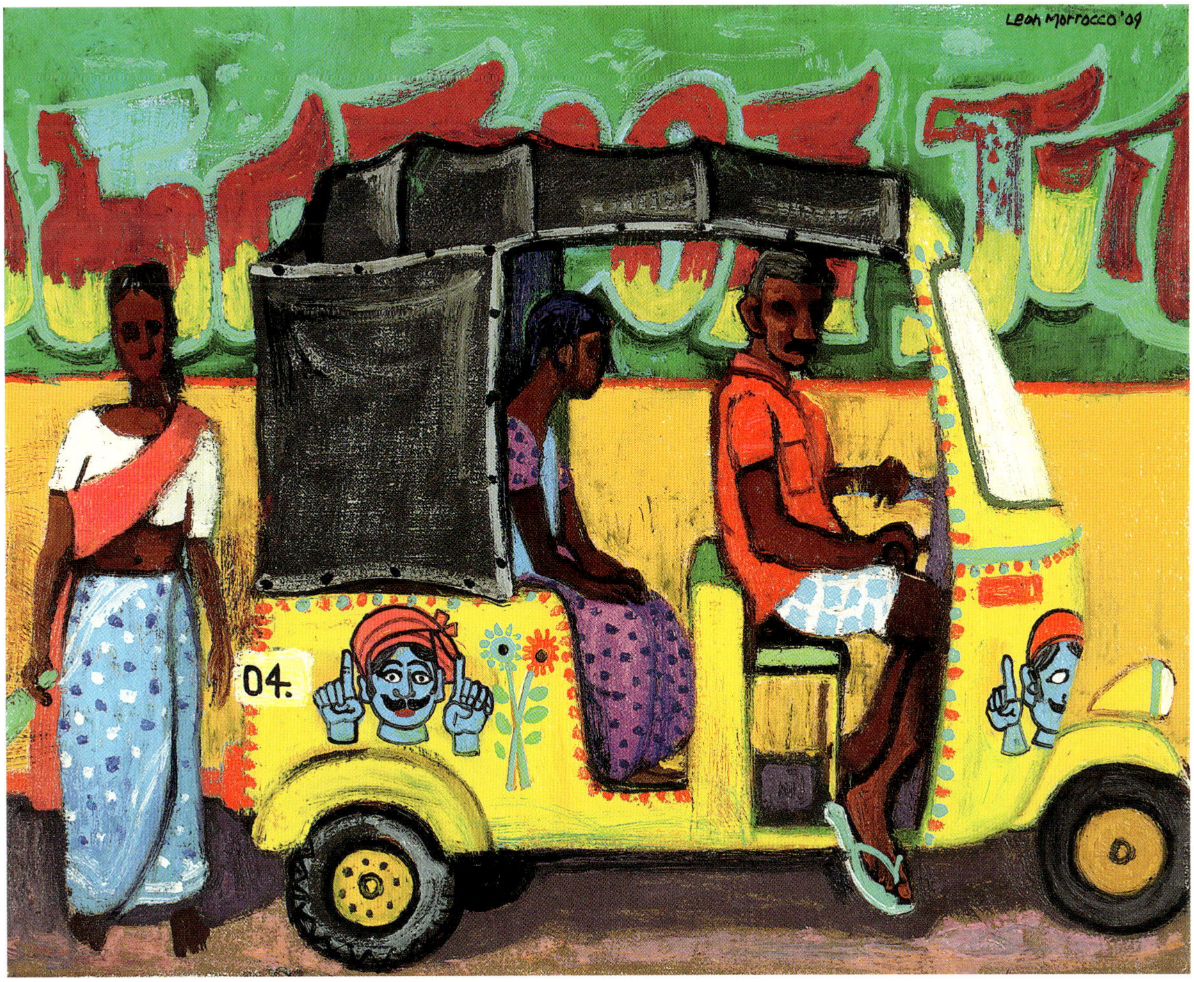
Leon Morrocco '09
04.

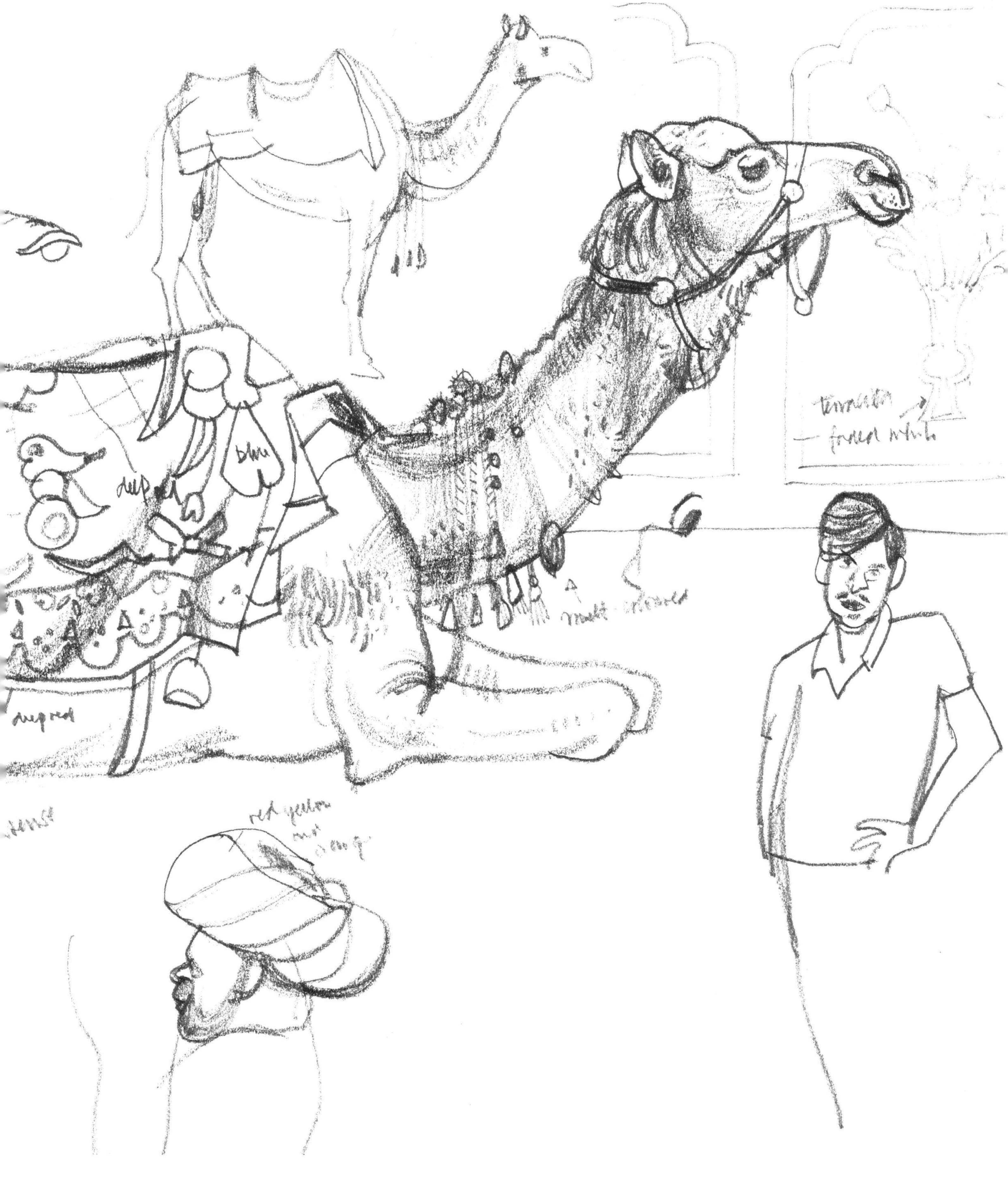
blue
deep red
terracotta
faded white

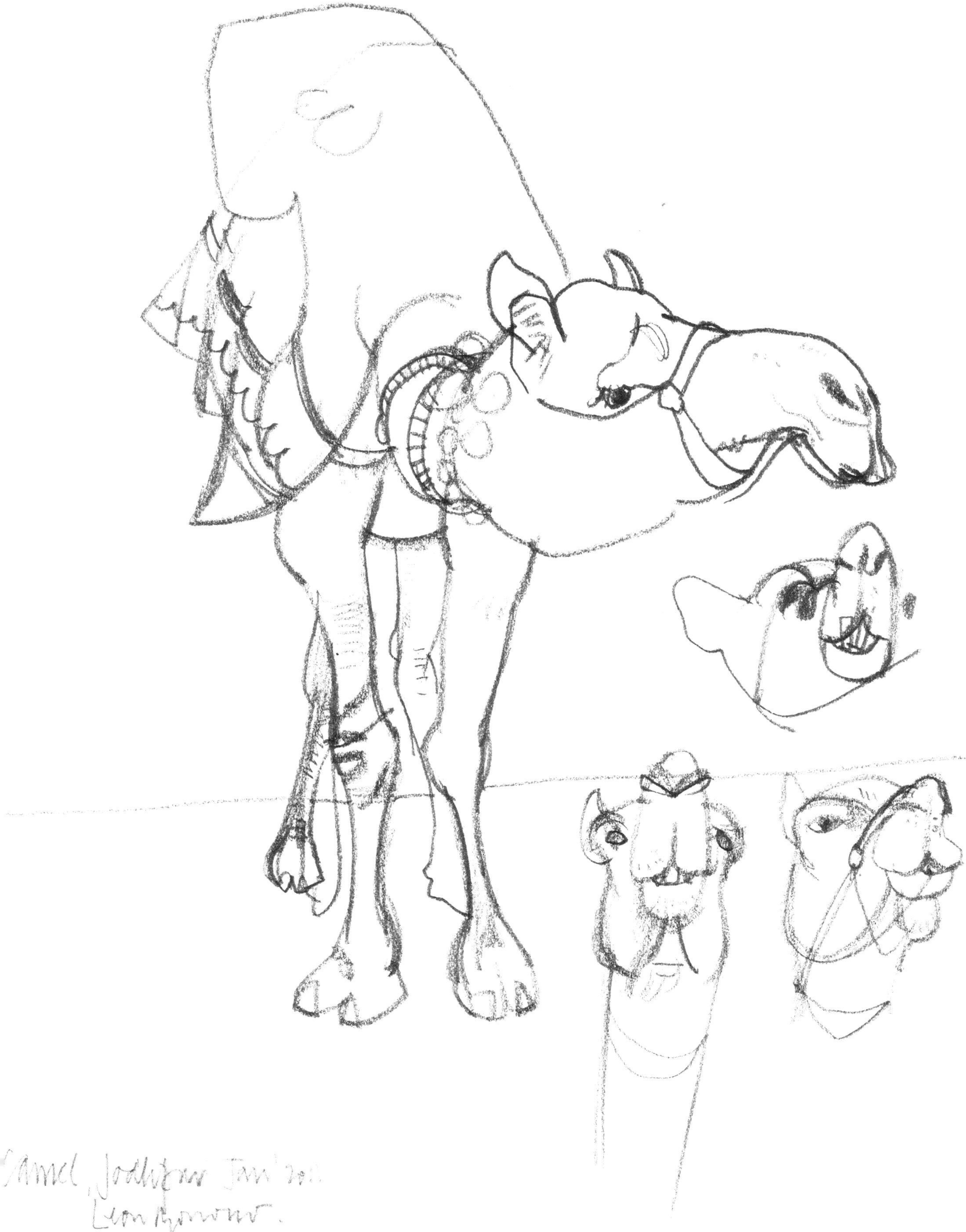
Camel, Jodhpur Jan

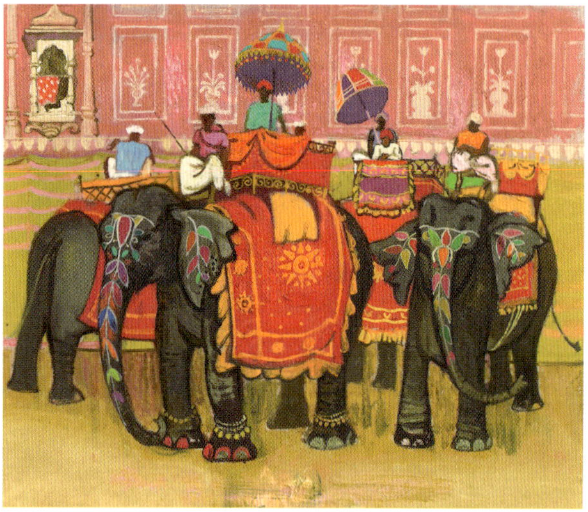

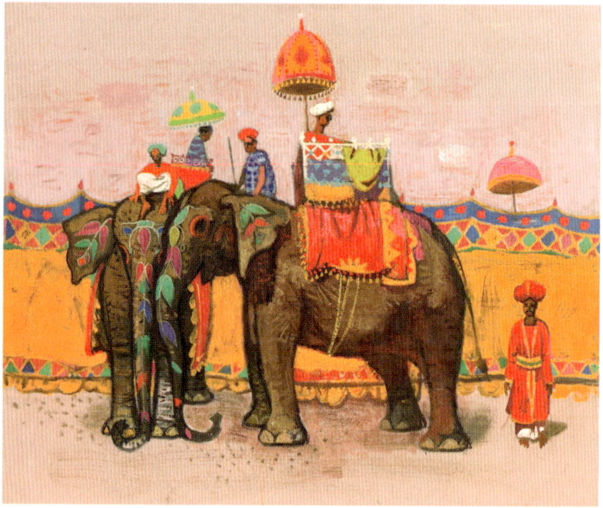

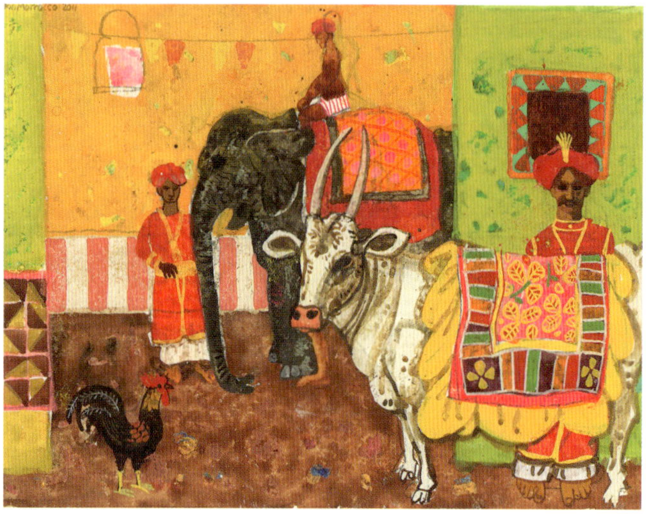

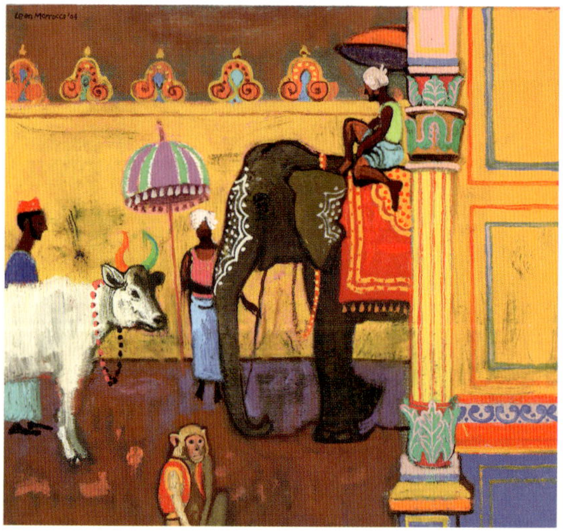

Page 136: **Waiting for Customers, Madurai 2009** oil on canvas 76 x 101.5 cm
Page 138: **Behind the Ghats, Varanasi 2009** oil on canvas 61 x 76 cm
Page 141: **Autorickshaw Madurai 2009** oil on canvas 40.5 x 51 cm
Page 142 and 143: **Camel studies, Jodphur 2009** pencil on paper 25 x 25 cm
Page 144 *clockwise from top left*: **A Circle of Elephants at the Amer Fort, Jaipur 2010** oil on canvas 86.5 x 81 cm
Two Elephants at the Amer Fort, Jaipur 2010 oil on canvas 91.5 x 86.5 cm
Elephant Leaving the Temple, Madurai 2009 oil on panel 51 x 56 cm
A Holy Cow with Elephant and Cockerel, Jaipur 2010 gouache 30.5 x 42 cm

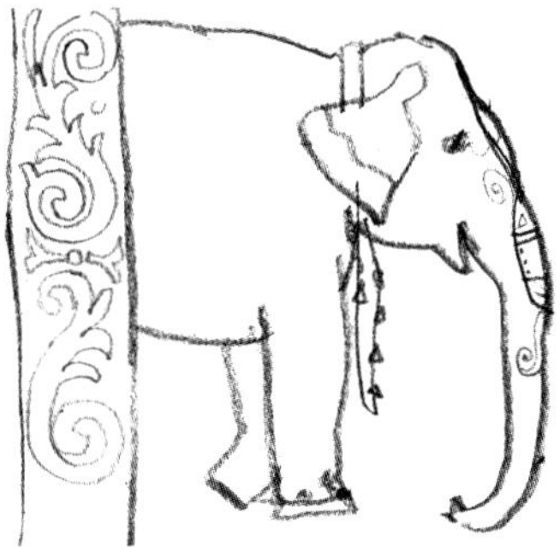

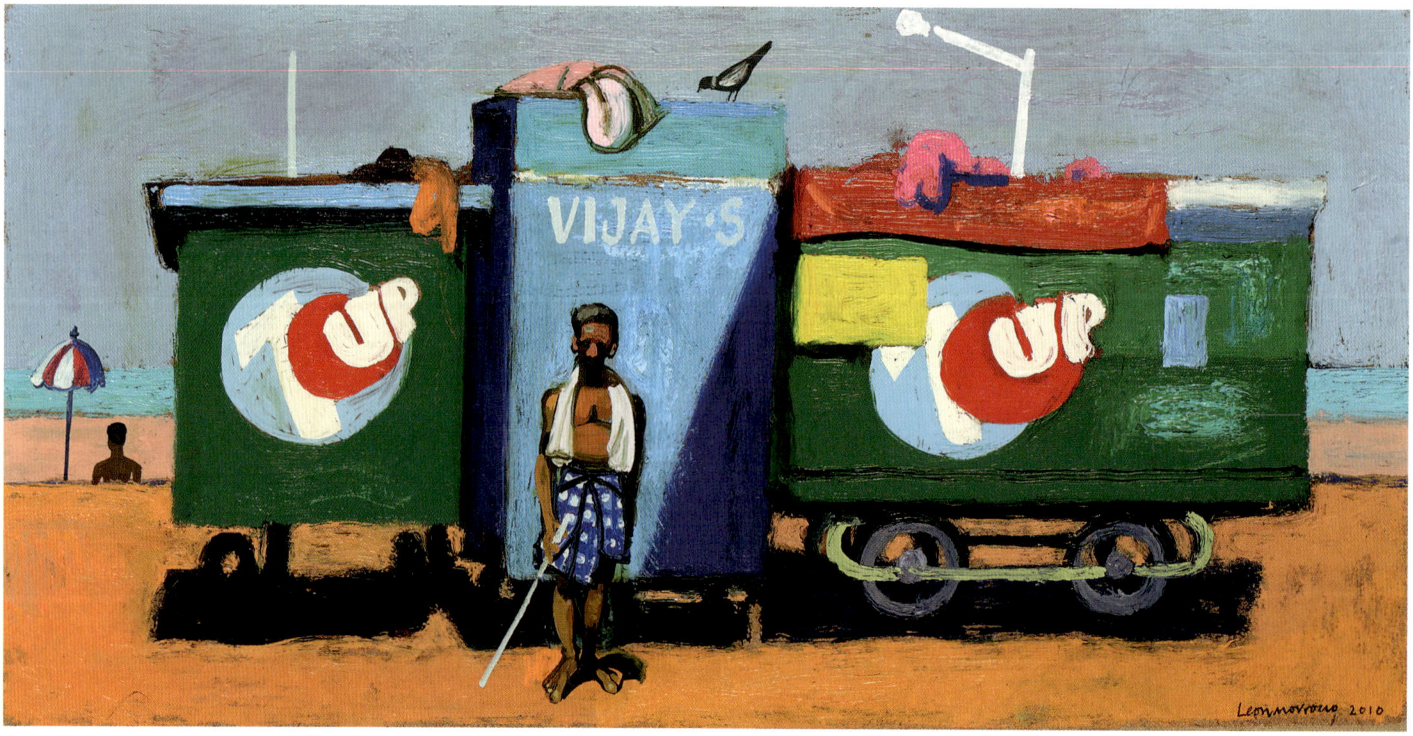
7UP
VIJAY'S
7UP
2010

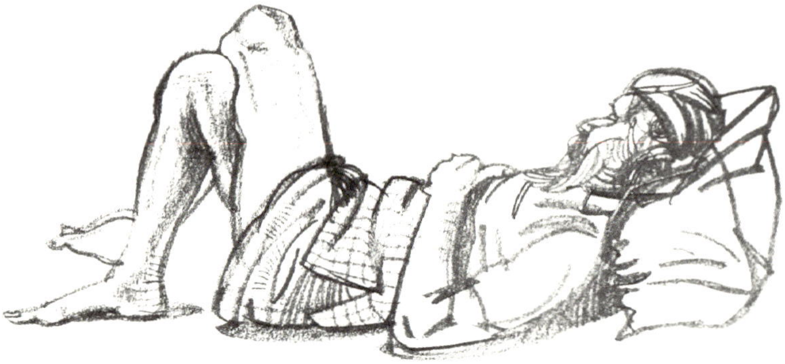

Page 146: **Vijay's Kiosks, Chennai (S1) 2010** oil on canvas 20 x 40.5 cm
Page 147: **Sleeping Man Against Fanta Sign, Kolkata 2010** oil on panel 38 x 20 cm
Page 148: **Maharaja of Benares, 2009** pencil on paper 11 x 15 cm
Page 149 from left: **The Maharaja of Benares 2009** oil on panel 25 x 25 cm
The Maharaja of Benares and His Coach 2009 oil on panel 25 x 25 cm
Page 150: **Farmer's Family – Vaigai River, Madurai 2009** oil on panel 25 x 38 cm
Page 151: **Holy Cow, Kolkata 2009** pencil on paper 14 x 21.5 cm
Page 152: **Temple on the Ghat, Varanasi 2009** pencil on paper 28.5 x 30 cm
Page 153: **Washing Saris, the Ghats 2010** oil on linen 150.5 x 160.5 cm

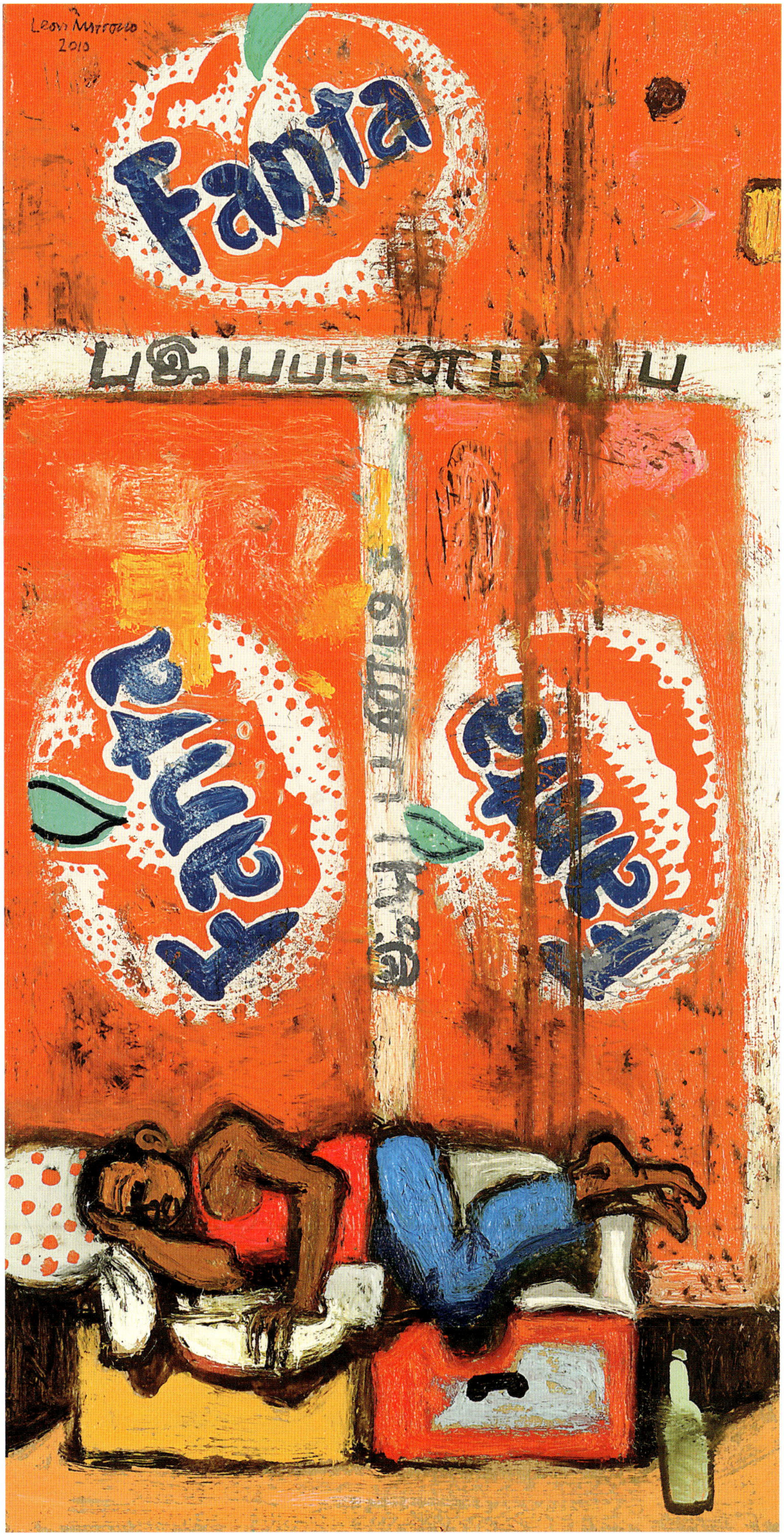

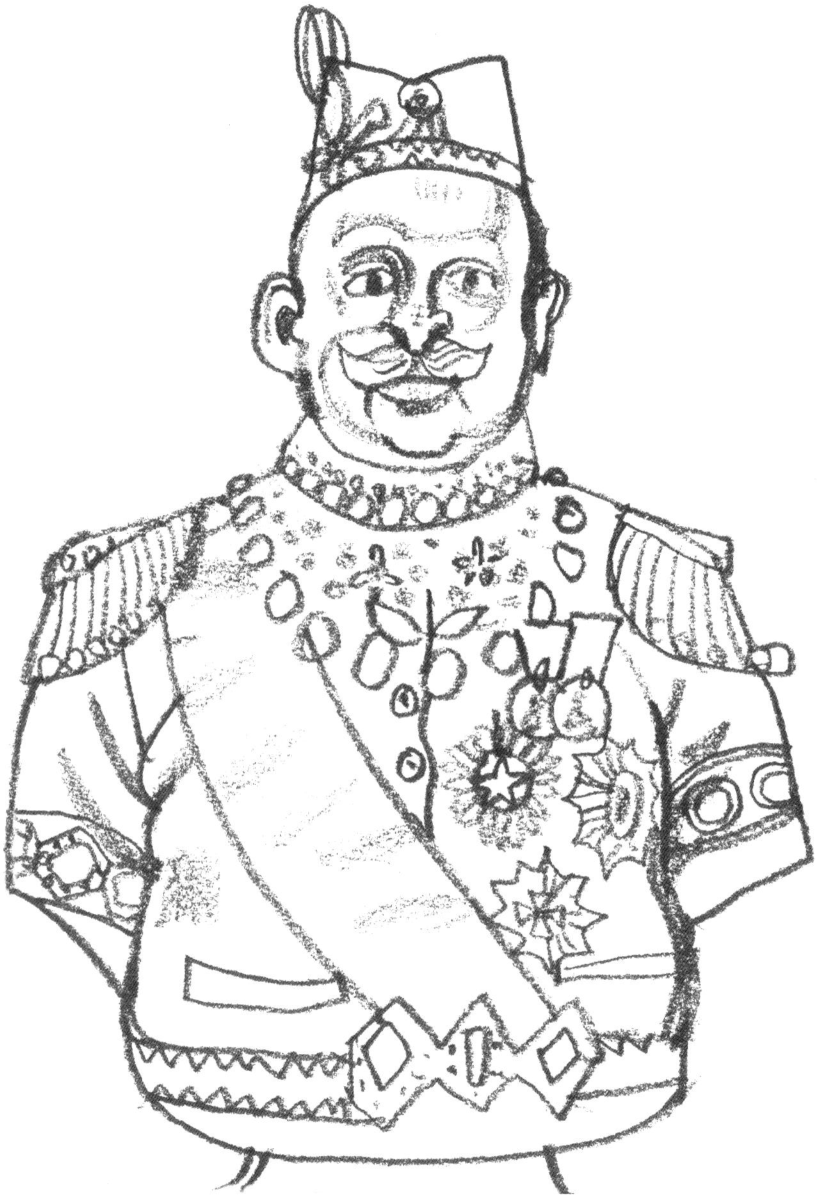

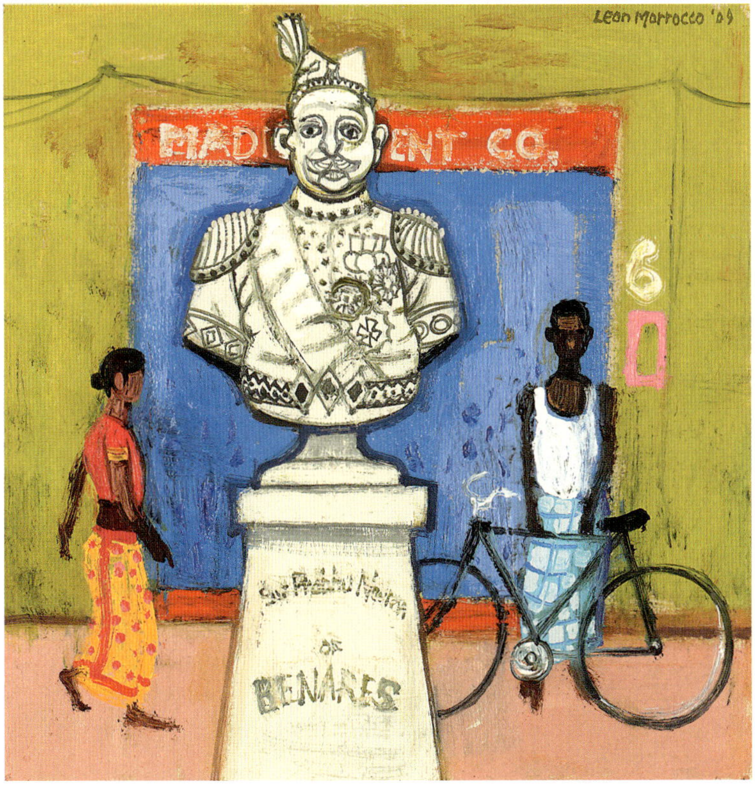
Leon Morrocco '09
ENT CO.
OF
BENARES

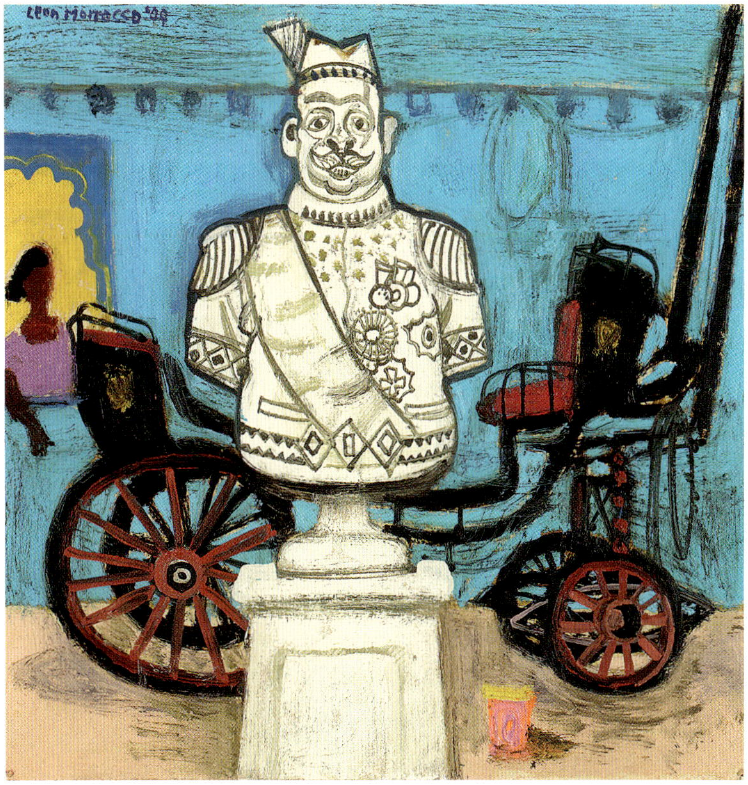

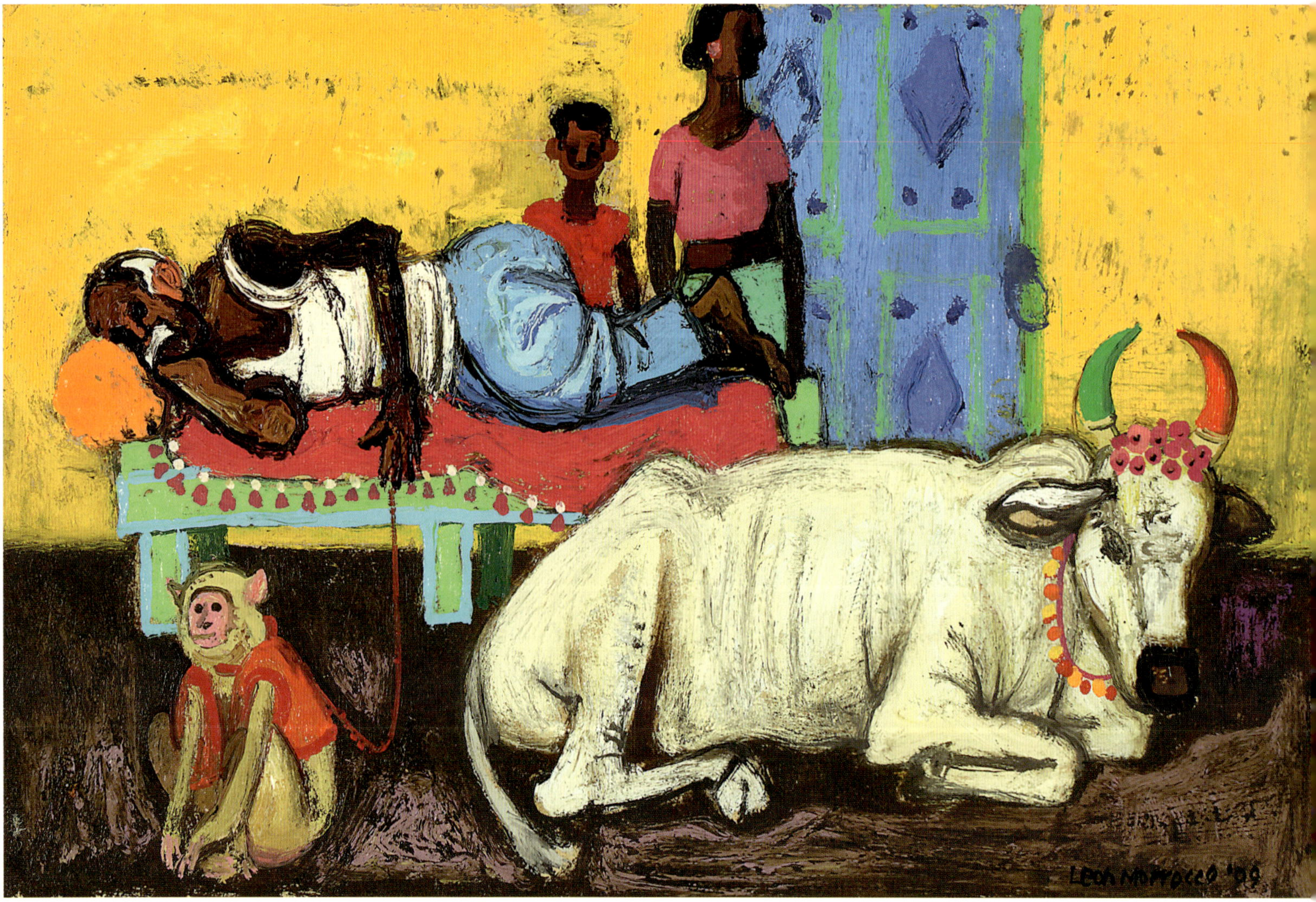

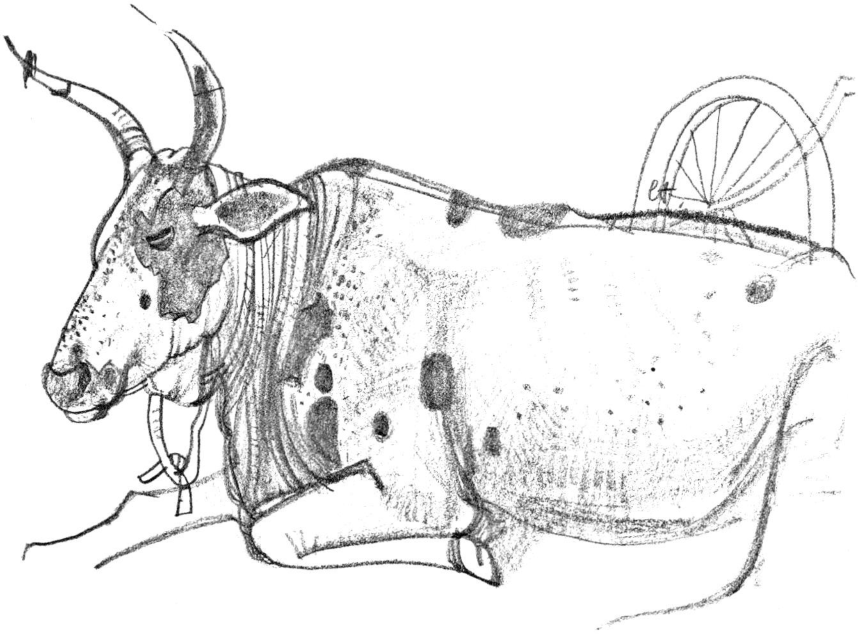

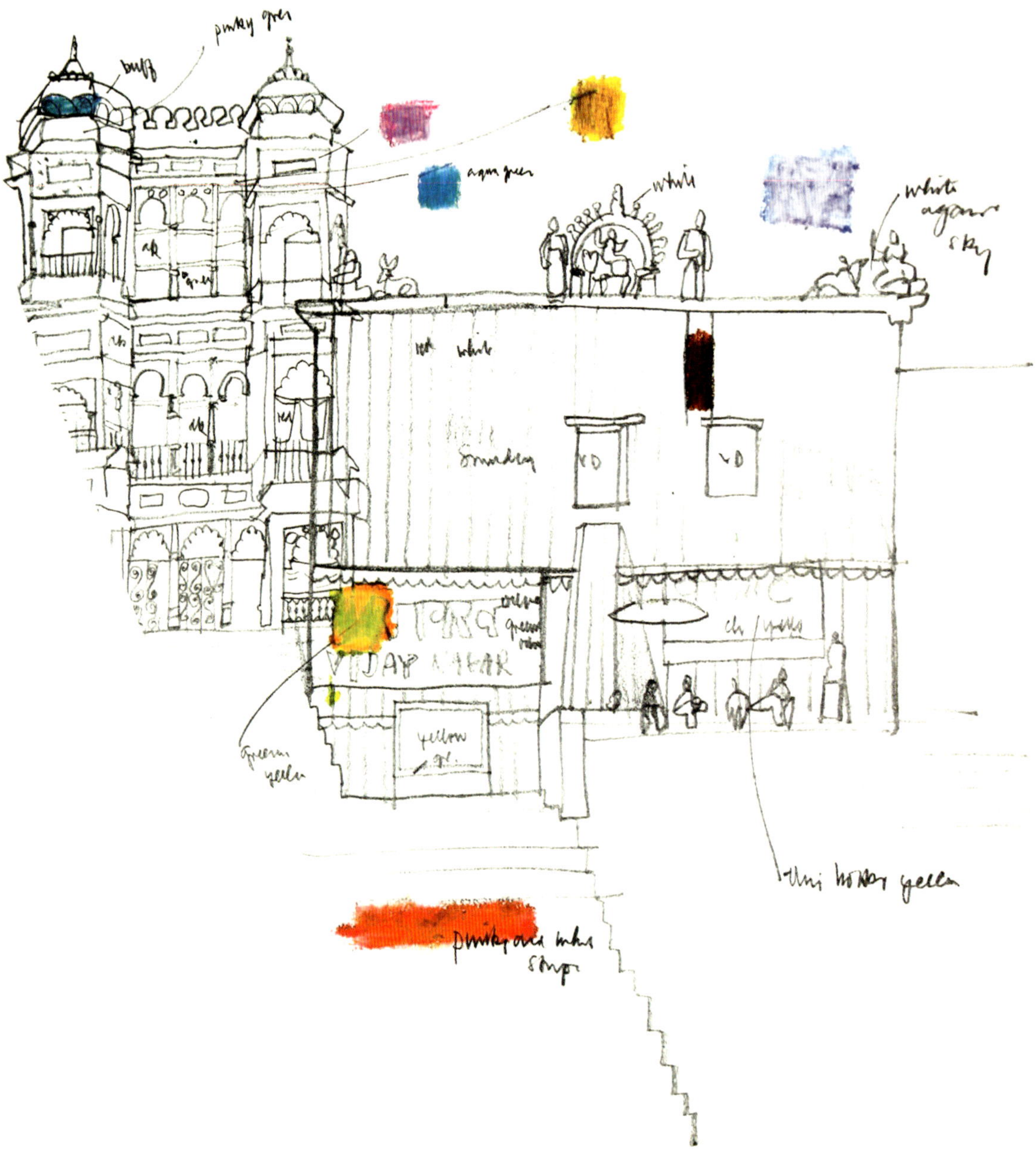
buff
aqua green
white
white against sky
yellow

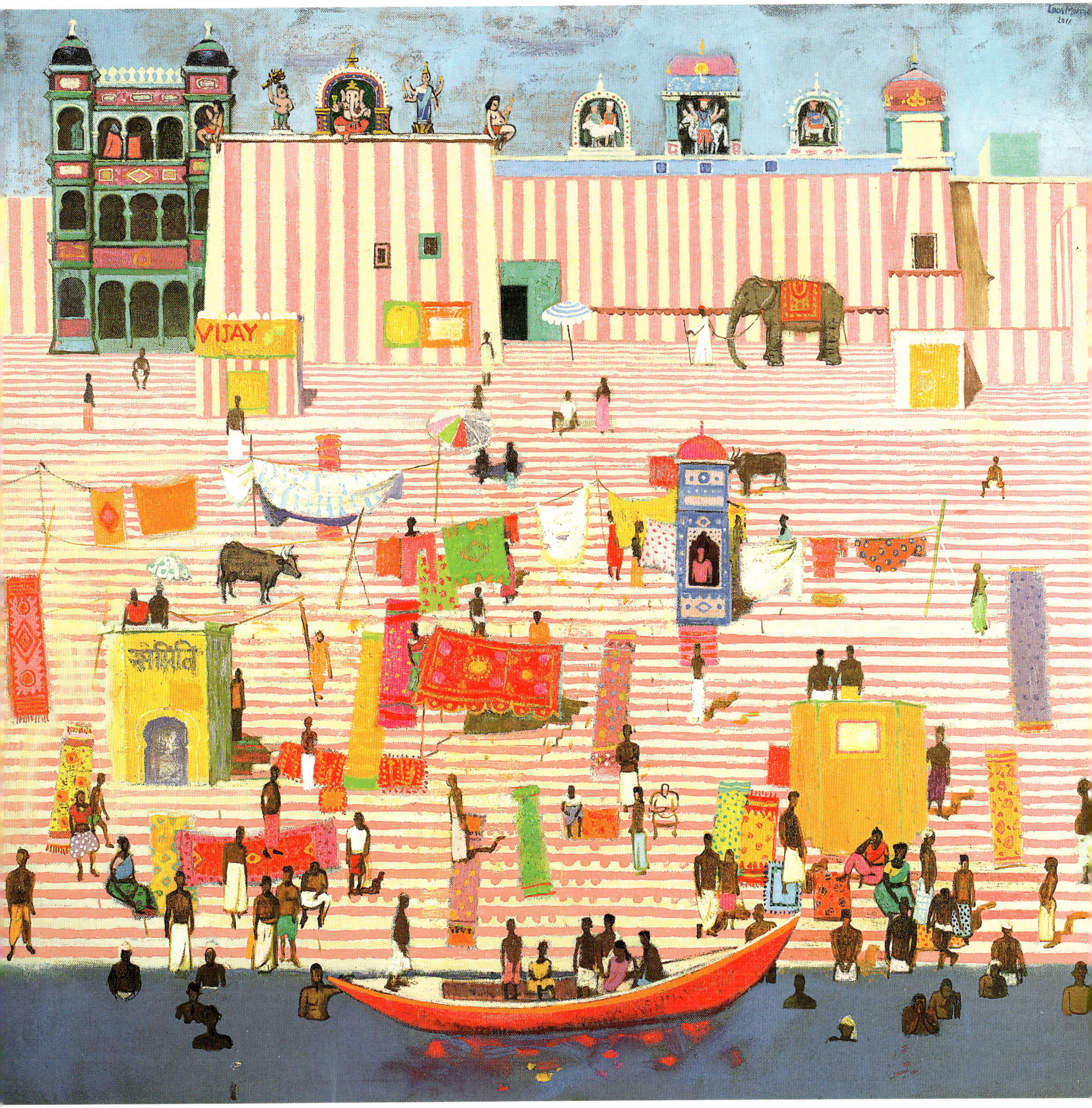
VIJAY

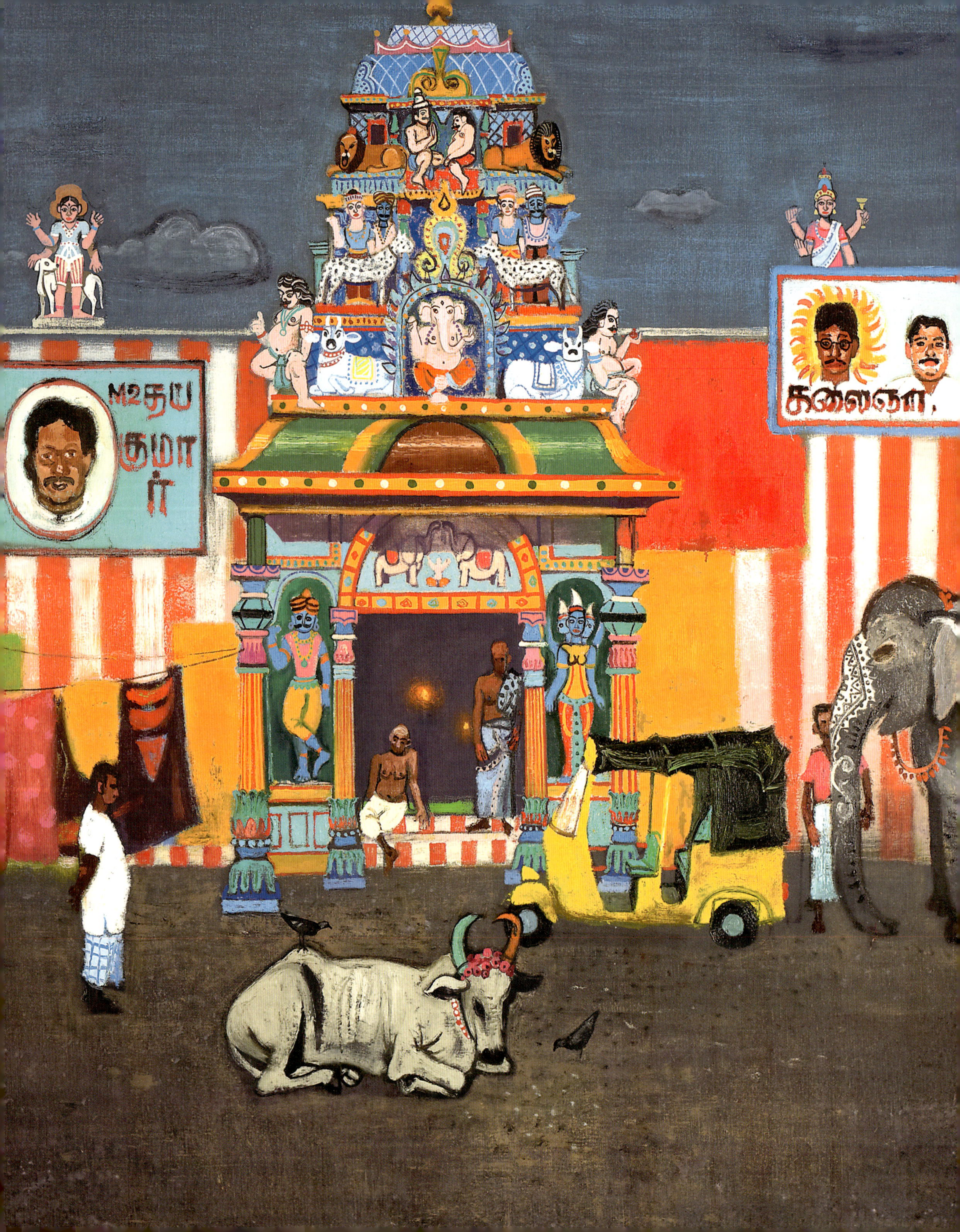

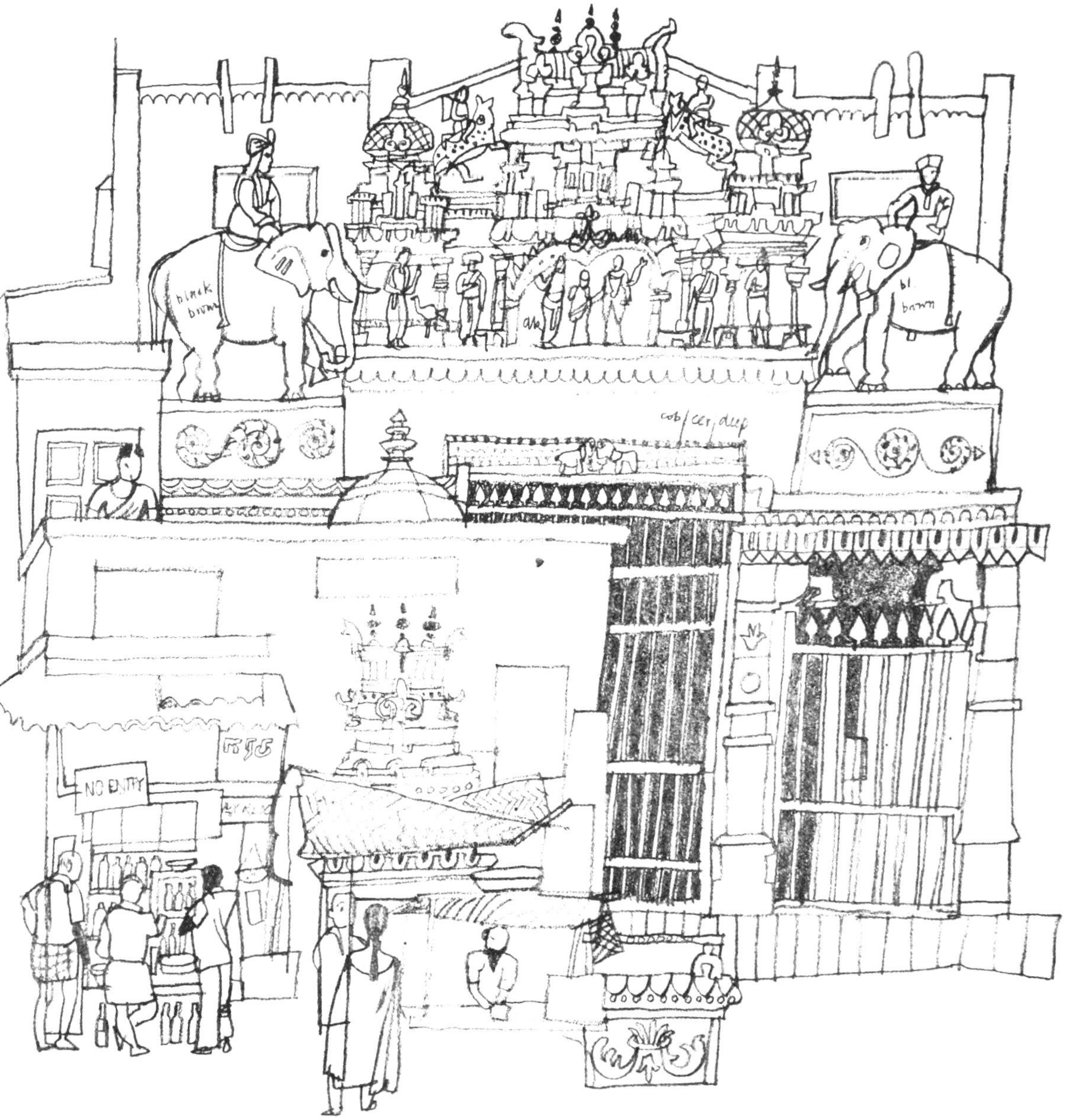
NO ENTRY

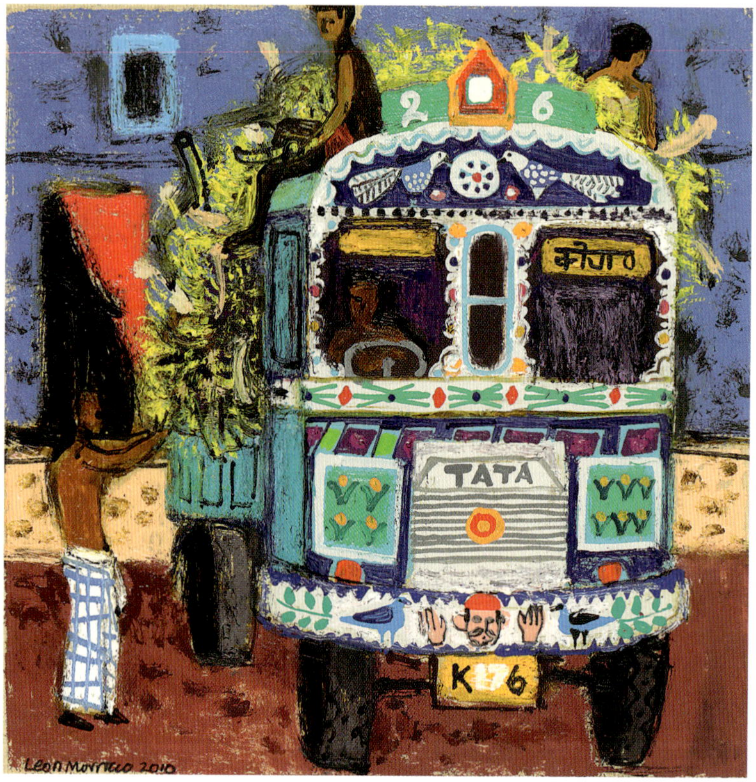
TATA
K 76
Leon Morrocco 2010

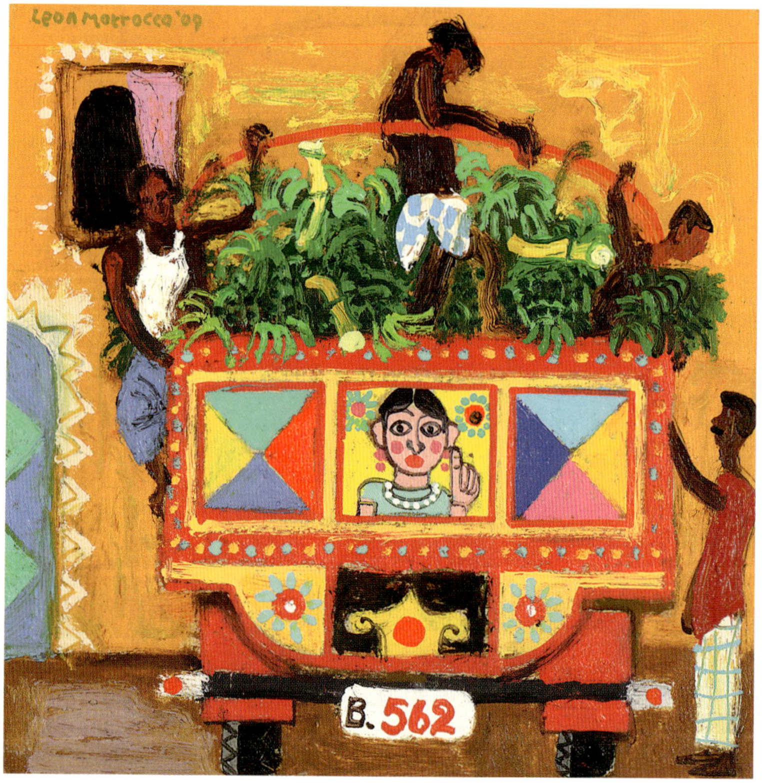
Leon Morrocco '09
B. 562

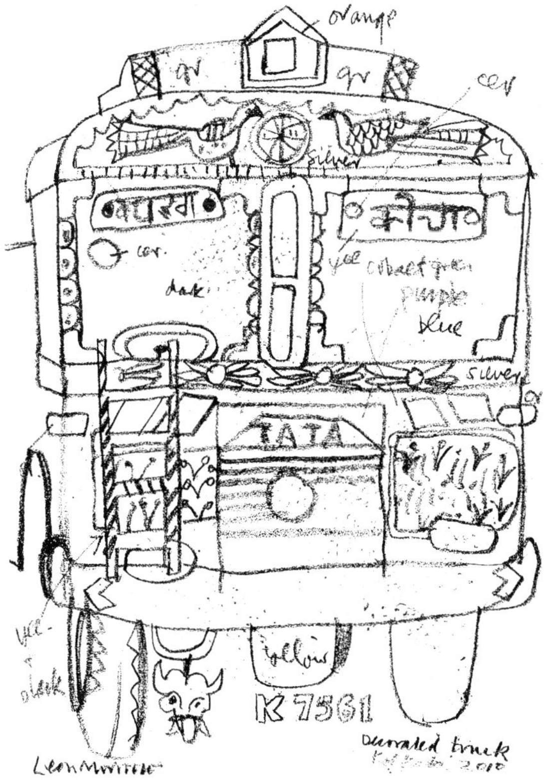
orange
silver
blue
TATA
silver
yellow
K 7561
Decorated truck

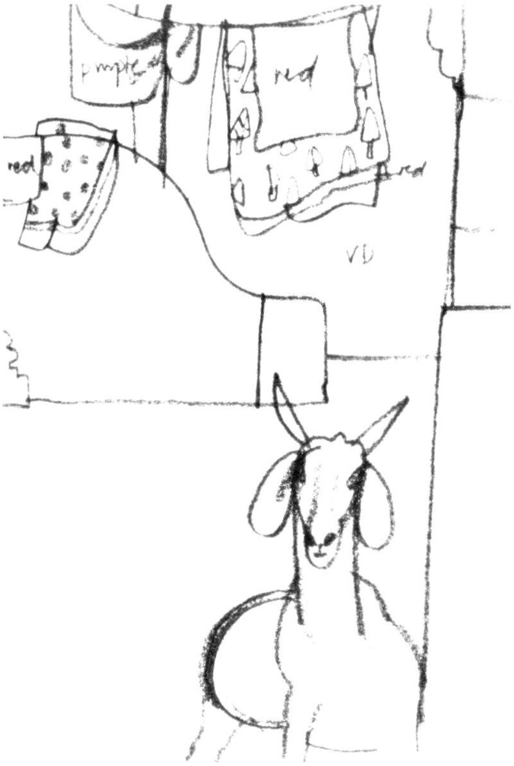

Page 154: **Temple in Madurai 2009** pencil on paper 28.5 x 30 cm

Page 155: **Temple in Madurai 2009** oil on canvas 127 x 127 cm

Page 156 *from left*: **Unloading Bananas, Kolkata 2009** oil on panel 25.5 x 25.5 cm

Loading Bananas, Madurai 2009 oil on panel 25.5 x 25.5 cm

Page 157: **Decorated Truck, Kolkata 2009** pencil on paper 14.5 x 10 cm

Page 159: **Startled Goat, Varanasi 2009** oil on panel 25.5 x 25.5 cm

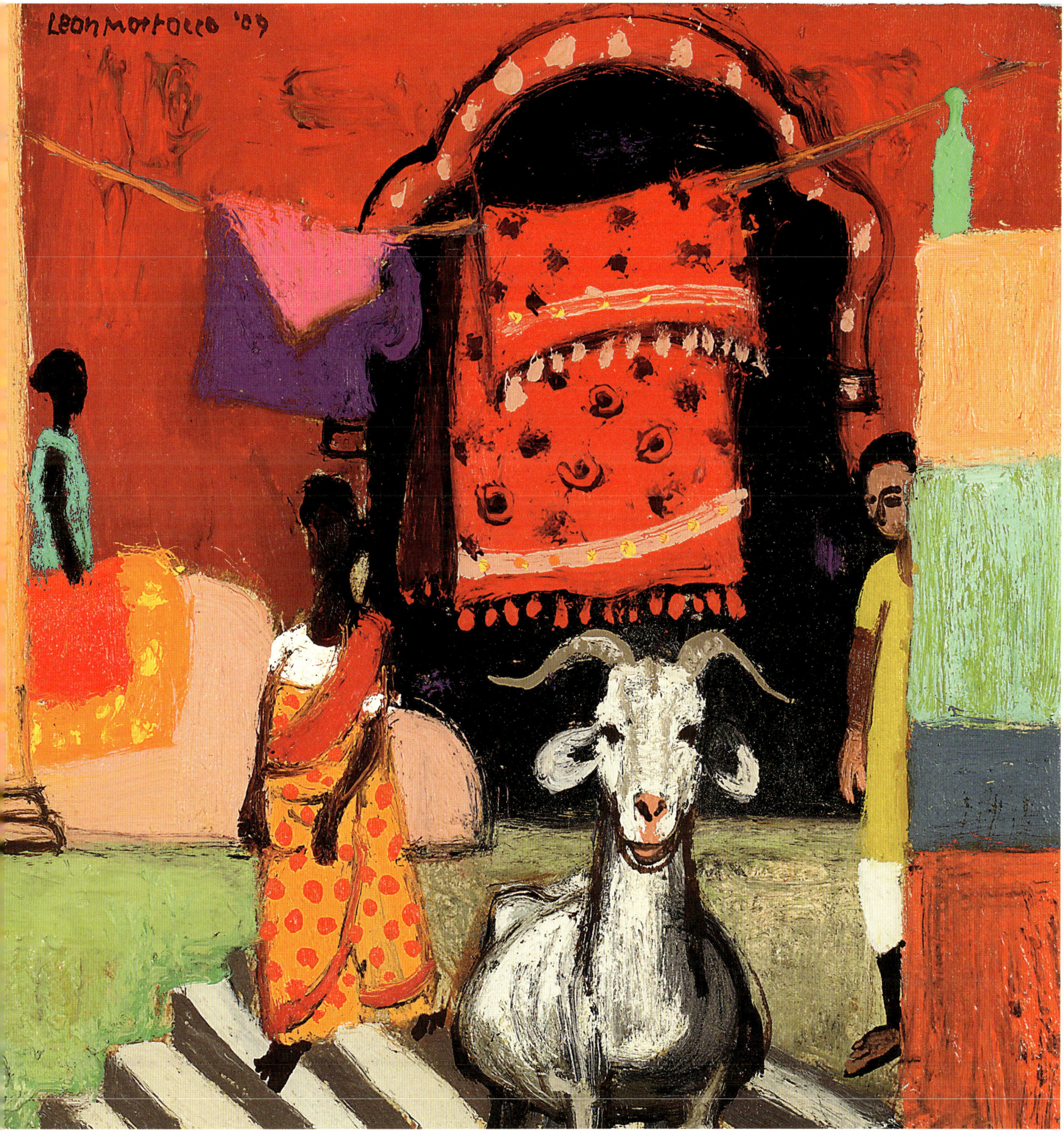
LEON MORROCCO '09

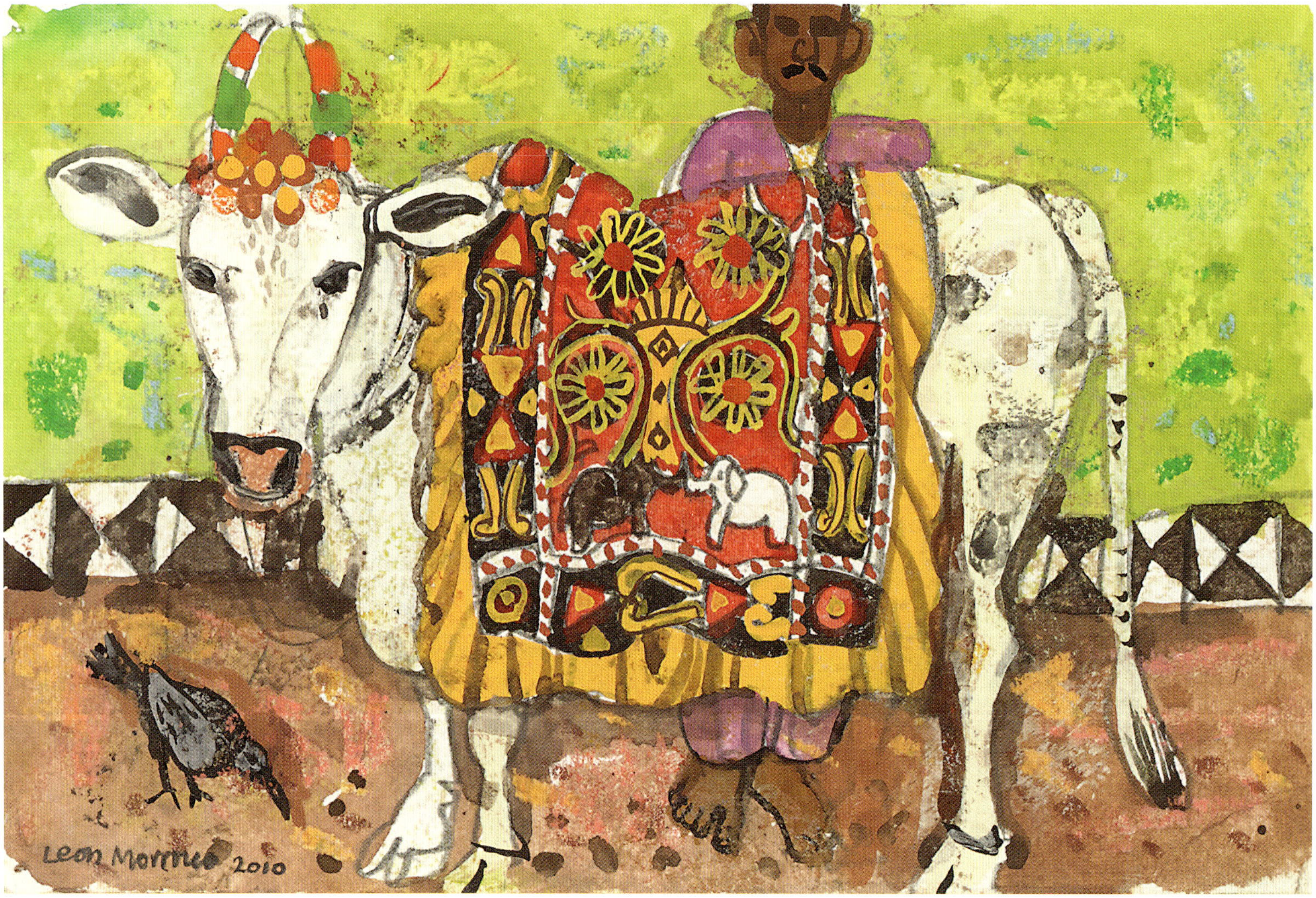

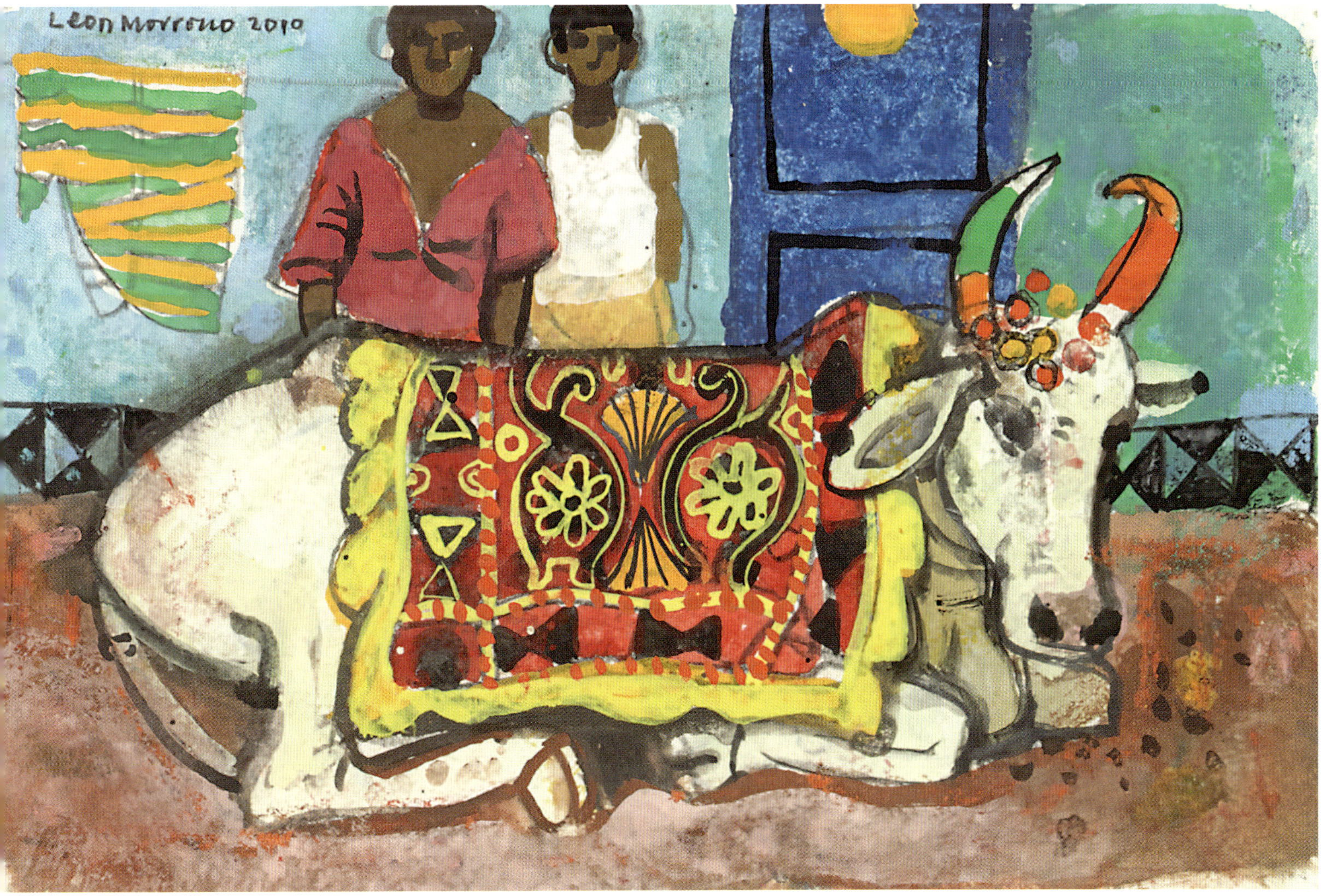
Leon Morrocco 2010

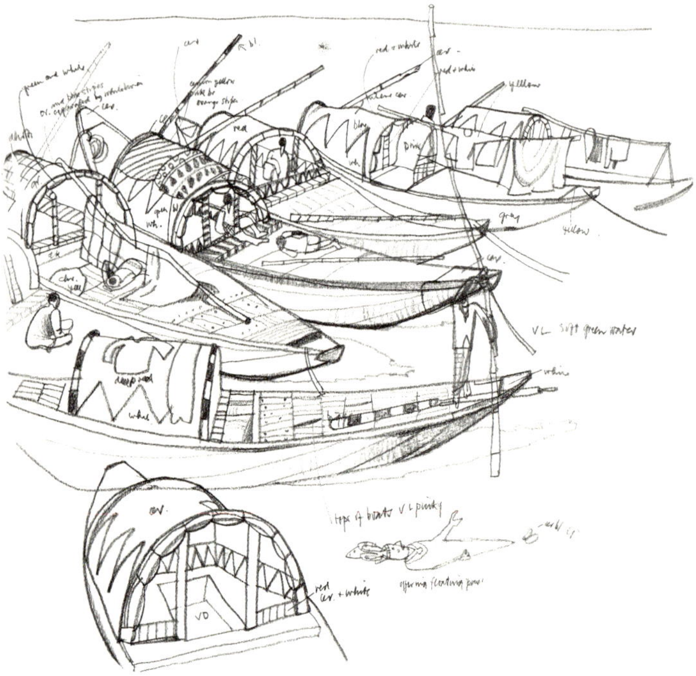
green and white
red + white
yellow
red
pink
gray
yellow
VL soft green water
white
deep red
tops of boats VL pinky
red
cer. + white
VD

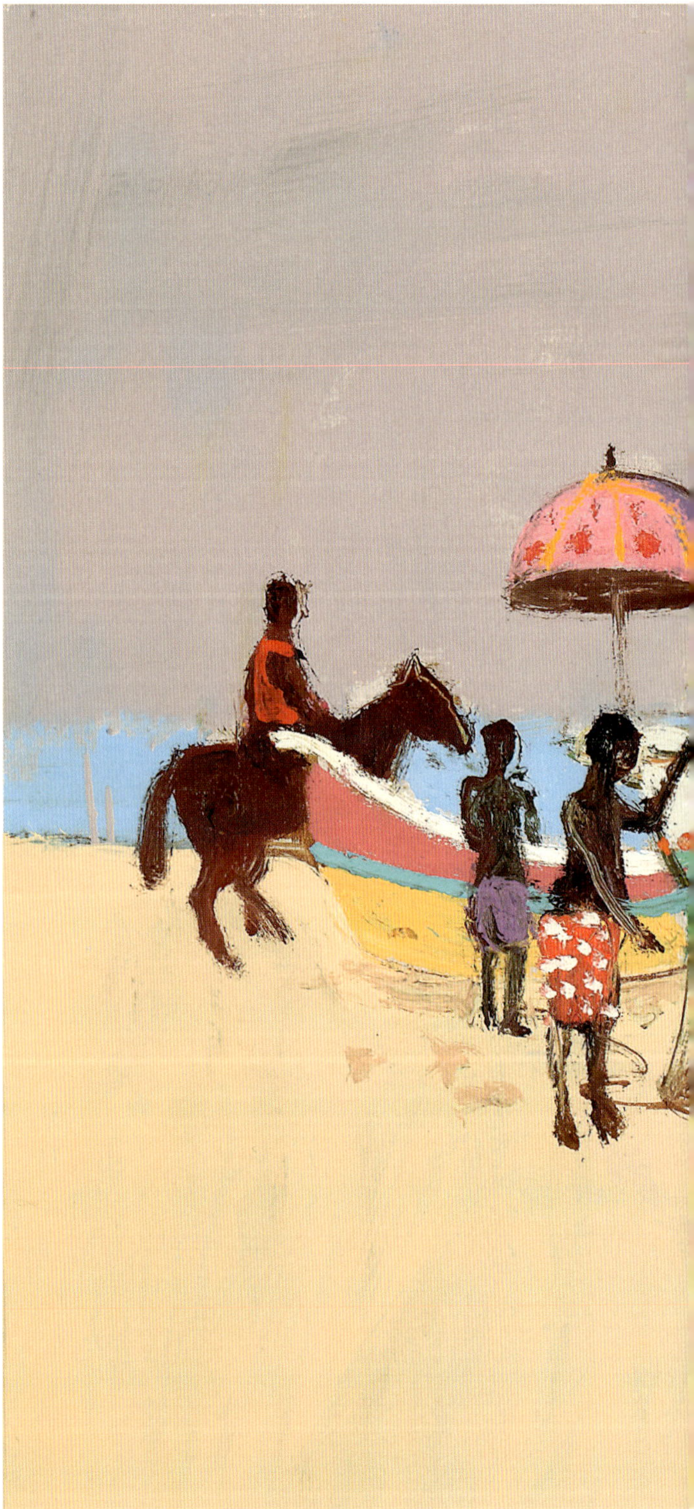

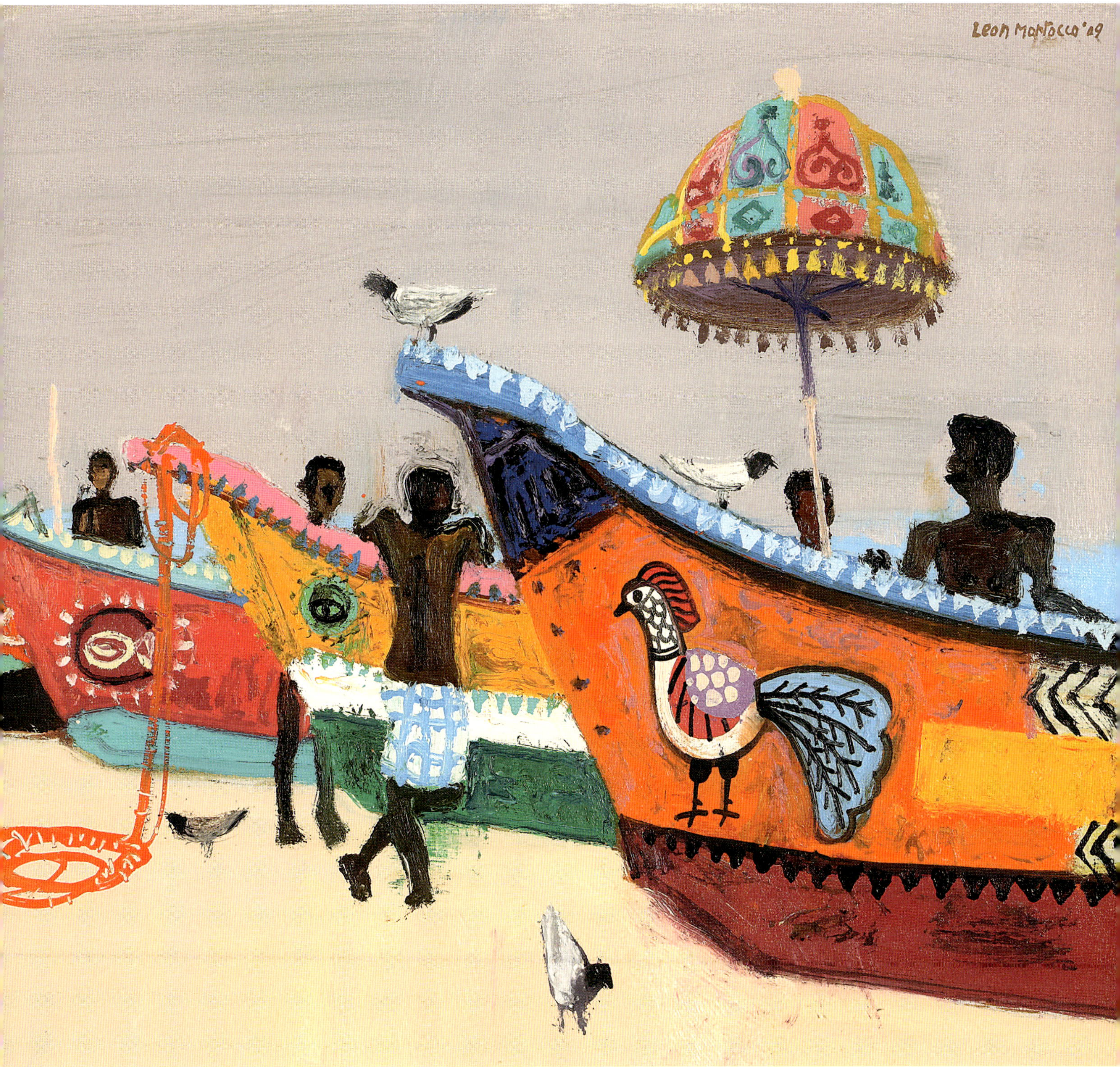
Leon Montocco '09

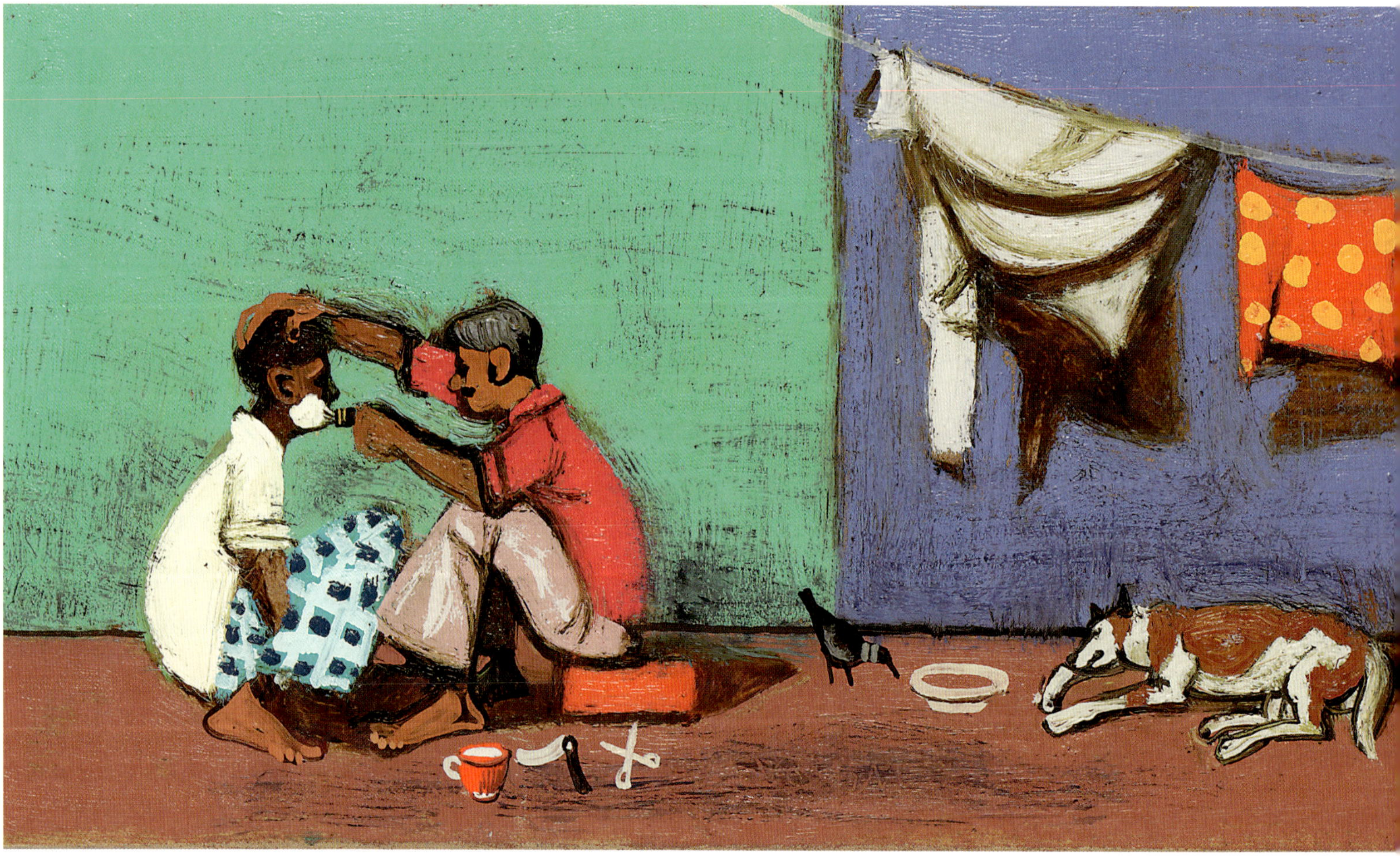

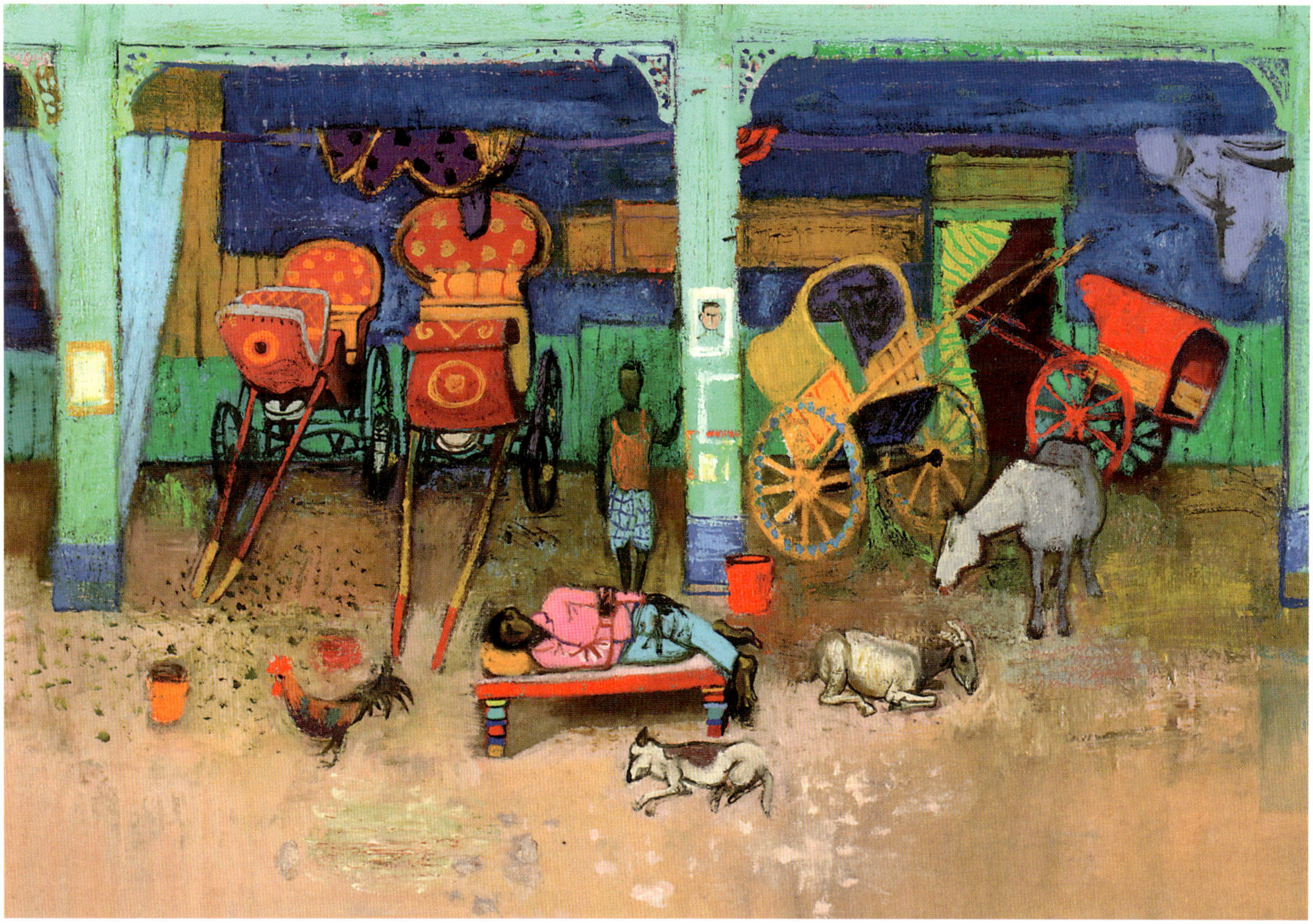

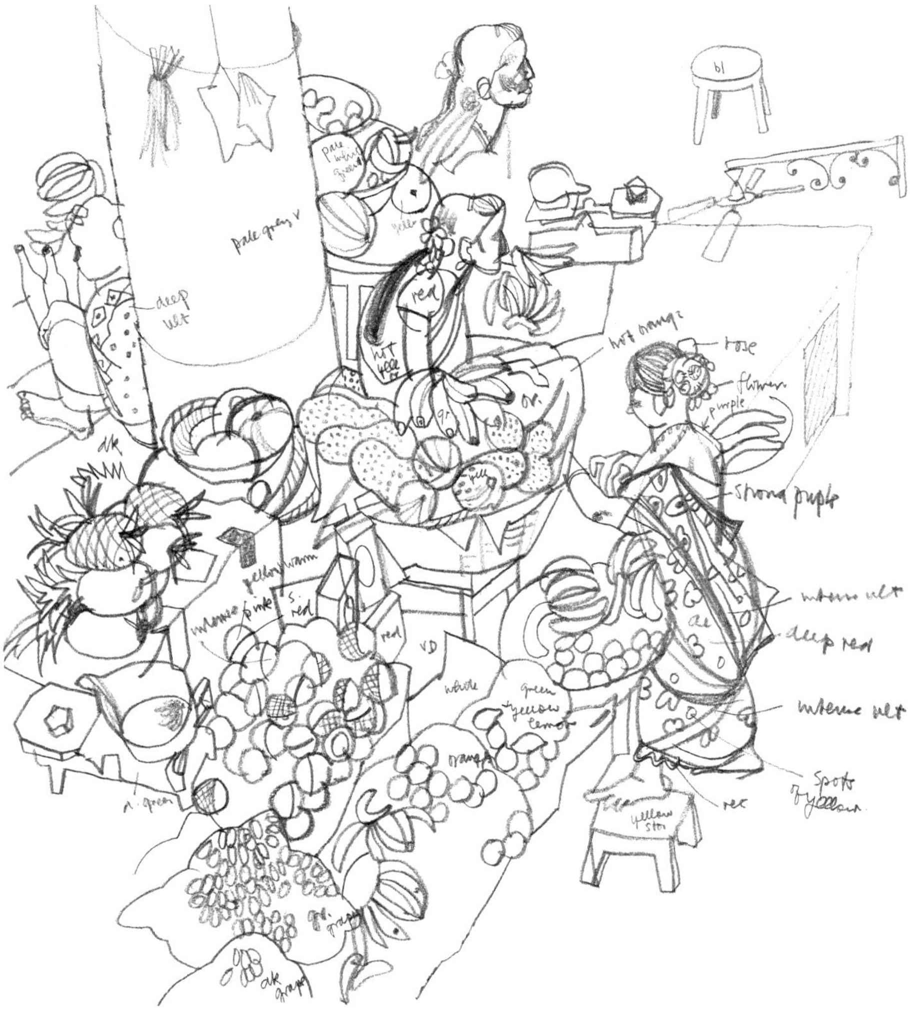

Page 160: **Holy Cow with Blackbird 2010** gouache 13 x 20 cm

Page 161: **Holy Cow Resting 2010** gouache 13 x 20 cm

Page 162: **Fishing Boats Marina Beach, Chennai 2009** oil on canvas 51 x 76 cm

Page 164: **Street Barber in Kolkata 2010** oil on panel 20 x 40.5 cm

Page 165: **Nap by the Marriage Carriages, Chennai 2009** oil on canvas 66 x 96.5 cm

Page 166: **Fruit Stall at the Market, Goa 2010** pencil on paper 29 x 30.5 cm

Page 167: **Waiting Outside the Market, Mumbai 2009** oil on panel 71 x 76 cm

Page 168: **Four Women Back to Back, Goa Market 2010** pencil & oil pastel on paper 27 x 39 cm

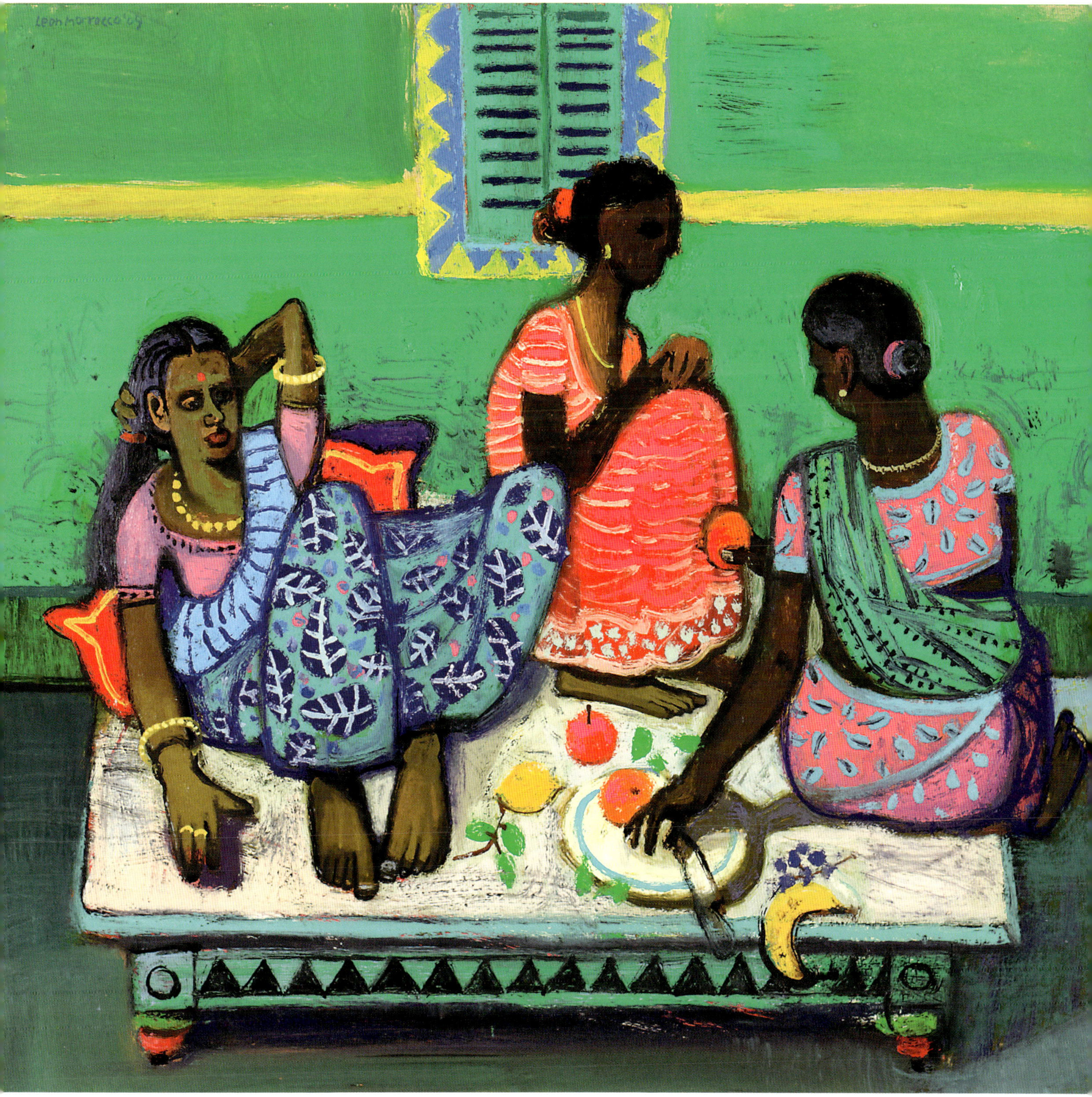
Leon Morrocco '09

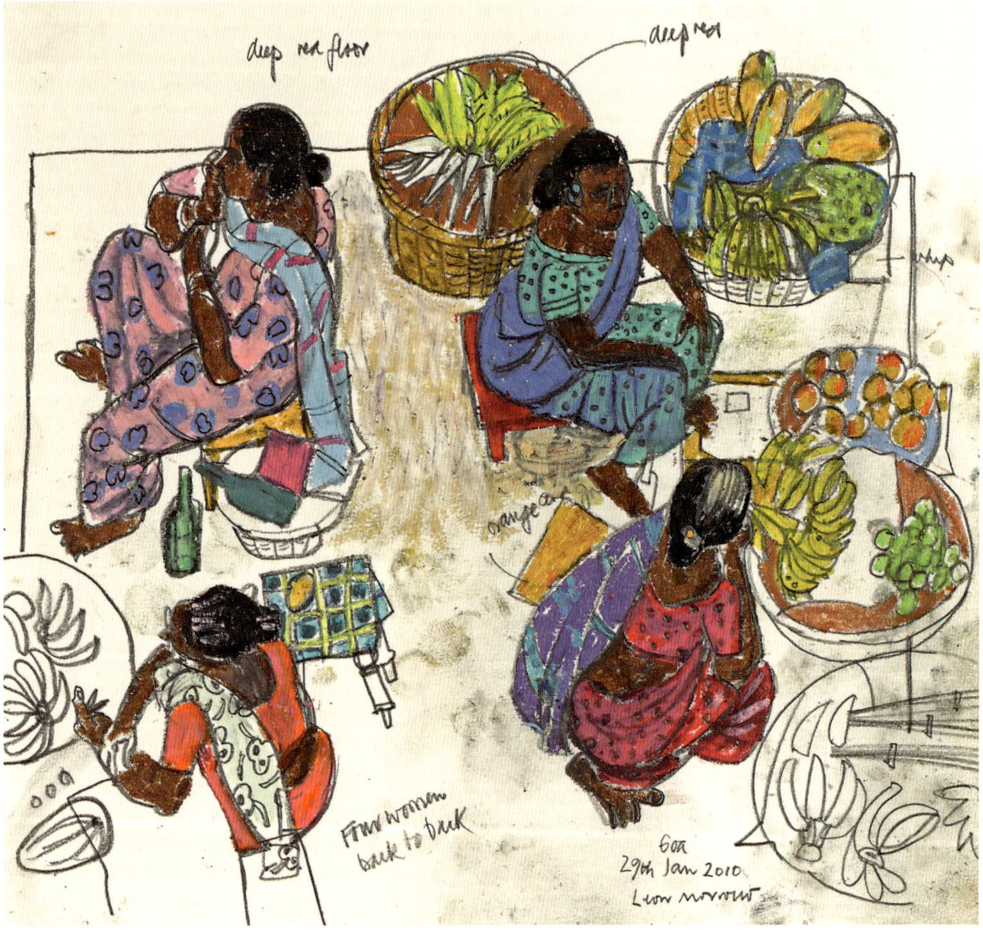
deep red floor
deep red
Four women
back to back
Goa
29th Jan 2010

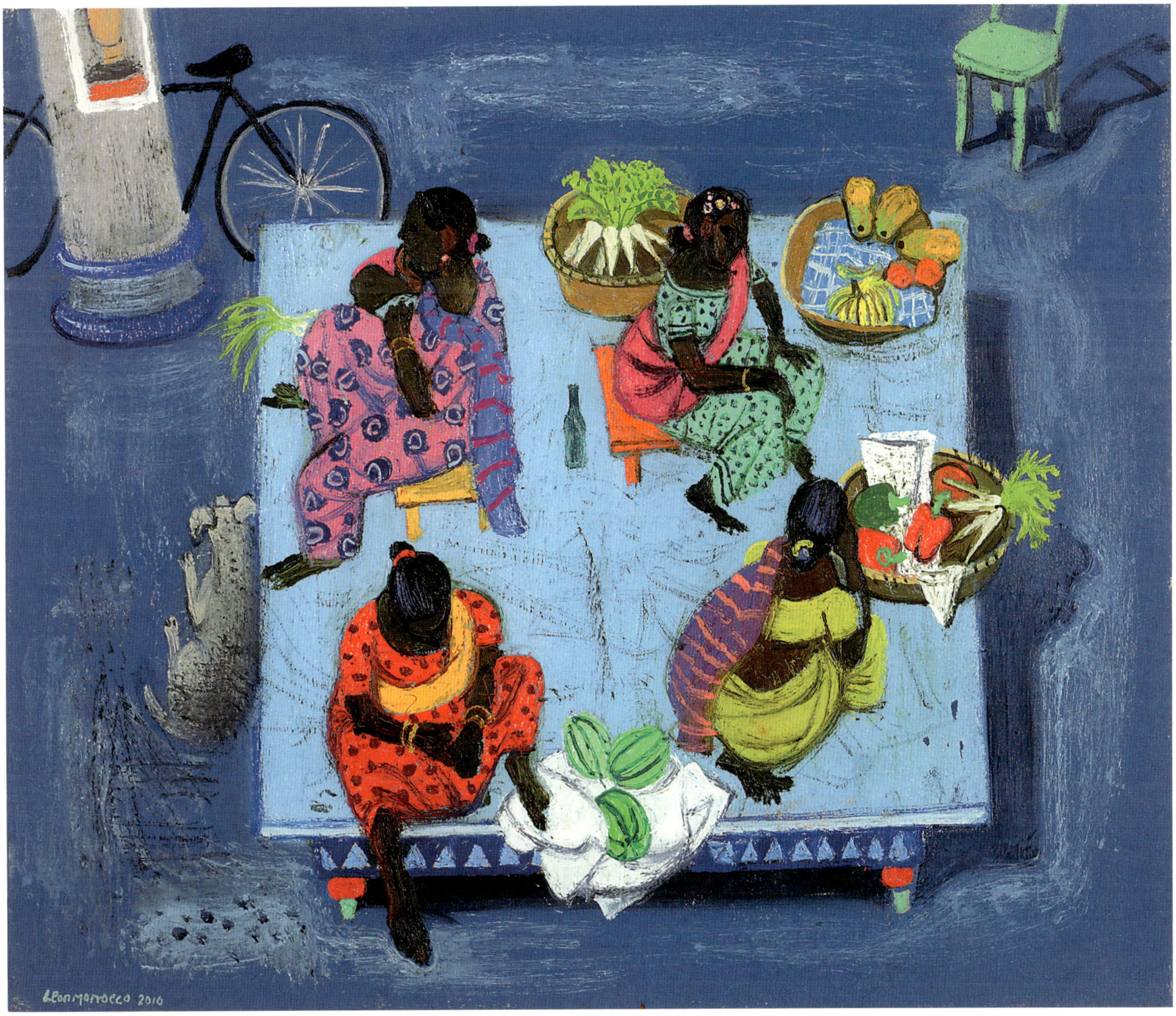
Leon Morrocco 2010

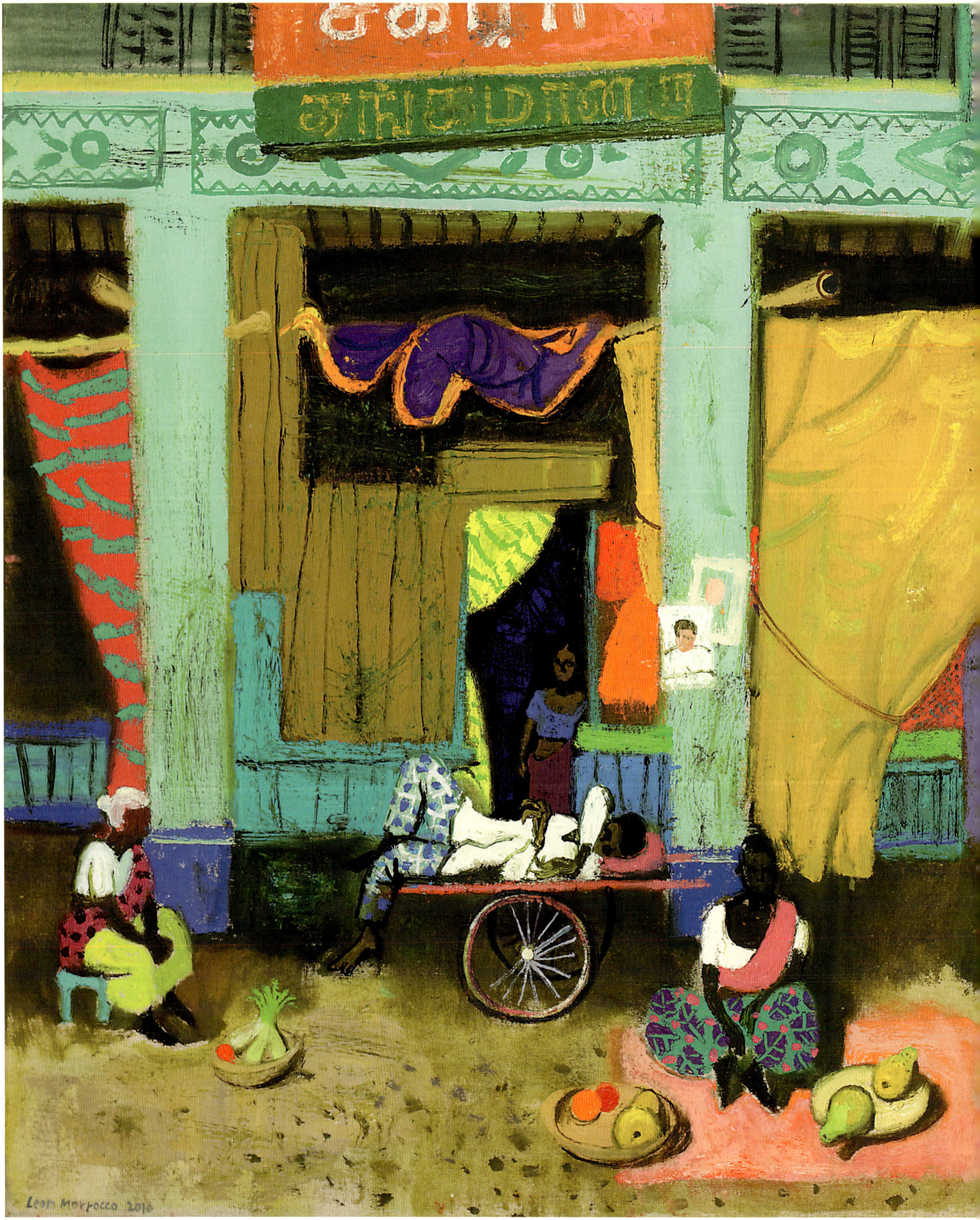
Leon Morrocco 2010

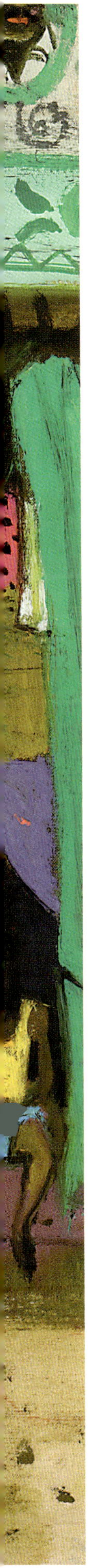

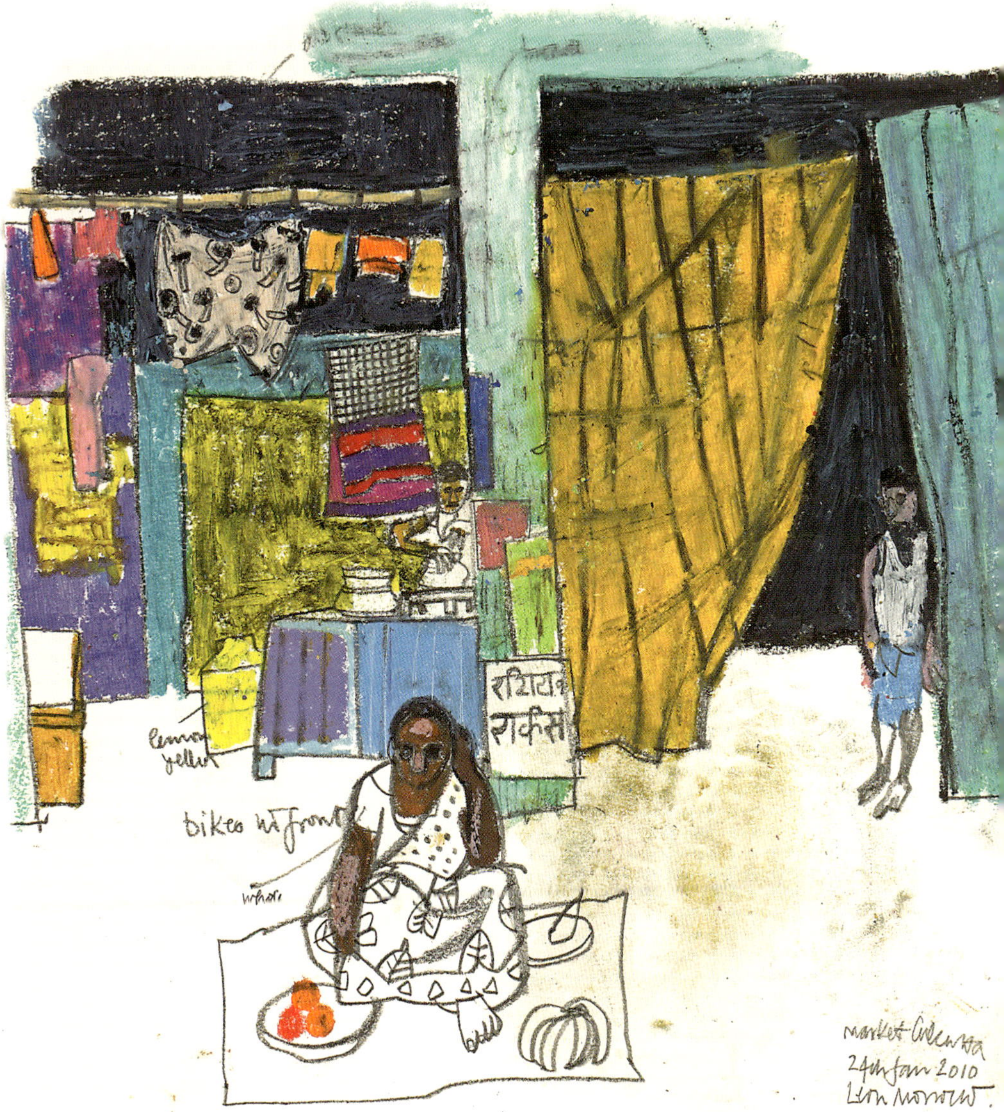
lemon yellow
bikes in front
market Calcutta
24th Jan 2010

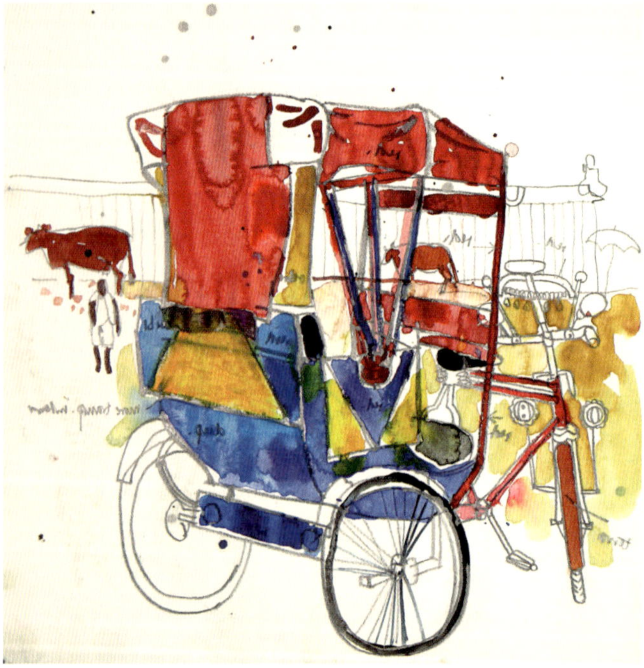

Page 169: **Women at the Market, Goa 2010** oil on canvas 51 x 61 cm.
Page 170: **Taking a Break, Kolkata 2010** oil on canvas 76 x 71 cm
Page 172: **Market Woman, Kolkata 2010** pencil oil pastel on paper 29 x 30.5 cm
Page 173: **Parked Rickshaw, Madurai 2009** pencil & gouache on paper 28.5 x 30 cm
Page 173: **Dusk at Marina Beach 2009** oil on canvas 61 x 107 cm

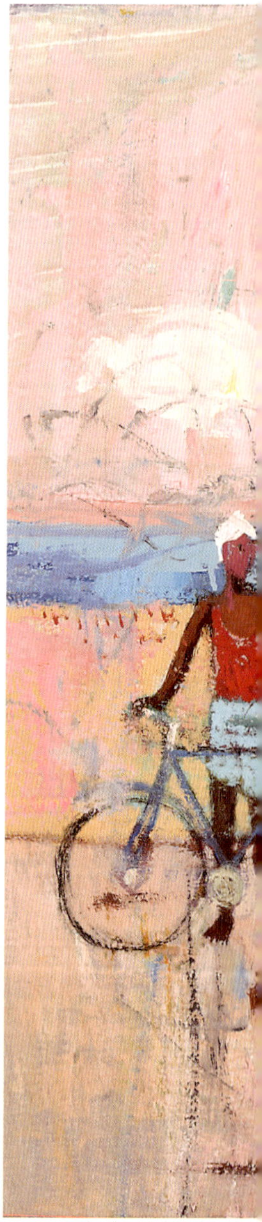

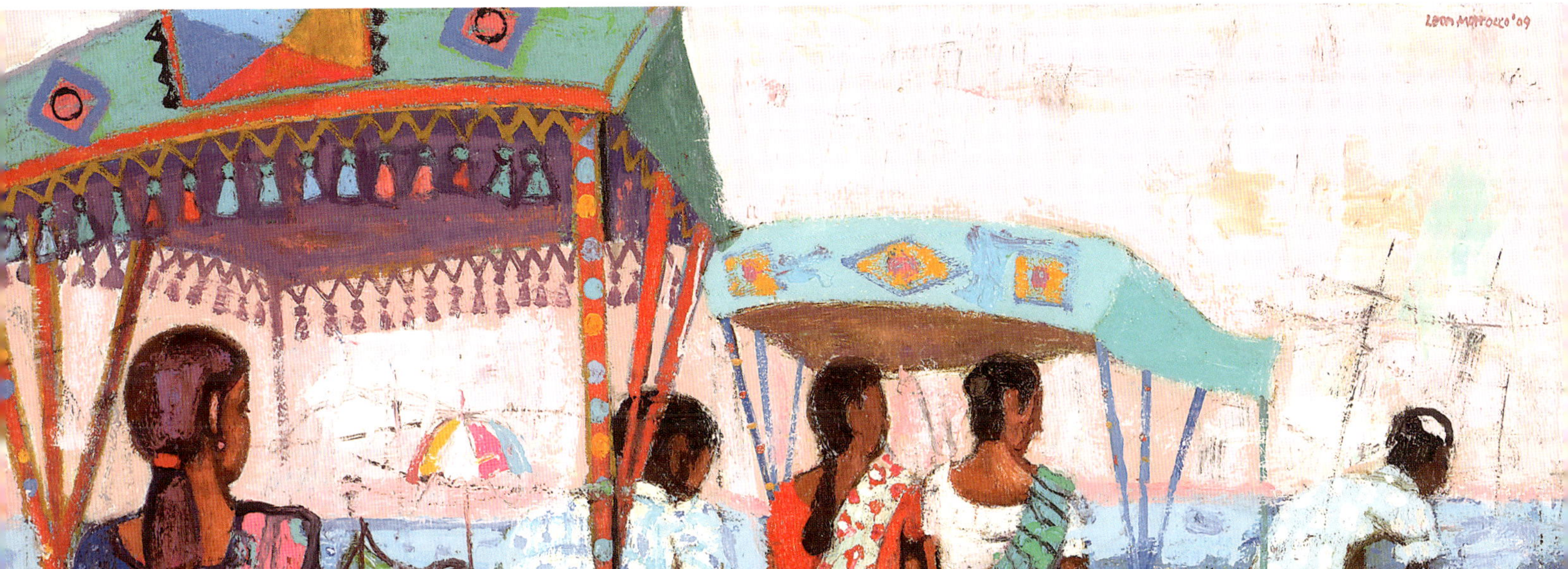
Leon Morrocco '09

LEON MORROCCO ARSA RGI

Born Edinburgh 1942

BIOGRAPHY

1959–60	Duncan Jordanstone College of Art, Dundee
1960–61	Slade School of Art, London
1961–65	Edinburgh College of Art
1965	Awarded Andrew Grant Scholarship
1965–68	Lecturer in Painting, Edinburgh College of Art
1969	Italian Government Scholarship to Academia di Brera, Milan
1969–79	Lecturer in Painting, Glasgow School of Art
1970	Latimer Award, Royal Scottish Academy
1971	Elected Associate of the Royal Scottish Academy
1972	Guthrie Award, Royal Sottish Academy
1979–84	Head of Fine Art, Chisholm Institute, Melbourne, Australia
1991	Lecturer in Drawing, Ballarat University College, Victoria, Australia
1992–96	Returns to live in London
2010	Made full academician at the Royal Scottish Academy

SOLO EXHIBITIONS

2016	What the River Knew, 1–25 June Mascalls, Gallery, Kent
2015	Paintings & Drawings, Open Eye Gallery Edinburgh
2013/5	Drawing the River Parts 1 & 2, John Martin Gallery
2012	Leon Morrocco, Open Eye Gallery, Edinburgh
2011	Paintings of India, Edward Cutler Gallery, Milan
2010	Chennai, Kolkata, Goa, John Martin Gallery
2009	From Mumbai to Madurai, John Martin Gallery
2009	Strade di Roma, Open Eye Gallery Edinburgh
2007	Morrocco's Morocco at Art London The Sketchbooks & Paintings of Leon Morrocco, Open Eye Gallery, Edinburgh
2006	Havana, John Martin Gallery
2005	Roman Drawings, Australian Galleries Melbourne
2005	The Open Eye Gallery, Edinburgh
2003	Roman Paintings, John Martin Gallery
2000	John Martin Gallery, also 1998, 96
1999	The Open Eye Gallery, Edinburgh, also 1999, 97, 95, 93
1998, 94, 93	Roger Billcliffe Fine Art, Glasgow
1995, 73	Loomshop Gallery, Fife
1993, 91	Portland Gallery, London
1992,89,86,84	Australian Galleries, Melbourne
1986	Bonython-Meadmore Gallery, Sydney
1982	Stuart Gertsman Galleries, Melbourne
1979	Glasgow School of Art
1978	Stirling Gallery, Greenock Arts Centre University of Strathclyde, Glasgow

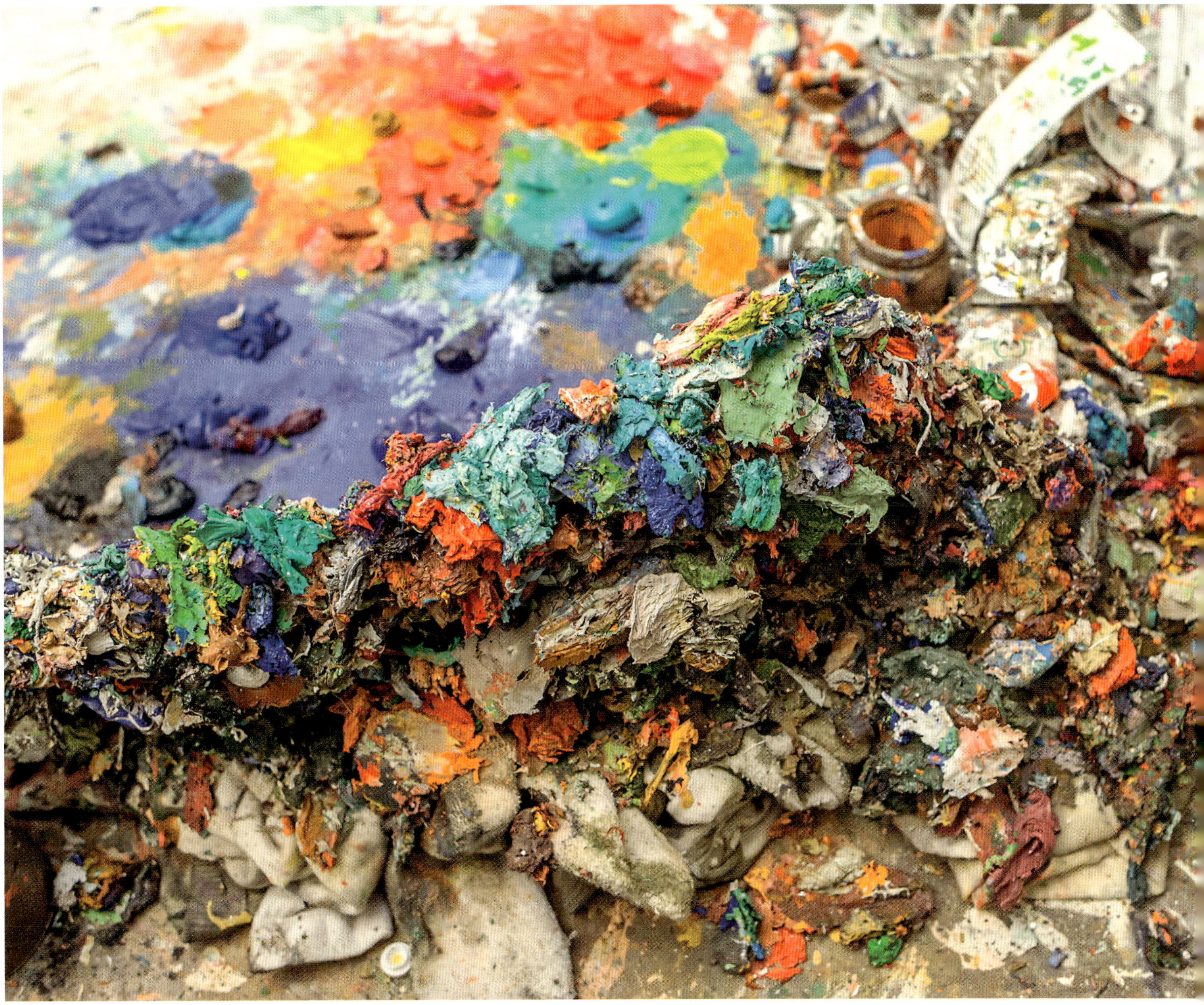

1976	University of St. Andrews
1975,71	The Scottish Gallery, Edinburgh
1965	Douglas & Foulis Gallery, Edinburgh
	French Institute Gallery, Edinburgh
	Traverse Theatre Gallery, Edinburgh

PUBLIC COLLECTIONS

The Scottish National Gallery of Modern Art, The Scottish Arts Council, Leeds Art Gallery, Lille Art Gallery, The Nuffield Foundation, Queensland Art Gallery and the Australian Government Collection.

FUTURE EXHIBITIONS & AWARDS

Leon Morrocco regularly exhibits works at the Royal Scottish Academy Annual Exhibition and in April 2017 won the William J. Macaulay/Scottish Gallery Award for an outstanding work.

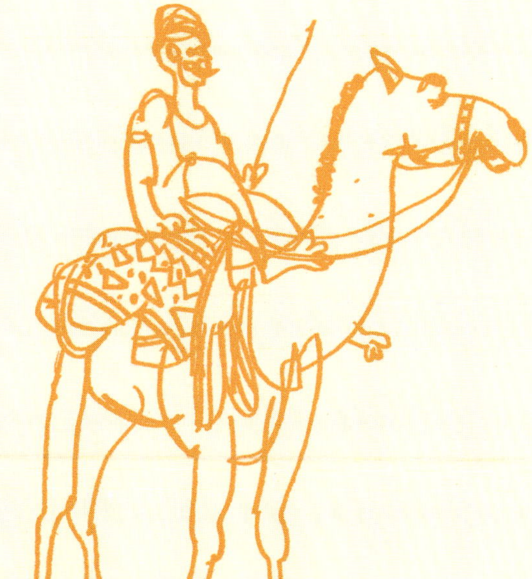

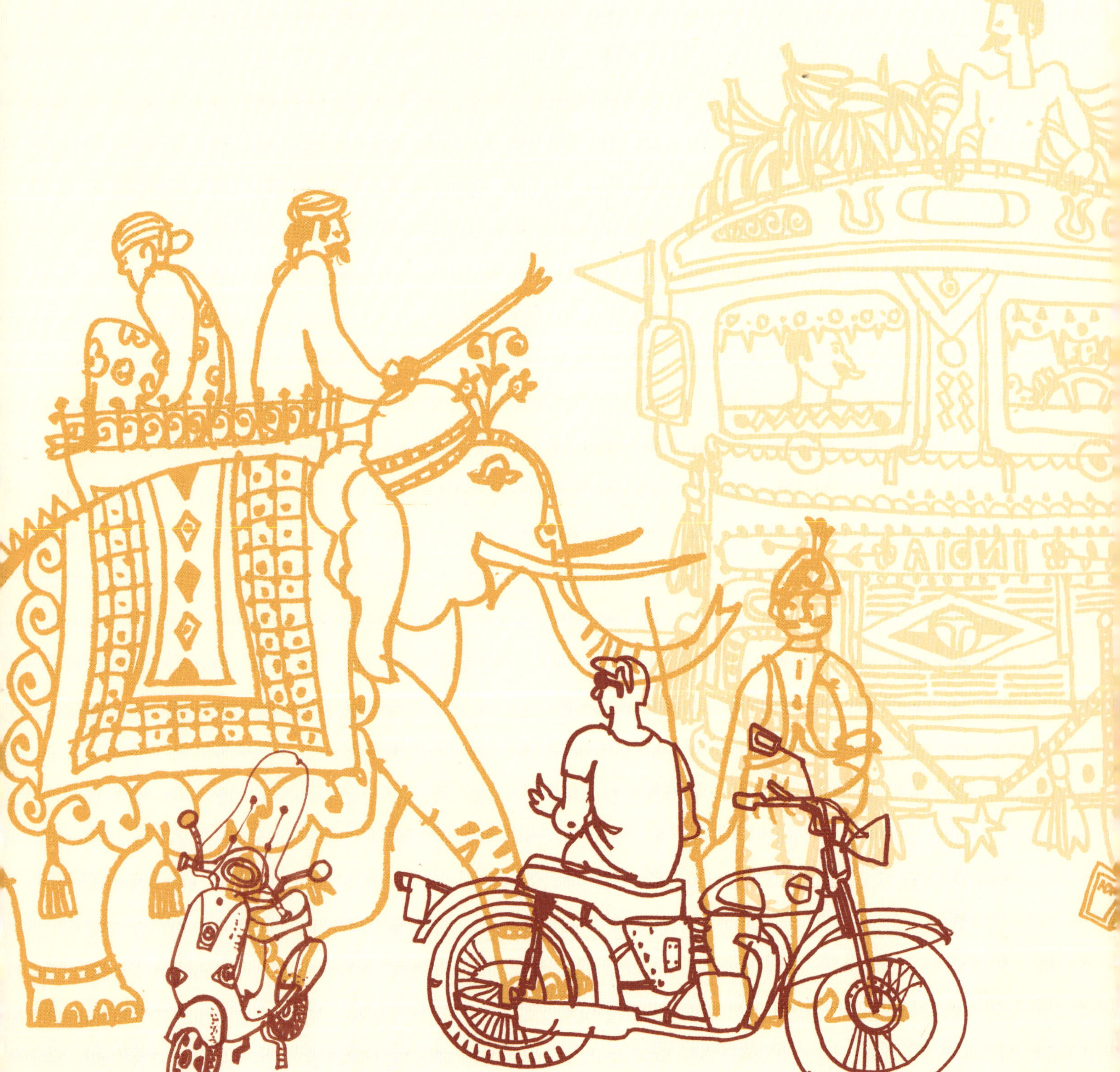
INDIA